QUEST FOR A CONSTITUTION: A MAN WHO WOULDN'T QUIT

By
Elmer Gertz
And
Ed Gilbreth

340.92 W788g

QUEST FOR A CONSTITUTION: A MAN WHO WOULDN'T QUIT

A Political Biography of
Samuel Witwer
of Illinois

By
Elmer Gertz
And
Edward S. Gilbreth

Edited
And With An Introduction
By
Joseph P. Pisciotte

UNIVERSITY
PRESS OF
AMERICA

LANHAM • NEW YORK • LONDON

University Press of America,™ Inc.

4720 Boston Way
Lanham, MD 20706

3 Henrietta Street
London WC2E 8LU England

Library of Congress Cataloging in Publication Data

Gertz, Elmer, 1906-
Quest for a constitution.

Includes index.
1. Witwer, Samuel W. (Samuel Weiler), 1908-
2. Lawyers—Illinois—Biography. 3. Legislators—Illinois
—Biography. 4. Illinois—Constitutional history.
I. Gilbreth, Edward S. II. Pisciotte, Joseph P.
III. Title.
KF373.W53G47 1984 342.773'0092'4 [B] 84-13226
347.730200924 [B]
ISBN 0-8191-4208-5 (alk. paper)
ISBN 0-8191-4209-3 (pbk. : alk. paper)

University Press of America
In Cooperation With
The Hugo Wall Center for Urban Studies
Wichita State University

To
Ethyl Witwer
A source of patient and continuing support
throughout the several decades of
her husband's quest for
constitutional reform in Illinois.

Special appreciation is expressed to the Louis Ancel Foundation of Illinois, whose financial support has made this volume possible.

PREFACE

E very book has more authors than those whose names appear on the title page. We owe a debt of gratitude to each of them, some whose names we mention, others who are anonymous.

First of all, we must express our gratitude to the remarkable man who is the subject of our book — Samuel W. Witwer. No one could have been more helpful in the insights and leads that he gave us without undue intrusion upon our editorial judgment. It is always a delicate situation to deal with a man who is living and has the sensitivities of a normal human being. Samuel W. Witwer was ideal both in his helpfulness and in his reserve. We were especially fortunate in being able to read passages in his constitutional convention journal and much of his correspondence.

Many of those persons who played a role in Witwer's career are, fortunately, still with us. Virtually all of those were helpful to us. We want to particularly thank Louis Ancel, whose kindness was limitless, Governor William G. Stratton, Rubin Cohn, Alan Jacobs, Ann Lousin and Roy Fisher. Some who were close to the subject of this book died even before we began our labors. They included such luminaries as Adlai E. Stevenson, Louis Kohn, George B. McKibbin, and Jacob M. Arvey. As to these persons we were fortunate in being able to verify our facts and characterizations in ways that will be apparent in the reading of this work.

Witwer has played a special role in the history of his *alma mater,* Dickinson College. We have been able to depict and document this role in several ways. Our co-author, Edward Gilbreth, spent time at Dickinson, interviewing many persons with first-hand knowledge and going through documentary sources. Current President Samuel A. Banks and former President Howard L. Rubendall were most helpful and gave willingly of their time and observations, as did Dr. Horace Rogers, J. Milton Davidson, Charles Coleman Sellers and Jack M. Stover.

Even without the marvels of computer technology, a volume such as this would not be possible without assistance from many people during the course of its preparation for publication. Our special gratitude goes to Dr. Joseph P. Pisciotte, our editor and a welcome source of inspiration and insight. Corinne Pardon of Sam Witwer's law offices made his materials accessible for us and provided administrative support. Robyn A. Bair, Sandy Marler, Barbara Telford, Connie Kennard, Fran Majors and Carol Hoaglan, all of the Hugo Wall Center for Urban Studies of Wichita State University, did the editing, computer work, word processing, copying and indexing that turns words into a manuscript. Daryl and Janet Standifer, Marilyn Rust and Gil Urick of the Graphicshop in Wichita provided the typesetting, layout and design.

Much of the Witwer story is told in journals and proceedings, such as the already mentioned Witwer diary, the *Record of Proceedings of the Sixth Illinois Constitutional Convention,* press reports, transcripts of speeches, correspondence and the like. We have familiarized ourselves with all of this material.

We have known our subject intimately for some years — Edward Gilbreth in the course of his career in journalism, particularly as political editor of the former *Chicago Daily News* and now of the editorial staff of the *Chicago Sun-Times* and Elmer Gertz as chairman of the Bill of Rights Committee at the Sixth Illinois Constitutional Convention over which Witwer presided. This has given us insight not otherwise available. We have tried to restrain the deep feeling of respect and affection for the man and the public figure that has been engendered by our personal contacts with him. We have tried to let the facts speak for themselves — objectively and fairly, without effusiveness.

Of course, we absolve all of our collaborators from responsibility for what we say in this book. We gladly proclaim that it is our book.

ELMER GERTZ
EDWARD S. GILBRETH

CONTENTS

PRELUDE
TO CHANGE

By Joseph P. Pisciotte

It is often said that the measure of a man is in the legacy of his deeds. Perhaps the greatest legacy can be measured in terms of change — social and political change that impacts the lives of many and opens the way for a new order of things. History records such change, often in terms of events and often on a national or global scale. In today's fast moving, high-tech, computerized society, seldom are events recognized as having impact much beyond tomorrow's headlines; even less frequently are events chronicled at the state level — as having a profound and lasting impact on large numbers of people. In this small volume, Elmer Gertz and Edward S. Gilbreth have done just that. Theirs is a book about change and the political role that one individual — Samuel W. Witwer — played in bringing about a new order of things for one state — Illinois.

Illinois is more than simply one of fifty American states. It is rural, urban, industrial, commercial and one of the largest states in the union. It annually battles Iowa for the top position in corn and hog production and challenges other top-ranking states in beef production, meat packing and soybean harvest. It ranks at the top in exports, contains two of the nation's busiest tourist attractions, is part of the Great Lakes waterway shipping system, is recognized as an important banking and finance center, and has a metropolitan center which is known throughout the world.

Geographically, Illinois is located in the center of the nation, midway between the Atlantic and Pacific oceans to the east and west, and almost halfway between the Canadian border to the north and the Mexican border to the south. The state stretches nearly five hundred miles from its northern Illinois-Wisconsin boundary down to its southern tip at Cairo. While Illinois is considered a midwestern state, it begins at a latitude as far north as Boston and extends southward to a point as far south as Newport News-Hampton, Virginia. Its people and social institutions reflect its geographical diversity, and its history and development have been shaped by its geographic location. Illinois has been proclaimed as the best state because it is so American. It is the heartland. Many feel that because of its diversity, its location and its importance, it is a true cross-section of the nation at large. So goes the nation, so goes Illinois; so goes Illinois, so goes the nation.

The framework for change for the authors is a new (1970) constitution for Illinois, replacing its 100 year old document about which the late Professor Kenneth C. Sears, a leading constitutional scholar said, "Illinois, everything considered, is in the worst position of any state in the nation." The "event" on which historians might focus could be several on a continuum: the Sixth Illinois Constitutional Convention itself; the final days during which 116 delegates battled for survival of values, goals and aspirations; approval of the document by the electorate by a substantial margin; or any of dozens of important post-convention dramas that have unfolded in the General Assembly, in the courts or among the voters as a result of the new document. The process goes on; as long as the 1970 constitution remains in effect, it will influence and be involved in the daily lives of millions of Illinois citizens now and for some time to come. Adoption of the 1970 constitution, put in this perspective, makes it the most significant single political event in Illinois in the twentieth century.

Only the final chapter of *Quest for a Constitution* deals specifically with the constitutional convention and its product, but the remainder of the volume, as Sam Witwer's life has been, is a preface to the convention. By reading the last chapter alone, one can learn a great deal about the unique politics of constitutional conventions. They are the only deliberative bodies in the United States which are *de novo*, without a tomorrow, and which involve all the complexities of the society of which they are a part. The authors underscore the extreme difficulties faced by the delegates and Witwer as their president. It had to be with mixed feelings that Witwer gaveled the convention into action, as he knew there would be a time of trial, before triumph could be realized. There would be the traumas of leadership, not only those that accrue to any chief executive, but Witwer's would be exacerbated by the times, the personalities of the delegates, the diversity of the state and the fear of failure. There would be only one index of success or failure — adoption or rejection of a new constitution by the voters. Trial was indeed turned into triumph, and there are lessons to be learned in this volume, not only about successful constitutional revision, but also about political leadership. The importance of such factors as an open convention with full debate and compromise, hard work, adherence to rules and schedules, the responsibility of proposing broad principles rather than statutes and ordinances, and the appointment of balanced and representative committees, to name but a few, are highlighted by the authors as Witwer's prescription for success in the convention itself.

The 1970 Illinois constitution did not simply happen nor did Sam Witwer suddenly appear on the scene. Both are a continuum with a long past involving many direct and indirect activities toward an end goal. The 1870 Illinois constitution had an historical record of numerous revision attempts and as Gertz and Gilbreth relate in Chapter V, revision had been a struggle frequently marked by delay and failure. A wealth of information has been brought together which heretofore ran the risk of being lost to history. Sam Witwer began his involvement in constitution revision some 25 years before the 1969-70 constitutional convention, and as he is quick to emphasize, it has been an involvement shared by a great many people. His was often a role of leadership, but he also had mentors, colleagues, adversaries and detractors. The authors bring it all together, and as such, make yet another contribution to the important literature on constitutional change in Illinois.

Sam Witwer may have begun his formal involvement in constitutional change in 1945 but in many respects he began preparing for his ultimate role much earlier, through many paths and through several regular institutions of our society — family, church, education, law and politics. A reading of this book is to further understand the importance of institutions in one's life, an importance that establishes a strong value scale for the individual, which in turn lays the groundwork for a strong sense of purpose. Sam Witwer excelled in each of these separate institutions that are a part of his life. But the manner in which he blended them is much of what this book is about, and much of which has enabled him to survive in the demanding world of constitutional politics. He is strong willed and tenacious; why else would one stay so involved with one goal in mind — a new state constitution? Witwer, perhaps as much as anyone, must be who the late Chief Justice Arthur Vanderbilt of New Jersey would have had in mind when he observed that "Constitutional reform is no sport for the short-winded." Witwer is opinionated and vocal, but he has taken on a clear understanding of the need to compromise; why else would he push for not the perfect constitution, but the best that was acceptable to the voters. He is a change agent, but he has a deep-seated respect for the law and all its traditions; why else would he push for and be proud of a basic framework of government that is innovative without being revolutionary or radical?

In presenting Witwer's involvement in his family, his school, his church, his political party and his profession, Gertz and Gilbreth have given us an assessment not only of how institutions impact the individual, but also how the individual in turn affects institutions. Institutions are the fabric of society which provide continuity, but which also tend to overshadow the importance of the individual in the grand scheme of things. This is a political biography in which the individual did count. Like Chapters V and VIII, Chapters IV, VI and VII can be read as separate entities and are snapshots of education and of elective partisan politics. Witwer's many years of leadership on the board of trustees of his alma mater remind us that the politics of higher education may well be the most difficult brand of politics. It brings to light the many problems involved in higher education development and all the conflicting pressures that are brought to bear on those problems. Similarly, the church has its own brand of politics and during the course of his many activities, Sam Witwer has experienced them as well.

In 1960, Sam Witwer was the Republican candidate for the United States Senate from Illinois. Chapters VI and VII are separated into campaigns through the primary and general elections, but together they give the full impact the campaigns had on Witwer, and how he dealt with the ups and downs, the rewards and deprivations of high level, partisan and elective politics. By themselves, the chapters are useful to students of Illinois history and government and contribute to further understanding of parties and politics, and campaigns and elections. The chapters are also basic reading for anyone contemplating elective politics, particularly those not well steeped in party politics. By reading these chapters, one is able to get a clear understanding of the euphoria and power (or near power) that accrues to the candidates, but also a painful awareness of the disappointments, loyalties (or disloyalties) that are ever present. For the defeated candidate, one cannot help but think about "what might have been," but in Sam Witwer's case, the campaigns offered him a chance to learn about himself, his relationships with others, and most importantly they prepared him for later political battles, albeit not of the partisan, elective type. The reader also is able to pick up bits of historical serendipity, for example, the events of the evening Witwer spent with Richard M. Nixon, the night before the first of the famous Nixon-Kennedy debates.

Within the recent history of Illinois, there have been many successful lawyers, many successful leaders in higher education, many candidates for higher elective office, many devoted fathers and husbands, and many men who have taken leadership roles in their church. But there is only one person who has combined all those things with long-term, effective leadership in constitutional revision to bring about a new constitution for the state of Illinois.

xviQUEST FOR A CONSTITUTION

That was a feat no one else was able to achieve during 100 years of Illinois history. Granted, Sam Witwer did not accomplish that task by himself, as there are a great many who played highly important roles and without them the total effort could not have been accomplished. Nor can we say unequivocally that ultimate success took place because of or in spite of Sam Witwer. But his specific role in the constitutional convention, together with the other roles he played throughout his life, is what sets him apart from some eleven million other people in Illinois, and one of the more important reasons why this book has been written and published.

The Sixth Illinois Constitutional Convention marked the high point of Witwer's life. In many respects it was his Rubicon; everything that preceded or followed this culminating event was in its shadow. Of course, as the authors point out, he did not cease living or achieving in other areas; indeed he continues to excel in the many institutions that have made up his life's activities. Note for example his work on behalf of the United Methodist Church in the Pacific Homes cases in which he was once again on the cutting edge of establishing new law. There have been weeks and months and years, indeed, in which he fought to have the new constitution understood, adopted, implemented and protected, but the measuring rod remains the successful convention and its work product, as it will no matter what his additional accomplishments. That is understandable, for as Niccolo Machiavelli has written, "there is nothing more difficult to take in hand, more perilous to conduct, or more uncertain in its success, than to take the lead in the introduction of a new order of things." Sam Witwer's legacy, as this book so well chronicles, has been a new order of things in Illinois.

The late Adlai E. Stevenson was descriptive and prophetic in 1949 when he referred to Witwer as "a man who never quits."

TO CLIMB
STEEP HILLS

The distinction blurs between those things that are impossible to change and those that are not impossible, but nearly so. Samuel W. Witwer seems always to have appreciated the difference. He devoted the larger portion of his adult life to an undertaking most of his contemporaries viewed as hopeless. The challenge: To rewrite the basic legal charter of his home state. The Illinois State Constitution was obsolete, it was replete with inequities, it fostered a multitude of legal contrivances to circumvent its rigid barriers. As such, the document spawned widespread contempt for the state's legal framework. Despite its horrors (shortcomings is too soft a description), few Illinois leaders believed it possible to amass popular approval of a new Constitution. Sam Witwer was among those who believed it *was* possible.

There are no heroics of the chest-thumping, epic scale in the story of Witwer's accomplishment. His success in getting the Constitution rewritten — after a century of dormancy and failures at revision — represents the sum of thousands of days, hundreds of meetings, scores of arguments, articles and speeches in which Witwer painstakingly and relentlessly built a consensus for change. The struggle persisted for decades. It tested Witwer's stamina and dedication more severely than any other battle in politics or education where Witwer left indelible marks.

Persistence emerges as the most dominant personality trait from a study of Witwer's life. Some might call the quality stubbornness; a few, bull-headedness. Whatever its characteriza-tion, the trait weaves through the Witwer story and gives it an even texture. As a boy, adolescent or adult, Witwer, once fixed on a goal, would not quit. The lad who brazenly confronted his church elders and demanded that he be admitted to full membership despite not having reached the minimum age; the youth who trekked back to Harvard with only a fistful of dollars, lacking tuition fee, unsure of lodging and with no prospect of work — only a grim determination to complete his final year of law school and get his degree; the alumnus who wrestled with the forces of reaction to trigger a monumental turnabout in the direction of his two-hundred-year old undergraduate school; the political neophyte who fought to unseat a United States Senator revered by many as an idol — this was the same individual who developed a virtual obsession with constitutional reform in Illinois. Sam Witwer did not "develop" into the person capable of winning that battle for reform; he had always been that person. His was the genetic and environmental blend that was to produce, in the cliche of historical hindsighters, "the right man at the right time at the right place."

Of course, Witwer did not spring full-blown onto the Illinois landscape to rescue the state from the legal dark ages. The lasting achievement crowned an accumulation of successes, some more ephemeral than others. As Shakespeare wrote in *Henry VIII*, "To climb steep hills requires slow pace at first." But each achievement is tied to the one that preceded it, and to the one that followed, as tightly as links on a chain.

Witwer's personality and inherent capacity for work fueled his productivity far more than did qualities of character, although all combined to make up the intricate individual. The point is, men or women just as "good" as Sam Witwer have existed, do exist and will exist through eternity. Yet many of them, attempting the same struggles Witwer undertook, would have faltered, or did falter. Witwer persevered. He achieved significance not for who he was, but for what he did. As one of his sons remarked to him in later life, his offspring derived pride from their father's emphasis on accomplishment, not on self-aggrandizement.

Is there a value to chronicling the life of a man like Sam Witwer? The authors of this biography believe there is, emphatically so. His was not a name that became a household word, but he was foremost among those who crafted dramatic change in hundreds of local governments affecting the lives of millions of Illinoisans for generations to come. He did not win bold headlines in national scandal sheets for eccentric behavior — a formula for riches that fascinated 20th Century readers. There is no sensual titillation in the Witwer saga. But his life encompassed more meaningful experience than that confronted by glamorous, "jet-set" denizens or those figures of notoriety whose fame flashes as briefly as a meteor.

Yes, there is an intrinsic value to tracing the roots of a Sam Witwer, reviewing the highlights of a life responsible for remarkable change in our and future times. He was a proud man, an intensely private man. Above all, he was dogged in his pursuit of an objective. Persistent. Stubborn. And, yes, sometimes a little bull-headed.

This then becomes the story of an individual obsessed with one overriding ambition, an obsession he wouldn't shake until he had triumphed. We hope a reader may infer from this story how that obsession shaped his life and continues to affect countless other lives.

Stripped of its diversions and trappings, this is the story of a man who wouldn't quit — Samuel W. Witwer.

A TALE
OF
TWO CITIES

In its early years, Gary was an immensely exciting place to live. The town was in social ferment. With the huge influx of steelworkers, it was a veritable 'melting pot'.... When we moved to Cumberland (Md.) in 1921, we entered a social milieu far different. The town was divided between a small number of persons who considered themselves 'old family' and those who had to work hard for a living in the railroads, steel mills and mines. It was a charming, sleepy Southern-like town which watched the years come and go.

— Samuel W. Witwer
1979

I t is rare that a man, rummaging among the years and anecdotes that form the aggregate of his life, can pluck from memory one incident that permanently shaped his personality. But, Sam Witwer could do so. With the certainty that comes from full confidence in one's ability to be objectively introspective, Witwer pinpointed one morning in the fall of 1930, when he as a graduate student in law at Harvard underwent a crushing humiliation.

Young Sam was seated in a huge lecture hall in the company of more than 200 other students. They were listening to Dean Roscoe Pound, a legendary expert in American Jurisprudence, then teaching criminal law. It was their second or third lecture from

Dean Pound, and the students were familiar with his habit of consulting a chart with little squares that showed where each student was seated. When he wished to pose a question, the lecturer would stab at the chart with a forefinger and call out a name.

Under discussion this morning was an introductory book on law, by Edmund Morgan, which had been sent to students even before their arrival at Cambridge. Witwer, "feeling totally frightened" by Pound's intimidating style, sat in one of the last few rows of the lecture room in Langdell Hall, hoping to avoid attention yet all too aware there was no safe refuge.

Suddenly, he heard Dean Pound bellow out his name, "Witwer!" Sam snapped to attention. "Mr. Witwer," Pound repeated, "will you please state the facts in the case of the People versus Brown?"

"I don't recall whether that was the actual name of the case," Witwer said in recalling the incident, "but it was something like that. Well, I had read it. I got up with fear and trembling, my voice a little husky, and I started out.

"In this case," Sam answered Pound, "the declaration charged manslaughter — "

"Wait a minute, Mr. Witwer," Dean Pound interrupted. The class grew quiet. Pound said, "You may start over again."

Believing Pound hadn't been able to hear him, Sam raised the volume of his voice, "In this case, the declaration charged manslaughter, the facts being . . ."

"Stop!" Witwer stopped. "That's what I thought I heard you say the first time, Mr. Witwer. And would you like one more chance?"

Sam looked around him. He saw, or imagined he saw, more sophisticated classmates smirking, relishing the embarrassment of a newcomer who might be among the first to fall victim to Harvard's tough regimen. Witwer started reciting once again, this time almost shouting to be heard.

This time there was no mistaking the snickers and giggling from fellow students. Sam's obvious discomfort fueled their mirth. Pound raised a palm and cut Witwer off from continuing his recitation. "It is very evident to me" Pound said, looking with unblinking eye at Witwer, "that you have not read Professor Morgan's *Introduction to the Law* or you would not have recited as you have recited in this class this morning."

Sam made a final attempt to rescue himself, "Well, I beg your pardon, sir, but I have read it and I think I understand the facts of that case."

Pound looked away, his eyes searching for no target but roaming the walls or ceiling in the manner of persons accustomed to forcing others to gaze upon them without their having to return the honor. "It is very clear to me that if you understand that case, you understand something that legal scholars such as myself do not understand about that case," said Pound. Sam slunk into his seat, a noiseless movement that quickly caught Pound's notice. "I have not asked you to be seated. Please stand up." Sam slowly rose. He listened with unrelieved dread as Dean Pound confronted the class and made the speech he intended to make even before selecting the student to serve as his prop. Pound said:

> I want to make a statement to all of you, including Mr. Witwer, that Harvard Law School will not accept this kind of careless expression. It's quite evident that Mr. Witwer hasn't seen the point yet, that in the common law, the 'declaration' is the form that is used in *civil* proceedings, to launch civil proceedings, *not criminal proceedings.* He should have said 'indictment,' or I would have accepted 'complaint,' or 'information.' But he said none of these. It is very evident to me, Mr. Witwer, that if you are going to remain in Harvard Law School, you will not be able to perform as you have performed this morning.

After the class, Sam approached Dean Pound and expressed anger at the way he had been treated. Sam had heard that Harvard did not require students to recite in class, so he asked Dean Pound to remove the name of "Witwer" from his seating chart. Hereafter, the chastened student said, he wanted to be judged on his written examinations. "That will be your privilege," Pound told the student, "and (your grade) will not be prejudiced for having asked me to do that." As it turned out, months later, it was not.

It was not until months or years later that Witwer realized his experience was not unique; Harvard was known for its stern treatment of green law students as part of the ripening process. A movie and television series nearly half a century later ("The Paper Chase") dramatized this aspect of life at Harvard. The immediate effect of the treatment on Witwer, however, was to devastate him.

"From that point on, I made up my mind I wasn't going to waste my time 'outfielding.' We had certain students we called the outfielders, who wanted to get into the give and take of debate with their hands up continuously. But because I had been so thoroughly hassled, and this had hit me so hard, I became very introverted. In the three years I was at Harvard Law School, I doubt whether I spoke in classes more than half a dozen times in all courses combined."

Witwer grew more and more unwilling to stand and speak. "I would choke up, I would freeze," he said. He developed a personality the exact opposite of the fun-loving extrovert he had been in high school and undergraduate school. Some new acquaintances regarded him as stuffy, aloof. Throughout his life, when Witwer would overhear these or similar assessments of his personality, "I would trace it all back to Harvard, to that one day, that one professor."

In some ways it was odd that Witwer found his first clash with a professor such a shattering experience, because his first 22 years had not been sheltered. His emerging personality and character were being molded by social movements that were sometimes stormy, and he had seen first-hand the misery and indignity that accompanied class warfare and economic upheaval. Yet, for all of his experiences as a child and adolescent, Sam Witwer was nurtured by a close-knit family life which sustained him far more than he appreciated at the time.

Samuel W. Witwer's career as a lawyer, churchman, politician and constitutional expert developed after his Harvard years. What came before Harvard were thousands and thousands of experiences, most forgotten a few days later, that opened the way to adulthood. This chapter will concern itself with some of those experiences, for whatever illumination they shed on the personality and character of the man who emerged as an influential and persevering figure in the politics of his region, the development of constitutional reform, and the preservation of one of the nation's most respected Colonial era educational institutions.

Those experiences had as their backdrop the cities of Gary, Indiana and Cumberland, Maryland — communities as stark in contrast as any that might be compared between the sooty, industrial North and the leisurely Southland of privilege and tradition.

The Witwers were among the first settlers of Gary. They came to the new-born steel city in 1909, a year of economic panic that left Witwer's father jobless in Pueblo, Colorado. The senior Witwer and his wife sent their two oldest children to their maternal grand-father's farm in Pennsylvania while the couple took their three youngest — Marguerite, 9, Kathryn, 5, and Sam, 1 — to the fledgling industrial region at the southern tip of Lake Michigan. Their father, descendant of a Swiss immigrant in the 1700s, had started out trying to support a family by teaching in a one-room schoolhouse in Pennsylvania. As his family grew, he went into the steel industry, first as a "cinder snapper" (one who removes heavy formations of cinders from open-hearth furnaces), then progressed to open-hearth door puller and finally into supervisory ranks. He left Lukens Steel Company in Coatesville, Pennsylvania to join the Colorado Fuel & Iron Company in Pueblo, then headed for the Calumet Region when word spread that there might be jobs open at the Gary Works of U.S. Steel Corp., a huge plant on which construction had started only three years earlier.

The job-seeker, his wife and the three children arrived in Chicago en route from Pueblo to Gary. Exhausted from their travel, Mrs. Witwer and the youngsters were left seated in the old Polk Street Station, south of Chicago's Loop, while Witwer Sr. completed the last short leg of the trip to Gary. He had not wanted to inconvenience his family by taking them to Gary if there was no work to be found there; he also needed to save the pennies and nickels their commuter fares would have cost.

The vignette of a young mother and three youngsters huddled in a train station in a strange city, with meager finances and no assurance of where their next home would be, as later recounted by his mother, etched itself in Witwer's consciousness. In later years he recalled that scene with ironic relish because of the success all three children attained. From this most humble of beginnings on their first visit to Illinois, Sam was to carve a more lasting niche in the legal structure of the state than few of his contemporaries; Kathryn was to achieve fame in the world of opera, appearing with such stars as Mary Garden and Ezio Pinza at the Chicago Civic Opera; and Marguerite became a concert pianist, founded the Maryland State Federation of Music Clubs, and became one of that state's leading figures in the cultural arts, remaining active well into her 80s.

Twenty hours after having been left in the Polk Street Station, the family was rejoined by the senior Witwer, who bore the welcome news that he had secured a job working the open hearths at U.S. Steel.

They traveled to Gary buoyant and optimistic. As the train neared the city, the Witwers felt as though they were entering a Western frontier town. The train snaked its way through rows of shanties, tents and lean-to saloons. The train deposited the Witwers at a make-shift depot, a converted boxcar. There, Mrs. Witwer and the youngsters sat once again for long hours while Witwer scouted for temporary lodging. He found it in one of the many rooming houses that had sprung up to accommodate the hundreds of newcomers pouring into Gary each month seeking work.

The Witwers later moved into the first structure ever built in Gary. It was an old frame structure at the site where the South Shore Railroad later was to build a station on Broadway near Fifth Avenue. The building originally housed the first Gary Land Company office, and the city's first post office. In 1914, U.S. Steel relocated the building on the 500 block of Jefferson Street, and Witwer's father purchased it from the land company to convert into a family residence. (More that half a century later the building was still standing, delapidated and crumbling, in a city park near Broadway and Fourth Avenue, where it had been relocated by its later owner, the Gary Historical Society.)

Samuel W. Witwer, Jr. went through boyhood during the decade following the move to Gary. As his father advanced in the management of U.S. Steel, the son absorbed the flavor of life in a steel town. Sam's father was management-minded, but neither the father nor son were blind to some of the injustices of a giant corporation that was developing an economic stranglehold on the community. At the same time, Sam, Jr. was repelled by the violence stirred by union zealots in their efforts to organize the industry. He deplored the "cruel excesses" on both sides.

Next door to the Witwers lived a family with revolutionary politics. They displayed a red flag during labor demonstrations and expressed their sentiments loudly on the sidewalk in front of the Witwer home. During a prolonged strike, Witwer's father was confined to the plant, living there with other supervisory personnel. When he ventured outside the plant once to attend a meeting at the home of the general manager, he escaped a kidnapping attempt by several union leaders. Another time, Sam, Jr. was awakened when strikers tried to break into the Witwer home to snatch Sam, Sr. on a night he stole home to visit his family.

At one point violence was so rampant Army troops were brought in to keep the peace. General Leonard Wood visited the troops in Gary highlighting the importance authorities attached to preventing civil unrest.

Troops were quartered in the local YMCA and other buildings near the Witwer house, and Sam, Jr. spent many meal hours listening to soldiers swap tales at their canteens.

Sam, Jr. appreciated the other side to the labor conflict. "My father's hours were long and exhausting," he recalled. "There were very few occasions when I was able to spend any time with him. He left early in the morning, worked a long day shift — it was 10 or 12 hours a day then — and got back after dark. When he worked the night shift, he would come home from the open hearths totally exhausted in the morning, sleep through the day, and be back at work before my return from school in the late afternoon. It wasn't until 1918 that the steel industry adopted the eight-hour day.

"From what I saw, on both the management and union sides, I came to have less than total respect for either of the contending forces. Management was guilty of cruel excesses. So were the unions. I suspect my position as a 'liberal Republican' in later years was influenced by those experiences."

Witwer suspected his moderate position on labor-management relations and other social issues hurt him when he ran for public office in 1960. "My balanced position did not make me overly attractive either to the hard-core political or financial forces whose help I so badly needed to win," Witwer said. "Nor was I acceptable to the so-called 'liberal' independents."

There were a few advantages to the paternalism of a one-industry town, however. One was the erection of a magnificent Gothic structure at Washington and Sixth Avenue, a Methodist Episcopal church whose construction was financed by huge sums from U.S. Steel. Sam, Jr.'s mother, Lulu Richmond Witwer, descended from German stock among early Pennsylvania settlers, was deeply religious and led her children into an early exposure to Methodism. Her mother and grandmother had been Mennonites and had worn the quaint bonnets familiar to their austere culture. Mrs. Witwer frequently reminded her son that the name Samuel, as explained in the Bible, meant "called of God," a sign that young Sam might tend to a career in the ministry.

Mrs. Witwer also displayed strong ambition for the education of her children, perhaps too aware that she herself had not been able to get all the education she desired, although she had attended Linden Hall, founded by the Moravians, and said to be the oldest female formal seminary in the country; also, the Cincinnati Conservatory of Music. She was determined that her children's schooling, at least through high school, would be uninterrupted. She hoped, of course, they would be able to go on to higher education. Universal education was a concept still young in the United States, an experiment not fully launched until the turn of the century. At the time Sam, Jr. entered first grade, most youngsters dropped out of school before completing the fifth grade. At the time he entered high school, in most urbanized areas of the country, fewer than half of the freshman finished their senior year. The rapid rise of organized labor led to the compulsory school attendance laws, with minimum ages set for being able to drop out; this was a device to keep youths from flooding the labor market.

In Gary, Sam, Jr. attended the city's first public school, Jefferson. He was taught under the so-called William Wirt system, named after an innovator in public education who stressed not only the traditional academic disciplines, but also vocational trade courses. Wirt became a highly controversial figure in the opening days of Roosevelt's New Deal.

At the age of 11, Sam began selling newspapers at the gates of the Broadway entrance to the Gary Works. It was a newsboy's best spot for sales anywhere in Gary, and Sam had to fight some tough youngsters to hold his location. Hawking copies of the *Gary Post-Tribune* for four years, Sam was able to save money for his first year of college tuition. At 14, he got a job as an errand runner for the newspaper and developed a fascination for newsroom lore.

By the time he entered his teens, Sam was becoming disenchanted with Gary. When Elbert Gary, as chairman of U.S. Steel, initially planned the city, widespread hopes had emerged for cultivation of a prosperous, socially responsible community teaming with the fine arts and free from the evils of corporate control epitomized by many coal towns of the Southeast and Midwest. By 1920, as Gary's population soared over 55,000, it was evident this dream was to remain illusory. The U.S. Supreme Court, in outlawing the "company town" that had been Pullman City, Ill., only 20-some miles west of Gary, prevented U.S. Steel from developing company-owned stores, libraries and pre-empting other commercial and public functions. But the influence of Big Steel was all-pervasive nonetheless. Gary politicians became increasingly corrupt, tawdry and cheap. (In the decade after the Witwers left Gary, the city was so corrupt that its voters re-elected a mayor who had been sent to prison on a Prohibition-related conviction.) At the same time, the street murder of a Gary schoolteacher so enraged the voters that leaders of organized crime, fearful that the outrage would spawn a "reform" movement, publicly offered a $5,000 reward for apprehending her killer. There probably was no city in the country so brazenly corrupt in the 1920s, unless it was Gary's big brother across the southern tip of the lake, Chicago.

The Witwers moved to Cumberland, Md. in 1921. Sam, Sr. accepted a post as superintendent of a steel mill in this town that had been an old Colonial outpost during the French-Indian War. The Witwers moved into an 18-room Victorian house, built shortly after the Civil War, that was nestled within the stockade boundaries of old Fort Cumberland. This fort had provided a refuge for George Washington fleeing the Redcoats during a skirmish preceding the Revolutionary War when the British General Braddock was ambushed and killed at nearby Fort Necessity.

Sam, Jr. quickly fell victim to Cumberland's Old World charm. The town, center of the Western Maryland bituminous coal fields, offered magnificent surroundings for an inquisitive youth to explore. Sam enjoyed trips into the nearby mountains, strolling along the Chesapeake & Ohio canal and the Potomac River. He frequently visited a "Lover's Leap" precipice under which passed Wills Creek and the Baltimore & Ohio Railroad as the opening to the West. He listened often to retellings of an Indian legend about a young brave and his beloved who jumped from the high cliff because their families, from opposing tribes, would not let them wed. Sam pondered the universality of the Romeo and Juliet saga.

Sam plunged into activities at Allegany County High School with an extrovert's zeal. He joined the debate team, played soccer, sang the baritone lead in several Victor Herbert operettas, and enjoyed such popularity among his peers that he was elected class president. He graduated with honors. "At that time, you would not have known me," Witwer said half a century later. "Strangely enough, those activities should have made me far less 'stuffy' than I am perceived to be. But I'm sure the change set in during my first days at Harvard Law."

Those were extraordinarily happy days for Sam. Yet, the stirrings of a social conscience that began in Gary continued to bother him in Cumberland. Because of his father's executive status, Sam and his family were embraced by Cumberland's "establishment," the ruling elite, of which some claimed blood ties to illustrious Confederate family names. But Sam did not appreciate the rigid class structure.

"It simply did not appeal to me in terms of its exaggerated social status," Witwer said. "Small towns like Cumberland have their Four Hundred. If anything, I believe that my Middle West democratic background steeled me against these blandishments, even though my new-found friends were rather intrigued by my background. There was much about Cumberland that caused young men to think a lot about the kind of world in which they lived. At least I did. By the time I completed high school, I was pretty actively involved in youth work at our Centre Street Methodist Church. I had come to feel greatly privileged and enriched in my pre-college years."

Sam's church-related activity refueled speculation he might enter the ministry. During his last year in high school, he attended a boys' conference at Annapolis held in conjunction with the Baltimore Annual Conference of the Methodist Episcopal Church. "Under the influence of a good deal of old-fashioned camp-meeting religion, I came close to deciding upon the ministry," Witwer said. He refrained from making an immediate commitment, he said, because he resented some last-minute pressure on him from church leaders. Sam was becoming his own decision-maker; he did not bow easily to pressure. A few years later, when he was a college student, local elders renewed the pressure. Witwer was offered a small parish in a country town near Carlisle and the use of a Model-T Ford to drive between the campus and his congregation. This time, Witwer did not delay making a firm commitment. He simply said no. He never again came close to the ministry as a profession, but he has always had great admiration for men of the cloth.

"At times I reflect on the kind of minister I might have made," Witwer said. "I suspect my middle-of-the-road posture — the same attitude that inhibited my success in politics — would likewise have gotten in the way there. I doubt that I could have accepted and preached in accordance with the 'accepted' word, the discipline and committed views expected to be held by the ministry."

An incident at church during his childhood in Gary may have foreshadowed Witwer's leanings toward procedural matters (law) rather than religion. When he was no older than seven, the Methodist church in Gary completed construction of its new building, and the Methodist bishop in Chicago was invited to join the congregation for its first services in the new church. The local minister, preceding each sermon, was in the habit of stopping at the altar and kneeling in prayer for a few minutes. It was natural that young Sam viewed this ritual as a necessary preamble to the rest of the service.

When the bishop arrived, however, the local minister accompanied him down the aisle and onto the elevated level behind the altar without either kneeling to pray. This disturbed Sam, seated alone in a pew (his mother watched from the choir, and his father was at work in the mills). How could the services go on, Sam reasoned, without the preliminary kneeling?

At some point early in the services, Sam rose and walked down the aisle toward the altar. Sam motioned to the minister to approach him; the minister did, and Sam whispered his misgivings about the procedure into the minister's ear. The clergyman smiled, retreated a few steps to where the bishop sat, and shared Sam's thoughts with the prominent churchman. Sam returned to his seat while the congregation buzzed in puzzlement about his behavior.

Later, when the bishop rose to address the congregation, he said, "Apparently you have a practice here in which the minister kneels to pray before the services begin," he said. "I want you to know that your minister and I prayed together earlier this morning, and that is why we proceeded directly into the services rather than kneeling after we entered." The bishop paused, then went on, "It did not escape the notice of one of your young men that we did not pray on entering." All eyes turned toward Sam. "I trust now we have assured him," the minister said. Sam leaned back, assured that now, everything was "legal."

Witwer accepted his religion as an article of faith. He felt enough intellectual freedom as a faithful practitioner, but he questioned his patience for subjecting these views to the scrutiny he felt would be necessary if he were to accept a calling to the ministry. Witwer's religion was an anchor that bound him to ethical and spiritual moorings. It sustained him through grief and occasional unhappiness. If offered him not only comfort, but also spiritual elation at the concept of union with the Deity. Beyond that, Witwer did not go. He did not dwell on whatever doubts arose. He was content with an unshakable belief in the Prime Cause, and he would not debate whatever trappings organized religion added to that bedrock. Deciding against the ministry was probably the most serious decision of Witwer's early manhood. He became a more dutiful layman for having come to grips with that decision, intellectually and emotionally.

During summers in the mid-1920s, Witwer worked for a while in a railway labor gang for the princely sum of 35 cents an hour. He worked 10 hours a day as a grease-monkey in the roundhouse of the Western Maryland Railroad Company some 20 miles from Cumberland in West Virginia. As a grease-monkey, he squirmed underneath steam engines in the roundhouse and packed hard grease into the couplings of axles and journal boxes. With passenger engines, he had to climb on top of the engines and shine to lustrous brilliance the metal steel casings that surrounded the cylindrical boilers. When he performed these chores, the engines were still heated from steam pressure ready to make their runs to Baltimore.

Once his grease-soaked overalls caught fire when he was working in the pit under an engine. Another time, a steam valve blew off, knocking Witwer from atop a passenger engine. He broke the fall by grabbing a hot steam pipe. "Those experiences taught me patience and stubborn commitment," Witwer remembered. "Many times I wanted to quit outright, but my pride would not permit me." These summers strengthened what was to become one of Witwer's most dominant traits — the refusal to accept easy defeat, the adamant reluctance to quit, for whatever reason. Once he embarked on a course, Witwer would be unwavering.

If he acquired strength and forebearance from his father ("He worked extremely hard all his life, but he never believed the world owed him anything") and if he developed moral principles through the religious training of his mother, it remained for another family member to acquaint Witwer with the depth of familial devotion that can exist only between kindred spirits. It is no disparagement of Witwer's love for others in his family to relate the depth of his affection for his older sister, Kathryn. This was partly because Sam saw much less of the elder Marguerite during their childhood, although the ties between Sam and Marguerite deepened in later years after Marguerite was established as a distinguished pianist in Maryland.

Sam and Kathryn, born four years apart, grew up as playmates in Gary. They shared the family love for music — in Kathryn's case, a passion for music. Sam felt enormous pride in her growing accomplishments as a singer. At the age of four, Kathryn was taken by a grandmother to hear Emma Calve in "Carmen."

"From that night on," Kathryn told an interviewer many years later, "playing opera singer was more important to me than playing dolls." She began winning local music competitions.

She learned to play the violin and piano while still a child and began studying voice after graduating from Emerson High in Gary. She worked as a Chicago secretary to help pay for her singing lessons. When she was 21, she competed with more than a hundred singers in a national contest in Chicago and won selection as the leading American amateur soprano. The following year, when the rest of her family moved to Cumberland, Kathryn remained in Chicago to pursue her career.

The year 1926 was a pivotal one for Sam and Kathryn. The brother, through a series of coincidences, settled on Dickinson in Carlisle, Pa. as the college of his choice. In September he arrived in Carlisle aboard the old Cumberland Valley Railway, which chugged up the main street in the center of town, and "fell in love with the place almost immediately." Toting a large, heavy suitcase, he trudged along the campus wall three blocks west to Old Conway Hall, where he was to share a modest room in the resident hall's second floor with Harold Bigley, a student from Clearfield, Pa. After outliving a few months of homesickness, he began taking part in campus high-jinks with a relish. It was the beginning of a life-long love affair between Sam and Dickinson. At virtually the same time, Kathryn made her professional debut with the Chicago Symphony Orchestra, setting in motion a career that was to estabish her for the next 15 years as a star of opera, radio, symphony and oratorio work.

During Sam's sophomore year at Dickinson, Kathryn made her operatic debut (ironically, in "Carmen") with the Chicago Grand Opera Company. "It seemed almost like being a modern Cinderella — to be on the stage with Mary Garden — the thrill of it all!" she said after the debut in Chicago's historic Auditorium. The next year (her brother's junior year at Dickinson) Kathryn became the beneficiary of a fund-raising concert staged by business and political leaders of Gary. The "Witwer Day" concert, featuring Kathryn in a recital of her favorite arias, opened Gary's new Municipal Auditorium; its official purpose was to raise funds for Gary's "hometown girl" to study music abroad and to gain experience in operatic repertoire.

The tribute to the young soprano was covered by newspapers from around the country. A front-page story in the *Christian Science Monitor* recounted how the mayor and 200 band members from Gary's public schools greeted Kathryn at the train station to escort her to the auditorium. "About 2,200 persons came to hear and help," the *Monitor* reported. "Miss Witwer fully repaid them. She looked and sang like the prima donna they all wanted her to be. Scarcely more than 21 years ago the site of this great steel city of 100,000 people was nothing but oak and sand. The intervening years had been filled mainly with the struggle to take root. But with this bit of giving (for Kathryn), Gary feels today it has come of age."

The euphoria wore off in the weeks that followed. In letters from home, Sam learned of mysterious "delays" by local politicians in relaying proceeds of the recital to his sister. The Witwers began to suspect the tribute was a fraud to enrich the promoters and Gary's crooked politicians. The *Chicago Tribune*, getting wind of the incipient scandal, contacted the Gary business and political leaders among the tribute's co-sponsors, and threatened full-fledged exposure unless the funds were handed over to Miss Witwer.

The Gary promoters scraped together about $3,000 (a small fraction of what Kathryn actually needed for study abroad) and turned it over. This seed money sent Kathryn on her way to Salzburg. The *New York Times* covered her departure with a photograph and caption that read, "The adopted daughter of Gary, Ind., Miss Kathryn Witwer, who made her debut with the Chicago Civic Opera last winter, sails on the *Olympic* to study music abroad at the expense of her home town." The scandal thus was neatly camouflaged.

The senior Witwers by this time had returned to Gary. The father found himself unemployed once again when the steel mill in Cumberland went out of business. After Sam, Jr. became relatively self-sufficient at Dickinson, his father came back to the Calumet Region to become a consultant for the Hunt Company, an engineering firm that sought advice on the quality of steel rail heats designed for the making of rails. The family found it necessary to help support Kathryn's continuing musical education in Paris, so Sam, Jr. discovered ways to supplement his own income at Dickinson.

A member of Sigma Chi fraternity at the college, Sam waited tables and washed dishes at the fraternity house, and he worked several nights a week as an assistant librarian in the college library.

Before long Sam devised more ingenious methods of raising revenue. He and a fraternity brother, William Graden, rented a horse and wagon at the beginning of one school year and decided they could make a small bundle hauling students' trunks from the railroad station to the men's dormitories. "As it turned out, the work was enormously heavy," Witwer recalled. "There were no elevators in any of the dorm buildings, and the trunks we hauled generally were loaded with heavy possessions, including textbooks." Near the end of their first day in business (charging 50 cents per trunk), and after hauling scores of trunks, Sam and his business partner were confronted by Carlisle police and accused of operating a moving and drayage business without a license. They were escorted to the local police station, held in custody for several hours, and finally released after promising to never again go into business without a license.

Sam's four years at Dickinson combined study, part-time work, serving as manager of the school's football team (which scored the worst record in its history in Sam's time, losing to Army, 89-7), serving as managing editor of the campus newspaper, and a year as president of his fraternity chapter. There was time, also, for the usual campus merriment — street fights between freshmen and sophomores, tugs-of-war across Letort Creek (Sam dragged one leg across rocks on the floor of the creek and permanently scarred the leg) and general horseplay. Sam was a good student but not a top scholar — a fact that disturbed him in later years, when he expressed regret at narrowly missing out on becoming a Phi Beta Kappa.

Witwer's grades, on record in Dickinson's archives, show he attained a four-year average of 82.87, which he later learned was one point less than the qualifying level for the lowest Phi Beta Kappa the year he graduated. His grades generally dipped in his sophomore year (when he scored an average of 79), which was no accident. Witwer was elected an officer of his sophomore class and took very seriously his responsibilities for disciplining and hazing the freshmen. By the time he was a senior, Witwer was getting his best marks, finishing fourth year with an average of 86.48. Interestingly, Witwer had no recollection whatever of taking trigonometry, the course he scored highest in with a grade of 95. He also got excellent grades in English rhetoric, psychology and philosophy. His worst subject was freshman French in which he scored 70.

Witwer received no high honor or award at his commencement in 1930, but the graduate derived great pride at the appearance of his famous sister to sing during the ceremonies. By this time Kathryn had returned from Paris (too early, by her own reckoning, but dwindling finances demanded it) and she was receiving national publicity with weekly appearances on a musical variety program carried by the old Mutual Radio Network. "She sang beautifully at Commencement," Witwer recalled, "much to the pleasure of the faculty and my classmates." And to the profound pleasure of her brother.

There was a near-tragic footnote to Kathryn's appearance at Dickinson. A few days later, Sam joined her nationally known accompanist, Henry Jackson, for the drive home to Gary. The old Ford they jointly purchased (to save money that would have been spent on rail transportation) spun out of control on a mountain road near Hagerstown, Md. The jalopy rolled over several times. Neither occupant was hurt, although both were deeply shaken. Witwer remembered, like a short snippet of a movie, the first thing he saw after the shock of the accident began to wear off. It was the sight of his companion, the pianist, flexing his fingers to see if any were broken. It was one of those vivid scenes remembered through life.

Witwer had chosen Dickinson for his undergraduate work for several reasons. His uncle Albert had attended the school and graduated around 1900, leaving a yearbook that Witwer found many years later while a boy in Gary, which whetted his interest. After the Witwers had moved to Cumberland, Sam's father returned home from a church men's club meeting one night and casually mentioned having heard an appeal to support a Dickinson fund drive. After his father became an active solicitor in behalf of the school, young Witwer decided to attend that college. He had a cousin, a son of his uncle Albert, who was graduating from Dickinson the year Sam planned to enroll. His cousin encouraged Sam to join Sigma Chi, which Sam did. "At the time it seemed like the most natural thing in the world that I would go to Dickinson," Witwer said, "but the conscious decision to do so had to be the result of all these family influences. No one ever 'pressured' me to do it. It just happened — for which I've always been grateful."

There was a great deal more methodology to Witwer's decision to attend Harvard Law. He wanted to attend either Harvard or Yale and applied to both. Surprisingly, he was accepted by both; Yale, the most selective of the schools, at that time admitted only about 125 students a year, while Harvard took in more than 700. Witwer knew that Yale had tough admission standards but was not known as unduly harsh in its demands of students once there. Harvard, on the other hand, was known for a rigorous weeding out of first- and second-year law students. The challenge of Harvard appealed to Witwer.

"Why are you going up there (to Harvard), Mr. Witwer?" he was asked by a Dean of Women at Dickinson. "Don't you know that everyone who has gone to Harvard Law School from here has flunked for the past seven years?"

Witwer was intimidated, but not persuaded to quit his plans for Harvard. Witwer never wanted to give up. But there were times when he doubted his decision. "I arrived up there, much to my discomfort, to see all of the newcomers twirling Phi Beta Kappa keys, speaking in very sophisticated fashion, and I had this great sense of being just essentially a small-town boy," Witwer said. Thus was the stage set for his humiliation in Dean Pound's class during his first week at Cambridge.

While at Harvard, Witwer lived in a little rooming house near Massachusetts Avenue and ate his meals in a restaurant on that street until his last year, when lack of funds forced him to make most of his own meals. His student life was Spartan. He studied 10 to 14 hours a day, had no regular social life, and dated only occasionally. He found it a grueling exercise in self-discipline. "It was a grind, grind, grind," Witwer said, with "very little joy or lightness."

Added to this was the constant search for school funds. Witwer was able to finance his first two years at Harvard with loans from relatives and fraternal groups, but his third year threatened to be one of outright poverty. The year 1933 was the most severe year of the Great Depression, and Witwer worked that summer at a Studebaker garage in Gary with the understanding that its owner would loan him funds for his third year at law school.

Three weeks before the start of the fall term, the owner called in Witwer and confessed that because auto sales had been so poor, he lacked the money to help Sam. "I just can't do it," he told Sam, who readily understood the economic devastation that gripped the entire country. Even his family was hurting.

"All I had to my name was $27.50," Witwer said, "but I was determined to get back to Harvard within the next ten days. He got as far east as Pittsburgh by purchasing for 50 cents a $7 excursion ticket from a Pennsylvanian who came to Gary and extended his visit beyond the period allowed by the round-trip ticket. In Pittsburgh he invested $3.50 in a bus ticket to New York City, where he looked up Ed Kohnstamm, a classmate from Dickinson. His family lived in well-to-do quarters on Park Avenue, and since the rest of the family was abroad, Ed invited Sam to recover from his trip at their residence and get a few good meals before continuing the trek to Harvard.

Renourished, Witwer arrived in Cambridge and scoured the community to find a job waiting tables or washing dishes. There was no work available. He trudged to his rooming house to tell its owners, Mr. and Mrs. Louis Conant that he wouldn't be able to afford staying at their house.

"Mr. Witwer, you can keep your room," Mrs. Conant told him. "Even if we have to wait until you get out of law school and start to practice before you repay us, that'll be all right with Louie and me. Won't it, Louie?" Her husband, a semi-retired New Englander, as sentimental as his wife, piped up, "Yes, yes, certainly." The couple, who slept until after 10 each morning, also told Witwer he could use their kitchen each morning for breakfast. This kindness encouraged Witwer to redouble his efforts to stay at Harvard, although he still lacked funds for tuition.

His third day back at Cambridge, Witwer received a letter, forwarded from Gary, that had been written to him by Professor Mortimer B. Campbell, the dean of Witwer's third-year class. "Dear Mr. Witwer," the letter began, "I am pleased to advise you that because of the excellence of your work during the past years, you have been awarded a faculty scholarship that will pay your full tuition. However, if you do not need this, please allow the funds to be loaned to a student in need."

Witwer read the letter with disbelief. Then he hastened to Campbell's office and exclaimed, "Do I need it?!" Witwer excitedly told Campbell the story of his fragmented return to Cambridge and his barren finances. "My Lord," Campbell said, "if you want to complete your last year at Harvard this badly, Harvard won't let you go home." Campbell grabbed his telephone. He called the Harvard bursar, "I am sending over one of our third-year law students. He needs a loan to buy his books and for his living expenses and his food. See that he gets it." Two hours later, Sam Witwer's final year at Harvard was made possible.

"It seems a miracle now, when I realize how close I came to returning home," Witwer said. "I was just very fortunate." Fortunate, and very strong-willed.

From the perspective of another half-century, Witwer's post-Harvard life seems to fall into convenient categories: his law practice, which fluorished into one of the most respected in the Midwest; his efforts in behalf of Dickinson; his efforts in behalf of Methodism; his foray into politics; and his dramatic success at achieving constitutional reform in his new home state of Illinois.

At various stages during and between these episodes, Witwer made many acquaintances among the famous and politically powerful. President Eisenhower, who appreciated Witwer's personal and political loyalty, wanted to reward him with appointments to several federal commissions, spots Witwer declined because the compensation was too low and he lacked the private wealth to make up the difference in providing for his family. Richard M. Nixon, with whom Witwer had many contacts between his service as Vice President and his election as Chief Executive in 1968, encountered Witwer and his wife while both were on tour in Hong Kong. Nixon knew Witwer on a first-name basis, and the two engaged in several conversations, then and in later years. Similarly, Witwer developed a professional relationship with Chicago Mayor Richard J. Daley, Illinois Gov. Adlai E. Stevenson, and others. Witwer encouraged Stevenson to enter politics and contributed to his campaign for governor.

These relationships were worthwhile and sometimes intriguing. They were not, however, building blocks in the construction of Sam Witwer's personality and character. Great truths, the late Governor Stevenson once said, are discovered in the small, quiet corners of life. This is surely true of Sam Witwer. No major political figure contributed significantly to the molding of Witwer. By 1960, the middle-aged Witwer was the product of crafting by places as much as by people. His mother, Lulu, who died in 1957 at the age of 85, and his sister, Kathryn, who died in 1964 after a serious operation in 1941 which left her permanently in frail health, were enormous influences on Witwer. Those relationships rank with the sooty environment and labor turmoil of early Gary and the class-conscious climate of Cumberland as dominant forces on Witwer.

The building blocks of Sam Witwer's life were the joys, hardships, fun and discipline acquired in the service of his school, church and public life, and the love and experiences shared by a wife and children who made Sam Witwer the center of their own existence. These experiences form the "great truths" in the small, quiet corners of Sam Witwer's life.

THE LAW, THE FAMILY, THE CHURCH

Young Witwer learned rather painfully that Harvard Law School was unlike Dickinson College. He never felt a great commitment to the school or any professor there because relationships at Harvard were so totally impersonal. No one, neither students nor faculty, seemed to have time to develop attachments. Where Witwer was outgoing, gregarious, a part of everything at Dickinson and supremely happy, he felt left out at Harvard, and not always happy. He did not believe he was excelling either as a scholar or as a person. He lost much of his self-confidence, his ability to speak out, and did not regain them for years. Still, he knew that they were doing their best at Harvard to make him a lawyer and were probably succeeding. He found the casebook method of teaching, originated at Harvard years earlier by the famous Professor Langdell, quite exciting. He liked the give and take based upon actual cases, a form of the Socratic method. Witwer had great respect for the famous Dean Roscoe Pound though the dean had given him a very rough time. Pound was obviously a man of great intellect and skill who had started as a scientist and then progressed to the law. There were professors who were appreciated by Witwer, a few of them for their immense sense of fun, even if they were essentially uncompassionate with respect to their students. He recalled that Edmund Morgan, who taught evidence and procedure, "had a dry, flat, tart New England wit about him." He found Felix Frankfurter, whom he had in

26

administrative law, to be very brilliant but impatient with anyone who was not brilliant. He felt that "Bull" Warren, celebrated now as the prototype of the John Houseman character in "The Paper Chase" was more legendary than real, perhaps because Warren was ill at the time. Warren was held out as the leading exponent of the Spartan educational system, which may have made tough lawyers out of those who survived. But the going was often rough in the atmosphere of intense competition and perfection.

There were others whom Witwer recalled in later years, some of them famous in their day, others largely forgotten. But from them he derived an instinct for isolating a legal problem and finding a response to it. Some have referred to this as the "common law nose." If he has been successful in his law practice, and he surely has, it has been due in large measure to that quality of perceptiveness which he acquired at Harvard.

By virtually universal agreement, Harvard has long been the most prestigious of law schools, and it is generally assumed that its graduates are quickly hired by the leading law firms in every part of the country and paid exorbitant salaries. These things may be true today and at times in the past; but in the 1930s in Chicago, even Harvard Law School graduates were not certain of quick, if any, employment, and they, in common with other beginning lawyers everywhere in the decade following the stock market crash of 1929 and the ensuing depression, were fortunate if they were placed anywhere, except possibly in the burgeoning federal government with very modest compensation.

Witwer had been a hard working and moderately good student. He was not one of the *Harvard Law Review* luminaries and not a member of the highest honor group, but he was practical enough to get from Pound a list of Chicago area firms having Harvard graduates with a propensity to hire Harvard products. He rushed to Chicago after the last third-year examination in 1933 in order to solicit a job before the "bright boys" would get started. Through financial necessity, he resided with his parents in Gary, Ind., and commuted to Chicago each day during June and July in order to be interviewed by the firms with Harvard graduates. All of them received him cordially, but none offered him a job. His ego was greatly frayed, and he scarcely had the means to travel to Chicago in that dire period.

Finally, in August 1933, he secured a job in the firm in which he is now the senior partner. The firm was founded around 1895 by Michael Francis Gallagher and thus has been in continuous existence, although under different names, for more than eighty-eight years, making it one of the city's older firms as a true continuum. Witwer joined the four-partner firm as the only associate, and was kept busy day and night as well as on many Saturdays, Sundays and holidays. When he was at work Witwer would look out his office window and across the court separating his office from an adjacent cubicle, he would see Morris I. Leibman, the law clerk for a then-prestigious law firm. The two almost excessively ambitious young men would wave to each other across the empty space or on elevators or on the street. Witwer felt very great admiration for this brilliant contemporary in the ranks of legal neophytes and felt certain he would advance in the highly competitive profession. Of course, Leibman did rise, becoming one of the most successful lawyers of his generation, but, alas, not with the firm for which he labored so unselfishly, doing some of their most important work. In the manner of the times, Leibman's firm decided that no Jew, no matter how brilliant and devoted, could become a partner. So, Leibman started his own firm and swiftly became more prosperous and prestigious than the firm which had allowed unreasonable prejudice to control its decisions. Witwer would remember this lesson as to the price of intolerance. He would strive to be free of bigotry at all times and would rejoice, ultimately, in helping to make non-discrimination a part of the basic law of the State of Illinois.

Just as Witwer believed in civil rights, he also suffered from no handicap of religion. He belonged to a good Protestant denomination, the Methodists, and he was associated with lawyers who had respect for his capabilities. He rose gradually but surely in compensation and in standing. He was paid only $15 a week at first and gradually progressed to about $225 a month when he and Ethyl

Wilkins were married in 1937. To conserve his limited resources, he continued to live with his parents in Gary until 1937, while working in Chicago. He was deeply in debt when he graduated from law school, because of the costs incurred while attending Dickinson and Harvard. Witwer's earnings during the first seven years of practice were just enough to pay the modest costs of living and permit him gradually to retire the educational debt. It was not until 1941 or 1942 that he was completely free of debt.

He respected the four members of his firm — Michael Francis Gallagher, Earl B. Wilkinson, Samuel N. Rinaker and Arthur R. Hall — and they held him in increasingly high regard. They were an unusual combination of extremely good lawyers, each with his own peculiar talents and style of practice. When Witwer was hired, Gallagher was in Asia on an extended vacation. Witwer, not yet sure of himself, awaited Gallagher's return with no little trepidation. He had heard that Gallagher was tough and frank in stating his views and would not hesitate to express himself to Witwer, Harvard background notwithstanding. When Gallagher returned from his vacation jaunt, he sized up the young associate, looking him squarely in the eye, and declared, unhesitatingly, "I think you're going to be all right." The young man and the older man became fast friends. Witwer worked closely with him, especially in Gallagher's declining years when his health was failing. Witwer and Gallagher worked well together while battling over legal issues.

Gallagher was a short, red-faced, fighting Irishman, on the exterior vigorous and hard-hitting. But he was deeply absorbed in cultural concerns and highly principled. His great passion was public libraries and he assisted everyone who was interested in their establishment and maintenance anywhere. He devoted countless hours to this absorbing interest. The firm, at his behest, spent much volunteered time in getting a big appropriation from the State for the funding of public libraries. Support of the Cradle, a child adoption facility in Evanston, was another major interest of the firm.

Gallagher was married to the niece of Thomas G. Masaryk, the President of Czechoslovakia. It was through this connection that

Witwer came to represent President Eduard Benes, the successor to Masaryk, on some income tax matters. In order to get in and out of this country, Benes had to have his taxes cleared, and Witwer helped him. Gallagher had other important clients whose business Witwer is handling to this day.

Gallagher earlier engaged another associate, Earl Wilkinson, tall, angular, looking a lot like Lincoln, and a graduate from Northwestern Law School in 1917. Wilkinson was a specialist in interstate commerce law and Gallagher had turned that part of his practice over to him. Wilkinson, unlike Gallagher and Witwer, was not active in public affairs. He worked exceedingly hard during the day. Then he would free his mind from the day's burdens and go home to his family in River Forest.

Next in line was Samuel Rinaker, grandson of Civil War General John M. Palmer. Rinaker treasured the old general's sword and kept it in the firm's vault where he would occasionally look at it. Rinaker had been a Rhodes scholar and had gone to Oxford and was about Witwer's height, rather stern looking and very precise in his speech. There was no doubt he was a Harvard graduate in his austere moments. He had gone there with Robert A. Taft, son of the rotund President of the nation, who remained his close friend and later Witwer's. Rinaker became very active in the English Speaking Union, and was socially very prominent in fashionable Lake Forest, where he lived with his artist wife. He was extremely meticulous in the social amenities, and Witwer, an eager student in such things, learned from him. He learned other skills as well from Rinaker, chiefly the art of legal brief writing. Witwer believes Rinaker to be the best brief writer he has ever known, and credits him with imparting to him skill in that great professional art. Rinaker sometimes would spend days in composing an essential paragraph, knowing that it might be the very point that would win a case. He represented important interests, such as the then successful Thompson restaurant chain.

Arthur R. Hall was probably the most likable person the firm ever had. Witwer, who cherishes him to this day, remembers Hall as a relaxed fellow, who loved to try unusual cases. He would take a tough case to get a student into the university when he was rejected by those in charge or he would defend someone who was being evicted by his landlord simply because he did not pay the rent that was unquestionably due. No wonder there might be as many as twenty people sitting in the reception room waiting for Art Hall, their friend in times of need, a sort of one-man legal aid bureau. He literally did not care at all about money and he cared even less about record keeping. Often he did not send out any bills. Almost absentmindedly, he would call in Witwer at times and casually say with respect to a client, "Sam, shouldn't we send out a bill?" Almost in disbelief, Witwer would say, "Yeah." Hall would say, "Well, send out a bill for $50." Witwer would protest, "Mr. Hall, don't you remember that there were some very unusual problems in that case. We had to go to court on that." Hall would say, reluctantly, "Make it $200." By the time they got through discussing the matter, the bill might be $500, still less than the real value of the services.

Hall liked to imbibe a bit and smile. He was a bon vivant, somewhat careless of his health and too concerned with helping others, rather than himself. He was burned out and dead at 55, remembered with affection by all who knew him. It was he who hired Witwer in 1933, in the absence of the senior partner, and Witwer was forever grateful.

These, then, were the varied men from whom Witwer learned law and life in his early days of practice. As he fully realized, he owed much to each of them. They set examples for him. One could analyze Witwer's character temperament and trace each quality to one or another of his associates.

It was Gallagher's wish to utilize Witwer frequently in important corporate work which the older man was handling for several major national corporations. This gave Witwer an auspicious introduction to Wall Street practice and brought him into contact with some of the outstanding lawyers of the country during the first few years of his service in the firm. Most of the trial work was done by the brilliant courtroom technician, Hall. Because of his virtual pre-emption by Gallagher, Witwer did not become involved in trial practice at that time or for many years thereafter, since most of his efforts were in the field of corporate, estate and federal taxation. This is not unusual in the legal profession where many good lawyers never participate in courtroom battles. It is only on television that all lawyers gambol before juries in melodramatic fashion. The law is often quiet, even austere, and that was the nature of much of Witwer's practice at that time.

Earl Wilkinson, second in line of seniority, was a nationally respected interstate commerce lawyer, specializing in coal rate cases. He was a good deal more private and withdrawn than any of the other partners. Witwer knew that he had to earn the regard of Wilkinson, and that it would not be bestowed lightly.

Until 1937, Witwer commuted to and from Gary via the old South Shore Railroad and the New York Central, generally returning home in the evenings around eight o'clock in time to have a late dinner, read the paper and retire in order to be ready for the early train the following morning. During those years his social life was limited to an occasional date on a weekend and escorting his talented sister Kathryn to musical events in Chicago. Many of those occasions were thrilling for a young and ambitious person like himself. They were sponsored by some of Chicago's leading citizens, including the Charles H. Swifts and other persons connected with the opera and the Chicago Symphony Orchestra. As Kathryn rose in the singing world, so did her ambitious brother rise by himself and in her reflected glory; Kathryn and Sam were exceedingly proud of each other, with good reason. Their relationship was a special one, differing in kind and intensity from his other familial attachments.

Witwer's work in the office advanced satisfactorily and he became a partner in name, if not in substance, approximately five years after his arrival.

One of the more favorable aspects of his association with the Gallagher firm, unbroken throughout his whole practice, was the willingness of the partners to permit him to be quite independent in the choice of extracurricular activities. While they worked him very hard, indeed, in the early years, they were never disposed to fetter any of his choices outside of the office. Had they done so, the chances are that Witwer would not have remained with them, so consumed did he become gradually with public-spirited activity. The larger firms in those days, in contrast to what the situation became a generation later, were unlikely to permit their young men to take on unpopular public causes to any great extent for fear of antagonizing clients. Many of his later activities consumed hundreds, if not thousands, of unpaid hours that might otherwise have been devoted to a profitable practice. While the firm was never as large and powerful as others in Chicago and provided Witwer no political or economic base of operations for his increasingly driving force, it did allow him freedom of choice and independence of personal action. During the period of his involvement in seeking a constitutional convention for the State when it was not popular in some circles, people wrote to the partners, trying to get Witwer's scalp. The partners, understanding Witwer's high motivation, were inclined to throw such letters in the wastebasket with irritation at those who could not appreciate the inspired young man.

Sometime in 1940, Witwer attended a meeting of the Chicago Literary Club with Michael Gallagher. Walking back to the office, they were joined by Dean Edward T. Lee of the John Marshall Law School. The dean, himself a Harvard graduate, inquired about Witwer's work at Harvard Law School and asked whether he was interested in teaching at John Marshall. Witwer eagerly assured him that he was in need of supplementing his income and would welcome the opportunity. That resulted in several years of service on the John Marshall faculty where he taught personal property law (bailments, gifts and related subjects). For a semester or two, he taught corporate law, when one of the older members of the faculty became ill. The burden of teaching two or three evenings a week for several hours, preparing written examinations and grading numerous blue books, at a time when he was the sole law clerk for four active partners, was a heavy load, indeed. He was paid $15 a night for his work at the law school. This did not include compensation for the preparation for lectures, the grading of papers, and the like. It was the same sort of work and compensation earned at John Marshall by another Chicago luminary, Arthur J. Goldberg, who was destined to go very high in the cabinet of a President, the Supreme Court of the United States, and in the United Nations. Witwer felt that he could not carry on any longer with heavy responsibilities both in the office and the school. Happily, his office income was improving. But he never ceased to look back with pleasure and gratification on those years of identification with the law school faculty. Years later he was given the honorary Doctor of Law degree by John Marshall Law School. He holds a number of similar honorary degrees from major colleges and universities, such as Dickinson, Illinois, Simpson, Lake Forest and DePaul.

Aside from this teaching experience and his activities in the Hyde Park Methodist Church to which he belonged, practically all of his time was devoted to the practice of law. He had not as yet become involved in public affairs and, in fact, it was the last thought he had during the first seven or eight years of his practice. In the same period he had little time or resources for Dickinson College and seldom, if ever, returned to the campus.

By the beginning of the 1940s, his professional life took a dramatic turn and became very stimulating. The excitement has continued with major litigation of national significance. Once he became a partner in the law firm, albeit a very junior one at a very modest level of income, he started to make contact with Dickinson College and commenced the unbroken series of trips to Carlisle to attend commencements, board meetings and to preside ultimately as Board President.

Since 1937, Witwer's life has been a romance, sustaining him through trials and triumphs. Until 1935 when he met the woman who was to mean so much in his life, he actually feared that he was going to remain a bachelor. True, he dated women now and then, but had met no one who really stirred him. One Sunday morning, he observed a young woman in the choir of the Methodist Church he was attending and he heard her sing a solo in a rich soprano voice. The woman and the song were beautiful. The song he could forget as it was the usual devotional; but the woman he could not forget.

Her beauty was of a lasting, even a haunting, quality. A generation later, she is still more attractive with an aura about her of physical and spiritual beauty. Witwer was naturally interested in music, as his sister Kathryn's career was blossoming. But the young woman projected beyond her song. He asked a member of the church to introduce him the following Sunday, which began a two-year courtship with Ethyl Wilkins. Ethyl, a nineteen-year-old woman, was dating others at that time. Sam soon learned that her father was an early settler of Gary and that he had been the superintendent of the huge Central Mills, which encompassed a varied group of mills between the open hearths and the steel and tin mills, stretching from east to west Gary. It was not of mills and fathers that he thought, but only of a remarkably appealing young woman, whom he wanted very much to make his wife. They were married on a warm August day in 1937 before he really could afford the luxury of a household establishment of his own. They rented a one-room furnished apartment in the Hyde Park section of Chicago and were as happy as if they were affluent. From this conveniently located apartment, Witwer would take the Illinois Central Railroad to his office. And his apartment was only several blocks from St. James Methodist Church, with which they soon became closely identified. In this church, Witwer made contacts which greatly enhanced his career. It was not as if he sought out these influential people; they were simply a by-product of his involvement in the church and of a personality which inspired confidence.

At first Ethyl continued to study music in order to refine her already superb voice. She studied with Witwer's sister, Kathryn, and a master teacher, Richard B. DeYoung, once well known in the city as the teacher of opera stars. Ethyl had sung, at the time of the marriage, at the Chicago Theatre in the Loop, with a group known as the Chicago Musicland Festival Septet. Soon she had to make a decision as to whether to be a good stay-at-home wife or an often absent professional singer. Coming home from an engagement, she was drenched in an almost torrential rain. It caused her to think through the vicissitudes of a career. To Witwer's great satisfaction, she preferred domesticity, with occasional amateur and charity engagements. Witwer was the kind of man who needed the quiet bliss of home life. Any bruises he received in an active professional life and later in public affairs could be healed by a woman like Ethyl. Others might be indifferent or worse; she would always show that he meant much to her.

The Witwers managed to upgrade their housing in Hyde Park, going from smaller to larger abodes. Finally in 1941, they moved to a very attractive, unfurnished apartment near the lake. It was a joy to finally acquire their own furniture and furnishings. They could feel themselves rising in the world.

The young couple, devoted to their respective parents, would journey in their lately acquired Ford to Gary and visit the families. As their children arrived — three boys and a girl — these parental visits increased. Friends sometimes gently chided Witwer saying that he spent too much time with his family rather than cultivating new acquaintances who could abet his practice. Surely, his growing family needed sustenance. Ethyl was in agreement with her husband rather than the well-meaning practical friends. They cherished every moment with those united by blood, and their warm feelings were reciprocated by their families. Later they observed that as their children grew and had families of their own, they developed the same close ties to them that they had shown to their kindred. Witwer was grateful that he and Ethyl had set such a good example.

An exciting family event occurred just before the Japanese attack on Pearl Harbor in 1941 — twin sons were born to them. It was double riches for them, they felt, while they speculated as to whose genes were responsible. They felt equally blessed with the arrival of a daughter and their third son, in four-year intervals thereafter.

It was at this time that it appeared young Witwer would join the Armed Forces upon the express invitation of Uncle Sam. He had given much thought to whether he would seek a commission by volunteering, but was deterred from doing so because of the then rather heavy burden under which he was laboring. His father had become seriously ill with tuberculosis. His sister, in 1941, had undergone emergency surgery and her life was spared by the promptness and skill of a leading Chicago physician and surgeon. Her health thereafter was never robust and she and the parents were dependent very largely upon Witwer's income. With six dependents, Witwer was not about to rush off to war before he had to, despite any patriotic fervor. In due course, he was drafted, assigned to the Navy and called up for induction at Great Lakes. Before that occurred, President Roosevelt declared that all fathers over a certain age would be deferred from service. Never again was he notified that Uncle Sam needed him, and by that narrow margin, he was spared for his family, rather than the Armed Forces.

While it was always a matter of some regret that he did not contribute in some manner at the time of World War II, he remained satisfied that he had done the right thing in staying with the family as its only means of support. The years 1942 through 1945 were transitional years in which he made the contacts and developed the interests which soon were to lead him into a highly active involvement in public affairs. It was then that he made his first contacts with the problems of Illinois constitutional revision which, in time, became the dominating interest of his career.

In 1942, George McKibbin was serving as Director of Revenue in the cabinet of Governor Dwight H. Green. McKibbin and Witwer had become very closely associated in the work of the St. James Methodist Church, and during the fall of 1942 Witwer was invited to hear a talk given by McKibbin in support of a constitutional amendment proposed by Governor Green for the purpose of deleting the Retailer's Occupational Tax on food. McKibbin explained to the Men's Club of the church the difficulties in getting a favorable vote on a constitutional amendment because of the fact that those who failed to vote at the election on the constitutional issue were automatically counted as if voting "no" in the test then required. It amazed Witwer to learn that the Illinois Constitution was badly bound to a straitjacket, and his amazement was compounded when the vote actually occurred — 979,000, or 32%, had voted "for," and 346,000, or 11%, had voted "against." But the measure failed because of the unreasonable constitutional requirement. Fifty-six percent of the people who voted in the general election did not vote on the amendment and were thus counted against it.

McKibbin and Witwer discussed the problem and the general inadequacies of the Illinois Constitution on more than one occasion and it was then, for the first time, that Witwer became convinced that here, indeed, was an immense challenge to our democratic system when a state such as Illinois could not even provide for the needs of its people because of the effect of the dead hand of the past. So, he became involved in other constitutional amendment campaigns, starting with the Gateway Amendment of 1946. As the great work of his life was underway, he could not then know where it would lead him in state and national affairs nor could he know that decades later he would still be actively involved.

This was the first of many instances in which McKibbin influenced the course of his career. McKibbin was dominant, too, in encouraging Witwer's interest in the United Methodist Church, which subsequently led Witwer into an active national role in the church. McKibbin had gone to Springfield as Governor Green's Director of Revenue at a time when he also had been serving as the lay leader of St. James Methodist Church. From his youth, he had been an active Methodist, as was his mother before him. McKibbin asked Witwer to be his deputy in the church and to be prepared to keep on top of problems that might emerge in the congregation during his absences in Springfield. He invited Witwer to meet with him every other week at the McKibbin law office in Chicago and, also, to contact Albert Harris, who was the dean of the Chicago bankers and one who was deeply involved in the local church with the Swifts and Armours and other establishment people, such as Roy O. West, who had served as U.S. Secretary of the Interior.

In consequence of those meetings, Witwer developed a broad acquaintance with the Methodist leadership, both within the local church and in the Northern Illinois Annual Conference, then known as the Rock River Conference. His service to the local church brought personal rewards and enrichments. In due course, he became a lay leader of the St. James Church and, throughout the

'40s and '50s, a delegate to the Annual Conference and to several of the jurisdictional and general conferences on the national level. It is unlikely that he would have been elected to these offices were it not for McKibbin. The latter put Witwer's name to the General Conference in 1964 in Pittsburgh when Witwer was elected a member of the Judicial Council of Methodism, the "Supreme Court" and the highest unit to which a layman may aspire in the international denomination. McKibbin and Witwer would frequently go to church conferences together, and many of their luncheon meetings at the Union League Club were devoted to consideration of the problems of the local church, the Annual Conference and the broader national level.

No one had a greater influence in Witwer's interests and choices than did George B. McKibbin. Witwer's activities in constitutional reform, Methodism and the Republican Party are all clearly related to the deep interest which McKibbin took in him as one potentially ready to serve. While McKibbin felt a strong personal regard for Witwer, his greatest concern was to find committed persons who would render services to Church and community. He encouraged many other young men, not necessarily Methodists, who were struggling to find opportunities for service. One of them was Rubin G. Cohn, whom he engaged for legal and drafting work when he was in Springfield and whom he pushed hard in all professional areas as a man of unusual talent and quality. Cohn was to become a leading University of Illinois professor of law and exponent of court reform. It was the fortunate relationship with George McKibbin which they shared that caused Cohn and Witwer to become acquainted, and to become colleagues in legal, civic and bar association matters.

Witwer is a deeply religious person, but he does not have the sanctimonious attitude of some religious people. There is nothing of the holier-than-thou in his makeup, nothing of the blue-nose, nothing of the Puritan. This is not to say that he has ever been intemperate — he is moderate in everything — although he has given some ministerial types moments of worry about his soul, in the context of his political involvements and pragmatic understandings. He was not surprised to learn that a study made at Boston University indicated that at least half of the persons of his religious faith were not teetotalers, and that they participated in social drinking in moderation. Nor were they opposed to dancing or dating. He and Ethyl enjoy their dancing. Witwer was never a strong drinker, even in moments of stress. But Witwer had become so thoroughly enmeshed in religion so early in his life that it had become an integral part of him. He sometimes asked himself, "Don't you accept too much too readily?" He sits in church sometimes and listens to the sermons and pulls them apart. In a different day and age people might have called him a doubter. Recognizing that the world is immensely complex and that he does not know the answers to all questions, he cannot deny that there is a purpose in everything, and not simply blind force or happenstance.

Witwer's father died after a rather lengthy illness at 79. He was in the Methodist Hospital for many weeks. The younger Witwer would go out almost every night from Chicago and sit with his father all night long. It was a time of spiritual regeneration and reflection. Witwer recalls, "He wanted to go to our home to die, and we brought him there. I was with him when he passed on. I'll never forget him. He was a very brave man. I turned to prayer, to me a form of communication with the Deity. I read the Bible rather closely. I found a Psalm that was very comforting in terms of what one generation owes to another in teaching the meaning of life. I thought to myself, 'My father's teaching me something here about the passing of the generations, I hope sometime I can teach my kids the same kind of a lesson as graciously as he's done. I have found that when deaths have come, there has come to me an inner strength that I never dreamed I possessed."

These were the reactions of a truly religious man and the devotion of a good son and brother, a family man. One does not know Witwer unless one understands this side of him. The man is revealed in his attitude towards both life and death, as serious, sympathetic and, somehow, devout.

Witwer's role in the affairs of the Methodist Church and the esteem with which he is held are well described by Professor

Emeritus Murray H. Leiffer who has known and worked with Witwer for more than two decades. Witwer was elected to the Board of Trustees of Garrett Theological Seminary some years after Leiffer started teaching there. Their rather formal and casual acquaintanceship became a very meaningful friendship after they were elected at the same time to the Judicial Council of The United Methodist Church, Witwer as a layman and Leiffer as a minister. The Council, the court of last resort in the international denomination, has nine members, four laymen and five clergymen, elected directly by the General Conference of The United Methodist Church, the body of delegates which come from around the world every four years.

Witwer and Leiffer served together for eight years. During that period the Council was faced with many highly important issues, including the integration of Black and white annual conferences, the uniting of the Methodist and The Evangelical United Brethren Churches, clergy responsibilities and church bureaucracies.

Witwer, recalls Leiffer, never missed the semi-annual sessions of the Council held throughout the country and, never declined responsibility for drafting a preliminary opinion on a case when requested to do it.

Leiffer felt Witwer was one of the most articulate and prepared members on the cases, rarely simple, that came before the Council. "There were frequently sharp differences of opinion among the members of the Council. Witwer always presented his views in a logical and forceful manner, as if he were in court. I have seen his face flush with the intensity of his exposition and occasionally with disdain for a presentation that he deemed illogical or casuistic. Yet, no matter how great the tension, I never saw him lose his self-control in the group.

"I have never seen Sam 'rattled'," Leiffer said. If the vote went against him in the Council, as it occasionally did, he never showed anger — at least not in public. He is a self-controlled person."

Gradually, those who had been Witwer's seniors and mentors passed out of the law firm, and Witwer, once the sole associate, became the senior partner and developed his own new team of partners. There was, first of all, J. Alfred Moran, who had been a well-paid executive of the Hearst magazines. Moran decided that he was going to be a lawyer and went to night school. Moran was a member of the same golf club as Witwer's then senior partner, Earl Wilkinson, who told Moran that when he was ready to become a lawyer, to see him. In due course, Moran entered the firm. Although Moran is older by a couple of years, Witwer is his senior in the firm by about five years. White-haired, stocky and of gentlemanly demeanor, Moran was president of the Oak Park Country Club and president of the Oak Park School Board during many of the years of his firm membership.

Then came Thomas D. Burlage. By way of contrast to Moran, he was tall, an active Catholic, the brother of a Jesuit priest who was on the faculty of Loyola. He had come to the firm through Walter V. Schaefer, later to become a justice of the Illinois Supreme Court. Burlage had told Justice Schaefer, who was then on the faculty of Northwestern, that he would like to practice a sophisticated brand of law without going to a big firm. He was told, "You'd better go and see Sam Witwer." He saw Witwer and was hired as a youngster fresh out of Northwestern. Witwer has held him in highest respect as an incisive lawyer.

Thus far the firm could not be accused of growth through family influences. But shortly after his 1967 graduation from law school, Witwer's son and namesake, Samuel, Jr., was added to the roster. At the time young Sam got out of Michigan Law School, he indicated he'd like to join the Witwer firm. His father wondered whether it would work given the necessary confrontation that comes between father and son, particularly if they're both dynamic and strong-willed. Also lying dormant was the imputation of nepotism. It was discussed among the partners who were pleased that the senior partner's son desired to join the firm. An arrangement was made from the outset that the son was not going to be actively involved in the father's work, and that he would work primarily for the other partners; they would give him the tutelage, and bring him up similarly to other young lawyers. In later years, father and son began working in close tandem with each other, largely because over the years Sam, Jr. became the firm's first trial lawyer. Both Witwers were deeply involved in the nationally important litigation involving the Methodist church. Sam, Jr.'s trial ability and background in United Methodism allowed him to join his father, not as son, but as able and significantly contributing counsel. In contast to the one associate when Witwer joined the firm long ago, there are now four associates. The firm is still relatively small, but thriving.

Witwer, Sr. came to the firm as a law clerk and has been with it ever since. And in the intervening years, he has had the encouragement of his partners in doing his work in his own way without interference. In addition, the partners respect each other. They concern themselves with trying to be solid, ethical and highly professional lawyers at all times. None have ever been with any other law firm; all came directly from law school and have remained with the Witwer firm.

Witwer has probably had his most active practice before the justices of the Illinois Supreme Court, possibly because of their familiarity with his constitutional work. He frequently is in the Illinois Supreme Court to argue cases of first impression and of major public importance. He is not the popular type of lawyer with the average Cook County circuit judge. He has had more limited contact with the federal judiciary in court proceedings, although he has had many close personal relations with the federal judges of the United States Courts through his years in public affairs, while they have moved up the legal and judicial ladders to positions of distinction. The younger Witwer, however, is an active trial practitioner in the Federal system.

"This lack of close contact has not exactly bothered me," Witwer Sr. said, "because I always feel a certain amount of embarrassment when I'm arguing a case before a judge that I know socially or who is my friend." Others may think in terms of "clout" in such situations.

After many years of immersion in legal matters, both public and private, Witwer has developed his own philosophy with respect to the law.

"I have a feeling that the administration of justice is the very foundation of government and society. When so viewed, there cannot be anything more challenging to a lawyer than being a leader in the development of the law. There's nothing more fundamental than respect for justice. We lawyers, since the days of Isaiah, have been the subject of all sorts of abusive characterizations, sometimes deserved. I feel that the fundamental law has got to achieve a greater degree of freedom for people in making their choices and meeting the needs of our changing society."

In carrying out his philosophy, Witwer relies on a strong background stemming from attendance at a good law school and an inherent trait of tough persistence. This latter quality, coupled with his philosophy, has shown itself in connection with his obsession with constitutional reform, and his willingness to stay with a lot of difficult matters over decades of struggle. He is perhaps more eloquent in expressing a legal position than expressing a political position. As is the case with most successful lawyers, a high batting average in the appellate courts is the result of hard work and detailed preparation, leading to the ability to give a strong and persuasive argument. There is also the continuing commitment to the law, the issues, and the clients. In Witwer's case, his persistence in the law has meant there was never a time when he ceased practicing, despite all of the distractions — political, educational and constitutional.

Witwer has been less sure of himself as a trial lawyer, particularly in cases before juries, but has had little reluctance about arguing cases in court and, when required, in contesting with leading trial attorneys.

But what interests Witwer most in the practice of law are the basic legal and particularly constitutional issues: an interest essentially in principles of law and their interpretations. His more recent work in defending the denominational interests of the United Methodist Church in the nationally important Pacific Homes cases in California, for example, illustrates the "new ground" involving significant organic or fundamental legal matters that excite lawyers such as Witwer.

Beginning in 1977, a number of class-action lawsuits seeking damages over $600 million in aggregate, were filed on behalf of the residents of retirement homes known as "The Pacific Homes," not only against the non-profit corporation which owned and managed the homes, but also against numerous units of the United Methodist Church. In addition, the plaintiffs sought to name as a separate defendant the entire religious denomination known as the "United Methodist Church," as distinguished from its 10 million members and literally thousands of separate units including local churches.

It was at this point that Witwer and his partner-son, Sam, were retained to defend the national and international interests of the denomination in an effort which continued until 1980. They saw action in numerous courts from the trial level to the Supreme Court of the United States in which grave constitutional issues became the focal points of national attention.

The suits were filed on behalf of approximately 2,000 residents of retirement and convalescent homes known as The Pacific Homes, a California not-for-profit corporation which owned and operated 14 such institutions. Local units of the religious faith, including the United Methodist Annual Conference consisting of churches in California, Arizona and Hawaii had, since 1912, afforded financial assistance to the Homes as a matter of religious mission. However, with inflationary increases, contracts for retirement services at $185 a month could not be performed; national costs had risen such as to require some $1,000 a month for comparable services.

In suing the entire denomination, the class-suit attorneys proceeded on the unprecedented theory that such a denomination was "an unincorporated association," usable in the same manner as if it were a corporation, not unlike General Motors. The effect of such a theory, had it been approved by the courts, would have made all units of United Methodism answerable in damages for the actions of individual United Methodists or of any one of the 40,000 or more local churches and units. In the history of American jurisprudence, no such pervasive theory of liability had ever been judicially applied to any major religious denomination.

Because of the far-reaching implications of this novel legal theory, the lawsuits were strenuously resisted in the state and federal courts of California and through the judiciary up to and including the Supreme Court of the United States. That Court declined to intercede as requested by a Petition for Writ of Certiorari, apparently because it wished to await further case developments.

After three years of intensive litigation and a partial jury trial of six months' duration, the plaintiffs reduced their damage claims from an aggregate of over two-third's of a billion dollars to the sum of $21 million and no longer insisted that the denomination as an entirety be held responsible. It was then dismissed from the case.

At the end of 1980 a settlement was concluded whereby the United Methodists advanced funds to permit a Federal reorganization of the homes, not unlike the plan of reorganization offered five years before by the Pacific and Southwest Annual Conference of the Church in an effort to protect the elderly residents. All lawsuits against other Church defendants have since been dismissed.

The constitutional questions remain unresolved, namely: (a) whether members and units of a major religious faith such as the United Methodist Church may be sued collectively as if it were a corporation; and (b) if so, whether liability for all damage claims arising at a local level will fall upon the entire denomination. Until such time as the United States Supreme Court issues definitive constitutional interpretations, these questions will plague all religious as well as fraternal and other voluntary associations operating on a national or international level. In the meantime, Witwer and his partner-son have been successful in securing favorable decisions dealing with these issues in cases in Montana and North Carolina state courts. The Montana Court recently observed:

> The United Methodist Church is a spiritual connection of millions of individual persons and thousands of representative church units which are collectively incapable of being sued as a jural entity. This Court is convinced that to subject them (the denomination) to jurisdiction would violate the establishment clause of the

Montana Constitution and the First Amendment of the United States Constitution.

A North Carolina state court similarly upheld the non-suability of the entire denomination, pointing out the far-fetched nature of the legal claim that it was an "unincorporated association."

Witwer has had a distinguished record of legal and public service in numerous other important cases. He has argued or worked on briefs in a number of cases in the Supreme Courts of both Illinois and the United States involving interpretation of the Constitution of 1970 and of the Federal Constitution. He has served continuously as a constitutional consultant to three Illinois Attorneys General who have been in office since 1970. In Witwer's view, no cases have been of greater importance to the future worth of the Illinois Constitution than two cases he and his close friend, Louis Ancel, successfully carried to the Supreme Court of Illinois in 1976 and 1982 involving the Legislative Initiative provisions of Article XIV, Section 3 of the new Constitution. These were the so-called "Gertz" and "Lousin" cases.

Ancel, whom Witwer views as the "unsung hero of Illinois constitutional reform," for decades had been deeply involved in substantially all of the constitutional campaigns headed by Witwer. It was not surprising that these two constitutional lawyers would team-up successfully to resist misuses of the Legislative Initiative procedure which, they perceived, would have gone far to destroy the stability of the Constitution.

During the Convention, it was believed that the General Assembly might be unwilling to submit future constitutional amendments to the electorate to reform or restructure the Legislature. Accordingly, the new Constitution provided for initiated amendment proposals for legislative restructuring which expressly were "limited to structural and procedural subjects contained in Article IV," the Legislative Article.

A substantial public revulsion emerged against "double-dipping" by legislators in holding dual offices, their advance drawing of salaries and other activities constituting conflicts of interest. A group calling itself "Coalition for Political Honesty," led by a young reformer, Patrick Quinn, circulated petitions dealing with these problems and sought to amend the Constitution accordingly. They received much public and media support and the petitions bore the required number of signatures.

When it became evident the proposals would be placed on the ballot and would likely create a precedent of interpretation which would open the Illinois Constitution to initiative change at every ensuing general election in almost any area of government, Witwer and Ancel filed a taxpayers' suit. The purpose of the action was to obtain a ruling concerning the constitutionality of the proposals, charging that the placement of them on the ballot at the forthcoming Blue Ballot general election would constitute a wrongful and unconstitutional expenditure of taxpayers' monies. Among the Convention delegates who served as plaintiffs were Elmer Gertz (the lead plaintiff whose name the case bears), Louis J. Perona (the delegate who in the Convention proposed Section 3 of Article XIV of the Constitution), Thomas Lyons and Elbert Smith (Vice Presidents of the Convention), Ann Lousin (former Convention staff member), Thomas McCracken (Chairman of the General Government Committee of the Convention), Lucy Reum (Vice Chairman of the Legislative Committee) and Maurice Scott of Springfield, a delegate who had much standing as an expert on taxation.

Ultimately in the Gertz case, the Illinois Supreme Court resolved the issue in favor of plaintiffs in a decision which has clearly limited, as Witwer and Ancel contended, the areas whereby the initiative system can be used in seeking future constitutional revisions.

The importance of the decision in supporting the stability of Illinois constitutionalism, could not then be foreseen. But, it was demonstrated clearly seven years later when a renewed effort was made by the Coalition for Political Honesty.

This time in 1982, the Coalition circulated petitions among the voters to place upon the general election ballot an amendment to the Constitution which would have removed the constraints of the earlier Supreme Court case interpreting Article XIV, Section 3. This time the Coalition sought to install a general system for writing legislation and future constitutional amendments by the device of the initiative and referendum. Once again, former delegates to the Constitutional Convention joined in filing a taxpayers' suit to enjoin the wrongful expenditure of public monies and to prevent the proposed amendments from being placed on the Blue Ballot at the November 1982 election. It is known as the Lousin case.

Again, Ancel and Witwer were successful in securing a decree of the trial court, declaring the improper application of the Constitution sought by the Coalition for Political Honesty and enjoining the placement of the unlawful propositions on the ballot. The Appellate Court for the First District affirmed the decision of the trial court and, thereafter, the Supreme Court of Illinois, on three separate occasions, denied review, thus allowing the injunction to stand.

There have been many other cases in which Witwer has been involved in interpreting the new Constitution and there may be many more. It is evident that the delegates and friends of the Constitution such as Ancel will continue to stand guard so that the basic intent and quality of the new Constitution will not be impaired.

*   *   *   *   *   *

No study of Sam Witwer is complete without an account, however brief, of his four children, now adults with personalities of their own, yet bearing the impress of their much concerned parents.

Samuel W. Witwer, Jr. arrived ten minutes earlier than his twin brother, Michael. During their last two years at the Riverside-Brookfield High School, the two boys worked as volunteers in the laboratory of the Augustana Hospital in Chicago, where the Witwer family's friend, Dr. Carl A. Hedberg, was in charge. Sam assisted in pathology and Mike in hematology. Somehow, this led Sam to decide to become a lawyer, like his father, and Mike concluded that medicine would be his life work.

Both young men went to their father's alma mater, Dickinson College, in 1959; but after two years, Mike transferred to the University of Michigan at Ann Arbor and Sam remained at Dickinson, graduating with honors in 1963. The same week Mike graduated from Michigan, Sam chose his brother's school for his law studies, and Mike went to the medical school at Northwestern University.

As already mentioned, upon graduation from the Michigan law school in 1967, Sam entered his father's firm and became a partner in 1975 on his own merits, rather than parental favor. Like his father, too, he developed a close attachment for Dickinson College, after serving on its Board of Trustees. The parallel between father and son does not end yet. Sam is an active Methodist layman and has served on the Administrative Board of the Chicago Temple, as President of the Methodist Bar Association, and on several Northern Illinois Annual Conference agencies. He has been active in Republican affairs and, as a Young Republican, chaired a large fund-raising effort with George Bush, now Vice President of the United States. Sam is a licensed airplane pilot who is devoted to the piano and the guitar. But his principal hobby is long-distance running, which he shares with Michael. Both men have participated in several of the 26-mile marathons each year.

Sam married Susan Stewart in 1971. They are the parents of two sons.

Upon completing his internship in 1968, the medical twin — Michael — was commissioned in the United States Navy, transferred to the Marine Corps and served in Vietnam in the field for over a year as a battalion surgeon. Throughout virtually all of his time in Vietnam, he served at the front, participating in many expeditions and being awarded the Navy Commendation for valor. Subsequently, he sustained injuries while stationed in Da Nang and returned home. He completed his residency at Northwestern's Passavant-Wesley Hospital and was appointed chief resident of the Veterans Administration Hospital. There followed two years on a fellowship study in La Jolla, California. He is now in private practice in Santa Rosa, California, in internal medicine, specializing in infectious diseases. He is the author of numerous papers on infectious disease and is a Fellow of the American College of Physicians.

As mentioned, he is devoted to the marathon, but has topped Sam in this strenuous hobby by running in 50-mile events and twice running a 100-mile race in the Sierras.

He has a son and daughter.

Carole Witwer Dalton, born in 1945, is the only daughter of the Witwers. At New Trier High School she participated in lead roles in the annual musical event known as Lagniappe. She, sharing the interests and talent of her mother and aunt, attended the School of Music at Northwestern and developed a soprano voice of rare beauty. She married Dr. Peter C. Dalton, professor of philosophy at Florida State University. Their family consists of three chidren.

The youngest of the Witwer siblings is David born in 1949. He, too, graduated from New Trier and then went to Dickinson College. He pursued graduate studies, getting a Master's Degree in engineering from the California Institute of Technology at Pasadena and an M.B.A. from the University of Chicago. He is a licensed professional engineer and a business consultant associated with a nationally prominent consulting firm.

He, too, has developed a strong attachment to Dickinson and to the California Institute of Technology where he serves on the alumni boards of both institutions. Unlike his parents, he is an active Presbyterian layman, serving as a deacon and usher at the Fourth Presbyterian Church of Chicago. Like his father, he is aligned with the Republican Party. He missed election as an alternate delegate to the 1980 national convention by only nine votes. He is not married.

Thus, the Witwers have been gratifyingly successful as parents. They have proven anew that successful persons need not neglect their families.

Nor have they neglected their friends. This narrative refers to a number of their friends, but two are especially important to Sam Witwer — the two Carls, as he calls them — Dr. Carl A. Hedberg and Carl P. Clare. At age 80, Dr. Hedberg remains in active medical practice and scarcely misses a day at Augustana Hospital or his office. It will be remembered that the Witwer twins worked as volunteers at the Augustana. Dr. Hedberg, vigorous, brilliant and devoted to the Witwers, is the recipient of honors from the King of Sweden and leading medical societies.

Carl P. Clare, a few years younger than Dr. Hedberg, has recently retired as top executive of a major electronics company. His inventions are highly important in the new computer and other scientific spheres which have proven essential in moon flights and trips to outer space. Witwer and Clare have been close friends for years, both active at Dickinson College. Clare has always encouraged Witwer in his efforts for constitutional reform and in other efforts to improve Illinois government.

Louis Ancel and Robert F. Spindell have also played momentous roles in the life of Sam Witwer. They have been close to him in his entire career in constitutional reform and have abetted him in all of his efforts. Although Sam Witwer does not gush since it is alien to his nature, he does, however, become sentimental when he talks of Ancel and Spindell. He has leaned upon them, and they have responded to his needs in an unselfish fashion. Both lawyers are men of civic affairs who have had the training to appreciate Witwer's role in the history of the state.

Witwer has demonstrated in his life that no one is an island unto himself. He has thrived on familial warmth and the concerned contact with friends.

LONG INTERLUDE IN ACADEMIA

Regrettably, today many people view the significance of educational institutions almost entirely in terms of job and vocational preparation. I believe in the importance of the liberal arts traditions and training for the general enrichment of the lives of people of cultivation.
— Sameul W. Witwer, 1980

Between Sam Witwer and the Pennsylvania countryside embracing Carlisle and Dickinson College there existed an affinity not unlike that which existed in a romantic fiction of the previous century, between Heathcliff and the moors. Even in his student days Witwer felt drawn to this region. After his graduation in 1930, he could not afford to return for a dozen years, but his longing to go "home" again never ceased.

Lack of resources was not the sole reason for his temporary absence from Dickinson. Witwer simply did not have the time to get involved as an alumnus. Immediately after Harvard, his time and energy were consumed starting a career in law, getting married, starting a family and helping to meet the financial obligations of family members who had become dependent on him.

In the early 1940's, however, Witwer succumbed to the lure of Carlisle, the rolling hills and rustic settings he referred to as his own "Currier & Ives country." He attended alumni festivities during the commencement weekend of 1942, the start of a Witwer tradition that remained unbroken through the early 1980s. For all those decades, he never stopped returning. His attachment to Dickinson did not go unnoticed and in 1948 he became a trustee of the college. This launched a second career for Witwer, a venture in education that immeasurably enriched Witwer's life and which, as others testify, proved crucial to the salvaging of colonial era-Dickinson as a respected institution.

Witwer found no ivory tower isolation in this new pursuit. On the contrary, he found himself enveloped in intrigue. From the beginning Witwer was involved in a tug of war between forces that wanted to take Dickinson out of any connection with the Methodist Church and those who wanted to nurture that connection for reasons of ideology or pragmatism. Witwer aligned himself with trustees who fought for academic freedom in the Communist witch hunt hysteria of the 1950s. He became a champion of higher salaries for faculty. He led the fight to pump millions and millions of dollars into a renewal of the campus. He was a liberal on issues dealing with campus life and its adaptation to changing mores. His leadership established a new rapport between the college administration and student activists during the campus turbulence of the Vietnam War era.

Witwer played key roles in several Board of Trustee fights before his election as President of the Board in 1964, but it was his ascension to the presidency that represented a turning point in the development of Dickinson. Two scholars familiar with the history of that period at the college assess Witwer's impact as enormously beneficial.

"I believe the meeting in 1964 where he was elected president to have been the most important of this century," said Charles Colemen Sellers, a prominent historian and official archivist of Dickinson who died in 1979. "It represented the difference between whether the college would adopt a very conservative, penny-pinching approach or whether it would accept the challenges of growth and adaptation.

"From the first meeting, Witwer was open and cooperative, and this itself was refreshing, because the Board had always operated in secret. It resented any intrusion in its affairs."

"Witwer was elected by one vote," recalled Howard L. Rubendall, at the time a new president of the college struggling with the forces of reaction and stand-pattism on the board.

"Witwer's election meant to me as president of the college that I had not only a strong and able leader under whom I could pursue my work, but one who shared with me the dream of bringing to our alma mater a renewal that would move us toward excellence. Over the years, there was a rebirth at Dickinson and Sam Witwer presided over it."

Rubendall had graduated from Dickinson in 1931, the year after Witwer's graduation, and had become a Presbyterian clergyman and head of two Eastern schools before the Dickinson board's nominating committee approached him in 1958 about the possibility of becoming president of Dickinson.

After his first interview with the nominating committee, Rubendall wrote Boyd Lee Spahr, a noted Philadelphia lawyer, then in his 27th year as board president, that he had sensed an "air of extreme conservatism" among the trustees who interviewed him. Rubendall said he feared such an atmosphere would stifle his goals if he stepped in as president of the college, because one of his first priorities would be to "create an environment of free and open inquiry" on campus.

In the spring of 1959, Rubendall formally withdrew his name from consideration at Dickinson, but Spahr kept after him, all the while finessing attempts by board members to promote other candidates for the job. Shortly before Christmas that year, Rubendall relented and the board elected him president, effective 18 months later when Gilbert Malcolm, chosen as an interregnum president in 1959, would be leaving.

Rubendall assumed the reins at Dickinson at a time when the college's fortunes were at low ebb. Campus housing was overcrowded and in need of massive rehabilitation. The college was under censure by the American Association of University Professors for firing an assistant professor of economics who invoked the Fifth Amendment when queried about alleged Communist affiliations by the House Un-American Activities Committee. The Middle States Conference of Colleges and Secondary Schools had withdrawn Dickinson's accreditation. There was growing unrest among faculty and students over what they regarded as repressive policies of the college administration.

This was the situation that Rubendall and Witwer confronted as each moved into leadership posts at Dickinson. The academic reputation of the college was at stake. The college's endowment was critically low. On all counts, Dickinson's prospects were bleak.

Rubendall, who took office a few years before Witwer became board president, was startled at one of his first meetings of the board to learn that many trustees did not share his zeal to erase the stigma of the AAUP censure.

"I wear that censure as a badge of honor," one trustee told him. Another trustee publicly denounced the AAUP as "a blatant, 'pinkish,' intransigent pressure group employing many reprehensible tactics of a labor union, including academic blackmail."

Witwer, as a trustee, supported most of Rubendall's struggles to liberalize campus social rules. When Rubendall won board approval to allow social drinking among students over 21 years of age, the Philadelphia Conference of Methodists withheld income to Dickinson from its endowment fund. As these monies remained frozen in escrow for years, the Philadelphia Conference escalated its conditions for freeing the funds. It sought the right to appoint trustees, for one thing. For another, it tried to stipulate that only Methodist students could benefit from the funds. When he became board president in 1964, Witwer was in a unique position to combat these demands. He had become a national figure in Methodism, widely known and highly respected. He argued Dickinson's case so persuasively that when the funds were unfrozen after six years, Dickinson was paid all accrued interest.

An episode preceding Witwer's rise on the board gave ample evidence of his capacity for leadership in sensitive situations. In late 1959, Witwer was named by Spahr to chair a committee of five trustees to improve the college's men's housing which was at the point of crisis due to overcrowdedness and neglect of campus buildings.

Another committee, appointed simultaneously and composed of representatives of the college's 10 fraternities, was to work with the Witwer committee on the problem of new buildings and the buttressing of the fraternity system.

Witwer's committee was spurred by the State of Pennsylvania, which condemned all but one of the school's fraternity houses as unfit for occupancy. Witwer concluded that Dickinson should erect several new and modern houses on a site west of Dickinson's Conway Hall, a site owned by the Pennsylvania Railroad and by a firm controlled by a Dickinson trustee.

To his dismay, Witwer met frustration and stalling tactics when he tried to win approval for his plan. After a year, Spahr and the board's executive committee trotted forth their own plan to construct a quadrangle of 10 fraternity houses on Biddle Athletic Field. Witwer was appalled at this plan to divide the field, which had the potential for development as a first-rate athletic facility. He also recognized the overriding motive for this suggestion which would keep fraternity men remote from the main campus and allow them to live and eat in splendid isolation from the "independents."

Witwer emerged as leader of a faction that fought the Biddle Field plan. Witwer had been flying East for monthly meetings on the buildings crisis and was growing increasingly irritated at the lack of any progress. Finally, he told his committee he would no longer tolerate "filibustering and dilatory tactics."

"This problem has been shunted back and forth for the past two years between various and sundry groups to the extent that Tinker, Evers and Chance were pikers," Witwer told them. "I am too busy in my office to establish a pattern of flying East once a month to participate in a round-robin, never-ending procedure." Then, calmly but quite firmly, Witwer announced his decision to resign the chairmanship unless action was imminent.

At a meeting of the board's executive committee a short time later, Witwer moved to start work on the first five new houses on the site he favored, the property to be acquired from the Pennsylvania Railroad. The committee defeated the Witwer motion, 6 to 3, and referred the subject back to the board's steering committee. Witwer, true to his word, resigned as chairman of the housing committee.

Ironically, Witwer's dramatic walkout proved to be a catalyst. The board's steering committee rejected Spahr's plan for the use of Biddle Field and wholeheartedly supported Witwer's plan. At the first meeting Rubendall attended as Dickinson president, he saw the board of trustees authorize the hiring of a Philadelphia firm of architects and engineers to do the survey work and draft blueprints for the new building program. Rubendall was mightily impressed that Witwer, four months after resigning in disgust, emerged winner of the fight.

It was not long before others appreciated the far-sightedness of Witwer's insistence to preserve the athletic field. The tract had been only six acres when it was donated to the college in 1909 as a memorial to an alumnus. At that time it possessed only a brick and stone entrance and iron gates. Over the next half century the college's athletic fund enlarged the field to double its original size. Less than a year after Witwer prevailed on the housing issue, the Washington Redskins football team, which used the field for pre-season practice, contributed funds for construction of a training and locker building for Dickinson. The field's grandstands were almost wholly rebuilt in 1967. By 1970, the field was fully equipped for intercollegiate athletics, with a football field, tartan track, tennis courts, lacrosse field, baseball diamond, full storage facilities and a press box. In 1964, the new residences for Dickinson's 10 fraternities had been opened, providing for 46 men in each residence. Because of Witwer, the college's fraternities were saved without sacrificing its irreplaceable athletic field; moreover, the fraternities were preserved without increasing their remoteness from the mainstream of life. (In fact, quite the contrary occurred at a later period when, in response to another housing problem, the fraternities were persuaded by the college administration to become "benign landlords" accommodating a percentage of non-fraternity men.)

Witwer's associates at Dickinson believe he never consciously sought the role of reform leader; yet, that role indeed was thrust upon him. It all happened quickly during two afternoons and one evening in the spring of 1964.

The day before the board's annual meeting that May, Sidney D. Kline, a leading Pennsylvania banker who had succeeded Spahr as board president in 1962, disclosed he did not wish to be re-elected. Spahr had held the position for 31 years, during which the board operated under the president's close personal control. Kline's succession was not seen at the time as an interregnum — indeed, under Kline, the board began serious consideration of the college's physical and academic growth — but his unexpected departure after only two years set off a chain of events to select a permanent "strong man" to lead the board.

Rubendall later acknowledged that his own career probably hung in the balance as trustees prepared, with only a day's notice, to select that "strong man."

The afternoon before the board election, Trustee Rolland L. Adams, as chairman of the college's fund-raising drive and publisher of a line of Eastern newspapers, called at the Carlisle office of Trustee Frank E. Masland. There, Adams found Masland conferring with Kline and Trustees W. Gibbs McKinney, George Shuman, and others about the question of Kline's successor. They planned to have the board's nominating committee, which was to meet the next morning before the annual meeting of trustees, recommend McKinney as Kline's replacement.

Adams didn't like the plan. He believed McKinney's supporters mainly opposed the reforms sought by Rubendall. Moreover, Adams suspected his own hopes for a significant boost in college fund-raising would have little chance for success under a fiscally cautious board run by McKinney.

So, Adams evolved a plan to counter the McKinney coup. That night he called together a group of the "liberal" faction of trustees, who were staying at the quaint and tree-cloistered Allenberry Inn in Boiling Springs, five miles outside Carlisle. Among those who answered Adams' call were Trustees J. Milton Davidson, who had been a roistering pal of Witwer in their student days at Dickinson, Professor Carl C. Chambers of the University of Pennsylvania and, of course, Witwer. They agreed upon a plan to nominate Witwer from the floor at the next day's meeting.

Both McKinney and Witwer were nominated, as contemplated, and both were excused from the meeting to roam the campus while debate raged over their respective qualifications. It is unfortunate that no written record exists of the debate; in the Dickinson archives, there exists not even a record of the number of votes cast for each candidate (so zealously did trustees guard the secrecy of their deliberations). But trustees who took part recalled the argument against Witwer as mainly a matter of logistics, although, of course, much more was at stake — the philosophical thrust by which the college was to operate.

The arguments were that Sam lived too far away to pay enough attention to what's going on in Dickinson (to many Easterners, Chicago is lumped with Omaha and Denver as "somewhere out West").

It was felt that McKinney (who lived in Baltimore) could get there in an hour in a real emergency.

Witwer prevailed by a single vote. Thus, as Dickinson archivist Charles Coleman Sellers expressed it, came an end to "that old, long-prevailing concept of sound ideals within a framework of littleness and parsimony" that had existed at the college.

The significance of Witwer's election became apparent a few months later. Rubendall and his executive assistant, Arthur Platt, met with a select group of trustees and faculty at a motel in Gaithersburg, Md., to work on refining a comprehensive plan for Dickinson's future. The plan, the product of efforts by faculty and staff under Platt's leadership, envisioned a decade of vast renewal for the college. It covered expansion of the college's physical plant as well as advancing economic, social and educational assumptions for the coming decade; it addressed the developing educational philosophy at Dickinson (Rubendall was ever insistent on his goal of creating a climate of "free and open inquiry") and the nature of the emerging student body. It also estimated the cost of implementing this program to be staggeringly high, in the multi-millions.

Witwer, Adams, Kline and Chambers were among the trustees that huddled with Rubendall and Platt and scrutinized the Ten Year Development Program. Murmurs existed that no cost estimate was reliable because of the unpredictable rises in construction costs. And, anxiety surrounded the plan's desire to double faculty salaries within several years — a cost item that was not a one-time shot but a constant in future years.

Rubendall remembered, "there was a long, painful silence as they pondered the unprecedented financial challenge."

As Rubendall tells it, "the silence was finally broken by the new board president, Sam Witwer, his voice was firm and clear. There was no equivocation. Witwer's words were: 'If the college is to achieve the excellence we cherish for her and have planned for her, there is no alternative. This is the way we must go. This is the road to excellence. We must accept this great challenge'."

The following December the full board followed Witwer's counsel and adopted the Ten Year Plan, which was renamed the Third Century Development Program with an initial goal of raising $6 million by 1970.

That figure proved modest. Under the program and during Witwer's presidency, Dickinson constructed 20 academic and residential buildings. Its endowment soared from $6 million to $19 million. The value of the college's physical plant almost quadrupled from $7 million to $26 million. Faculty salaries were beefed up substantially with the help of the establishment of annual-giving grants totaling $375,000. The college's enrollment experienced an orderly rise from 1,300 to 1,610 where it was stabilized by decision of the trustees.

The fear that Witwer's residency in the Chicago area would impair his effectiveness was proved false. During the 15 years of his presidency, Witwer never missed an important committee meeting or a board meeting. He regularly flew to Carlisle or Philadelphia for these sessions, and during some periods he was in telephone contact with Rubendall on a daily basis.

This communication was especially important between 1968 and 1970, the period of peak campus unrest due to the student disaffection with the Vietnam War. Student radicalism hit the campus in 1968. Like all protest movements, it reached out for targets totally unrelated to the circumstances which gave it birth. Students were demanding not only an end to the war, but abolition of the entire grading system at Dickinson and curriculum reforms.

On some days Witwer would be astonished to read in the Chicago newspapers some account of campus revolt at Dickinson. He would phone Rubendall. Invariably, Witwer would be surprised at Rubendall's calm. "You're not even mad!" Witwer would say, and Rubendall would reply, "Sam, I don't have time to be mad."

Actually, the closer one was to the campus, the less cause there was for anxiety because press accounts invariably exaggerated the student protests. Witwer himself was the essence of calm reason and cool reflection when he presided over board meetings during periods of campus strife.

Many trustees and a large number of Carlisle townspeople were disturbed greatly when Students for a Democratic Society (SDS) set up a Dickinson chapter. SDS had achieved notoriety for destructive rampages at other campuses, and many wanted to suppress the organization at Dickinson. Not so, Rubendall and Witwer.

Rubendall tried to mollify the board's fears. He told trustees that SDS was "not a group of Stalinists or Communists. Rather, it is a group of interested and concerned humanists who are intrigued by the philosophy of the early Marx." Witwer must have smiled to himself during that period as he thought of Dickinson's two centuries of existence . . . as he thought of the conflict between colonist and British soldiers in the shadow of the first buildings erected at Dickinson . . . as he contemplated how a later generation of students reacted with militance and patriotism during the War of 1812, as students fraternized with American soldiers in a military post at Carlisle . . . as he pondered how many students were activists during the Civil War helping runaway slaves find their way through the underground railroad, one stretch of which passed through the Carlisle area.

Witwer told the board, "As distressing as the present situation with SDS may seem to some, it represents nothing really new in

Dickinson's history . . . Revolution was in the air on the campus from time to time since the earliest days." Witwer had history and accuracy on his side. His viewpoint prevailed.

Shortly after radicalism had taken hold at the campus, the student senate elected a president, Jack M. Stover, who was able to build a valuable bridge to the board through Witwer. Stover led the students from February 1969 until the following February. Students staged a "Declare Day" on March 3, 1969, aimed at getting rid of the grading system. That semi-strike had been unofficial, however, and was not universally observed by the students. In May 1970, there came an "official" strike, as students reacted to the American invasion of Cambodia and the killing of several students at Wayne State University by members of the Ohio National Guard. Dickinson shut down.

Witwer knew there had to be some accommodation with the students, but he also knew the college could not afford to surrender its authority. Stover proposed that he and other student leaders hold a dinner meeting with the board. The board agreed.

"There was a very good dialogue," Stover said while retelling the episode ten years later. "You wouldn't say it was amicable, but it was civil. The dinner meeting between student leaders and trustees has become something of a tradition since then."

Stover (who ten years later had himself become a trustee of the college) said that Witwer "helped convince many students it wasn't a waste of time to work within the structure. I felt that throughout that period the board acted wisely — wisely, in that they were receptive to the students, but not necessarily acquiescent." In January 1970, Witwer approached Stover and asked him to appear at a board meeting to discuss student sentiment (it was a rarity for any outsider, let alone a student, to be allowed to attend a Dickinson board meeting in those days).

"I went before the board and spoke about what was happening on campus," Stover said. "That was a very critical time, but the board's listening to me was an obvious demonstration that the board was reactive to our ideas."

Under the guarded amity that Witwer and Stover set up between the board and students, the student viewpoint won out on two issues. The campus Reserve Officer Training Corps (ROTC) lost its academic credit in May 1970 (following the student strike), and faculty evaluation procedures were established. These concessions were not really deep; they had been granted on other campuses where far more concessions had been paid for restoring order. But the concessions served to dramatize the board's willingness to at least budge. Witwer knew the symbolic value of these concessions, because he appreciated that students regarded the board as too wed to the hide-bound conservatism that characterized trustees when Dickinson had been more under the influence of organized religion. Without the dialogue that had been opened a year earlier between Witwer and Stover, Dickinson could not have survived the post-Cambodia student strike with so little disruption and animosity aimed at the school.

Campus protests, at Dickinson and throughout the country, subsided after adoption of the all-volunteer Army in the early 1970s and the abolition of the draft. But a new problem was emerging to occupy Witwer's attention. Rubendall was about to retire, and Dickinson would need a new college president.

Samuel A. Banks had been a Methodist clergyman for five years while living in the suburbs south of Chicago in the late 1960s and early 1970s. A Duke University graduate of 1949, he received his divinity degree at Emory University three years thereafter and later obtained his Ph.D. at the University of Chicago. He became a psychotherapist on the university's staff while a graduate student, and it was during this period he preached as a clergyman at a church in Harvey, Ill. In 1974 he was living in Florida and was doing intensive research in the field of grief therapy, when he received a phone call from Witwer.

Witwer's voice was its usual low baritone, "Dr. Banks? Samuel Witwer calling. President of the Board of Dickinson College. We are engaging in a search for a president, and we're wondering if you would have an interest in this fine old colonial college . . ." A short time later, Witwer flew to Florida, had lunch with the prospective president in the Banks' home, then spent a few hours questioning Banks as the two men strolled through the woods around the house. "He did what any good member of a search committee would do," Banks recalled. "He probed my concerns, my background in education, my future career interests, that kind of thing. We had never met before, but I knew from the beginning I liked this man immensely. Since my election as college president in 1975, Sam and I have been very close. I would consider our relationship one of almost family."

Bringing Banks to Dickinson was one of Witwer's last major contributions to progress at Dickinson. Witwer views him as one of Dickinson's fine and influential presidents. Banks had no trouble picking up from Rubendall; both men were committed to the same general educational philosophy. Banks stepped into a campus situation in stark contrast to the one that existed when Rubendall took over. Student life was serene, political factionalism had all but disappeared from the board of trustees, and Dickinson was in excellent shape, academically and financially.

As 1979 approached, Witwer grew more certain that it was time for him to step down, to relinquish the board presidency to new leadership. He had been trying to do so for a number of years, but always an "unfinished project" kept him in the job. However, on May 18, 1979, Witwer presided over the board for the last time.

The board's annual meeting took place, as it usually did, in the double-storied, white-walled conference room on the first floor of Old West, a gray block-stone building that is the spiritual heart of the campus. Witwer, looking fresh and acting with the vigor of a man 20 years younger, strode into the room shortly before the scheduled 10 a.m. meeting time. After the usual hearty greetings of old colleagues and enthusiastic handshakes, Witwer seated himself behind a table microphone and called the meeting to order.

Banks began submitting his fourth annual report as college president, but interrupted himself partway through to introduce a resolution designating Witwer honorary board president for life. As his fellow trustees applauded, Witwer rose, graciously accepted an elegant plaque from Dr. Banks, and strove to keep his response limited.

He referred to his years of board service as spanning "a rather remarkable period in American higher education." He recalled the public and academic reaction to the challenge posed by the Soviet Union's launching of Sputnik I in the late 1950s. He alluded to the turmoil of student unrest in the later 1960s. He spoke with his hands clasped in front of his waist, his bearing erect but not forbidding.

"I don't want to lengthen this meeting with reminiscences," he insisted. "I wouldn't have missed my years as president of this board for anything, but I'm grateful you acceded to my requests (to resign)." Witwer was determined not to be maudlin, yet his voice took on a slightly more husky tone as he said his final words to the board as its president, "It's an occasion of tremendous sentiment for me. In your forthcoming meetings, I wish you Godspeed."

The following day, a Saturday, scores of alumni returned to the college for their annual reception at the President's House, a huge white frame house with green shutters almost hidden by foliage and set back on a corner lot of the campus. Banks, his wife, and Sam and Ethyl Witwer stood for a few hours greeting old friends, retired faculty and parents of students who would graduate the next day.

It was a time for nostalgia, for memories. Dr. Horace Rogers, professor emeritus of analytical chemistry, who taught at Dickinson from 1925 to 1971, chuckled remembering how Witwer, as a student, got an old Ford car positioned inside the college library as a prank. Dr. Rogers said, "I remember saying to myself after Sam Witwer graduated, 'That man's going to make his mark in the world. I've never seen such a born leader'."

Trustee Davidson, telling stories about his and Witwer's student days together, suddenly grew serious, "You know, in those days I was convinced Sam would become President of the United States. It didn't seem like such an outlandish notion. I was sure it would happen."

On Sunday of that weekend, the 206th Commencement exercises were staged on the John Dickinson Campus at Old West. In his last official act as board president, Witwer presented Hanna Holborn Gray, president of the University of Chicago, to the convocation for the conferring of an honorary degree of doctor of laws on her. Dr. Gray, who delivered the commencement address, began her speech with a tribute to Witwer for his service both to Dickinson and to constitutional reform in Illinois referring to him as Illinois' Lycurgus. It was not to be Witwer's final attendance at Dickinson commencement, but the occasion nonetheless marked the end of an era — for both him and for Dickinson.

When he returned to Dickinson the next year, for the 50th anniversary of his 1930 graduating class, Witwer confessed the experience did not buoy his spirits or particularly refresh him, as most visits to Dickinson had done. Perhaps this was due to his growing awareness of "my own mortality," as Witwer expressed it with a half-smile. Perhaps it was because he subconsciously was aware of classmates who had not survived for the half-century reunion. Most likely, his reaction was the normal letdown of an active leader who had been in control of events for many years, and who now was more of an observer, or a passive participant, than an instigator of action.

But there was another aspect to visiting Dickinson that never failed to revitalize Witwer which was touring the countryside around Carlisle. Witwer's maternal and paternal ancestors had settled in Lancaster County, Pennsylvania in the very early 18th century, and Witwer came to believe this genealogy fed his love of this region of the country.

Years previously, Sam and Ethyl searched for a family graveyard which Witwer thought might be found within a few miles of Blue Ball, Pennsylvania. They asked a farmer if they could inspect a small enclosure on a knoll on his farmland and when the farmer learned Witwer's name and the reason for the search, he directed the couple to a graveyard being cared for by the Mennonites about one-quarter of a mile away. There, Sam and Ethyl were astonished to find the marker of "Michael Witwer" and nearby, the marker of that pioneer's grandson, Samuel Witwer, "died age 20 years, 4 months and 3 days (1814)." Sam and Ethyl were dumbfounded at the coincidence of having named their twins Samuel and Michael without any realization that these surnames had been in the Witwer family for generations. They also learned that the farmer of whom they made the original inquiry was named Sensenig, which was the maiden name of the woman that Michael Witwer married when he emigrated from Switzerland in the early 18th century to start the Witwer line in America.

In early 1979, the Witwers learned of a second family graveyard in a mountainous area overrun with growth near Chambersburg, Pa. Witwer determined that a number of his ancestors from the Revolutionary War period were buried there.

The extent of his family ties to the region was not known to Witwer when he enrolled at Dickinson in 1927. He was aware, of course, that an uncle had graduated in the class of 1900, but he did not appreciate a regional genealogy dating back another 200 years. His three sons, Samuel, Jr., Michael and David, continued the Dickinson tradition, all graduating in the 1960s. (The Witwer's daughter, Carole, attended Northwestern University.)

Witwer was enormously proud of the growth of the college's academic stature between his student days and the end of his board presidency. By 1979, Dickinson was receiving six times as many freshmen applications as the college could accept. Dr. Stanley O. Ikenberry, vice-president of Pennsylvania State University who became president of the University of Illinois in 1979, appraised Dickinson as a "small Dartmouth." If I had a choice between Dartmouth and Dickinson for sending my son to college, I'd choose Dickinson," Dr. Ikenberry said. "The smaller student body makes it a more attractive college."

On occasion Witwer regretted that Dickinson had not reached such heights when he was a student. "It is possible had I gone to a somewhat more intellectually demanding institution — and Dickinson has since attained that status — that I might have been challenged to a higher intellectual achievement in the course of my career," Witwer said.

"On the other hand, my interest in people and public affairs was largely influenced by the breadth of my extracurricular activities at Dickinson. On balance, it probably worked out for the best."

In 1966, a $500,000 women's residence hall was built at Dickinson and named in honor of the Witwer family, but Witwer never thought of Witwer Hall as the measure of his legacy to the college. He saw his contribution as something not physically tangible. Witwer had become committed to a concept of education as an intrinsic value in its own right, not as a means to an end. He believed he succeeded in helping to preserve that concept at Dickinson, in helping the college to adapt to change without surrendering that concept.

In *Dickinson College: A History,* Professor Seller captured the essence of this concept. He wrote, "It is the essential duty of a college to preserve, impart and increase knowledge. Turbulence and ferment are needed from time to time to clear off traditional patina and give a new clarity to the old design."

Sam Witwer never quit fighting until he was convinced that he indeed had helped "give a new clarity to the old design."

1.

2.

3.

4.

5.

6.

7.

8.

9.

10.

11.

1. Former Governor Adlai E. Stevenson and Governor William G. Stratton with Witwer to celebrate the 1950 Gateway Amendment passage.

2. President Harry S. Truman greets Witwer on reviewing stand for Chicago "Bud Billikin Day" parade.

3. Left to right: Louis A. Kohn, Governor Stratton, Mayor Richard J. Daley, join Witwer in promoting 1958 Blue Ballot Judicial Amendment.

4. Witwer greeted by President Dwight D. Eisenhower in Oval Office in 1957 following 1956 presidential re-election campaign.

5. The Witwer family campaign in 1960.

12.

6. Governor Stratton and Chairman Witwer of Illinois Citizens for Eisenhower-Nixon, greet "Ike" in campaign rally.

7. Governor Stratton greets Sam and Ethyl Witwer early in 1960 in primary rally.

8. Witwer campaigns the Chicago neighborhoods with Pat and Dick Nixon in July, 1960.

9. Witwer visits Vice President in Nixon's Washington home in December, 1959, preparing for primary for U.S. Senate seat.

10. Witwer (left rear) joins colleagues of the Judicial Council of the Methodist Church (Supreme Court) following Pittsburgh General Conference of 1964.

11. Board President Witwer presents U.S. Senator Jacob Javits of New York for Dickinson honorary degree.

12. Witwer retires as Dickinson's Board President at 206th Annual Commencement in 1979, flanked by Past College Presidents: Howard L. Rubendall and Samuel A. Banks.

STRUGGLING FOR CONSTITUTIONAL REVISION IN ILLINOIS

The history of state constitutional conventions in this state and elsewhere — there have been more than 200 state conventions — demonstrates the futility of expecting soundly drafted constitutions to emerge from unsoundly structured conventions. The record is clear that conventions formed with partisan or sectional strife or controlled by or submissive to any interest other than the public interest, have little chance of succcess.

— Samuel W. Witwer
Union League Club of Chicago, February 13, 1969

During the years 1942 through 1945, Witwer, in his thirties, conscious of his growing position, was active with his professional colleagues in the Chicago Bar Association; chiefly as a part of the Younger Members Committee, then achieving importance in the affairs of the Association. He was chairman of the Committee for two years in 1944 and 1945.

Heads of committees in the Association generally serve only a one-year term. The added tenure was a recognition of the competence of his leadership. Thus, he came to know many of the top men of the bar, became keenly interested in professional and civic activities, and, for the first time since his days at Dickinson

College, emerged from his shell to a considerable extent. He was becoming extroverted. One of his first public appearances in Chicago, following his relatively quiet period at Harvard Law School, was an address he delivered at the National Junior Bar Conference, held in conjunction with the annual convention of the American Bar Association in Chicago in 1944. As chairman of the Chicago Bar Association Younger Members Committee, he welcomed the participants and presided at the opening of the conference. His talk had the felicitous ring that was to characterize all of his later public appearances. While Witwer never became a spellbinder, he could generally hold the attention of an audience.

Often in his life, Witwer observed that much he did was inspired by men whom he respected, as in the case of his fellow Methodist George McKibbin. His activities in the Chicago Bar Association were in part the result of his close acquaintance with Morris Leibman who preceded him as chairman of the Younger Members Committee. Leibman, then as now, was a dynamic person who inspired response and emulation; he liked to advance others, rather than himself, although he, too, had a dramatic rise in the profession. Thus, Witwer was soon elected to the Board of Managers of the Association, an unusual privilege for a young man only a decade out of law school.

It fell upon Witwer during this exciting time for him to draft a report of the Association censuring John F. O'Connell, the Probate Judge of Cook County, for his acceptance of travel benefits and entertainment every year from the Stanley McCormick incompetent's estate. The rich but unfortunate McCormick resided in Arizona in comfortable circumstances. The Bar Association investigation revealed that the judge felt that he had to make a trip each winter to look into the welfare of the wealthy ward of the court and that he took with him members of his family and billed a substantial part of the cost to the estate. This was unprecedented in the conduct of a court known, since the days of Judge Henry Horner, for its solicitude for those dependent on its watchful care. The result of the disclosure and the stinging report of the Bar Association led to O'Connell's defeat for re-election as probate judge. Witwer recalled writing in his draft a statement of censure that a judge should avoid not only evil but the appearance of evil, and he, the devout Methodist, quoted from Deuteronomy! O'Connell was succeeded by Judge William Waugh, who served with distinction for a few years and then died suddenly while addressing the Executives Club at the noon hour one day when Witwer happened to be in the audience seated in front of him.

It was these and similar activities which brought him to the attention of the leadership of the Bar Association — men like the legendary long-time secretary, Clarence P. Denning, and the current president, James F. Oates. And, in 1946, resulted in Witwer being made a co-chairman of a special committee of the Association which pressed for the adoption of the so-called "Gateway Amendment" to the Illinois Constitution, on the ballot once more that year. The co-chairmen with Witwer were Adlai E. Stevenson, who had served with the Secretary of the Navy Frank Knox and at the formation of the United Nations, and attorney Austin L. Wyman, Sr. The other members of the committee appointed by Oates were all distinguished lawyers: Walter V. Schaefer, Erwin W. Roemer, Henry A. Gardner, Harold A. Smith, Albert E. Jenner, Jr., Floyd E. Thompson, Walter F. Dodd, Judge Harry M. Fisher, Charles O. Loucks (who then was the nationally outstanding "Methodist law" expert), Eldridge B. Pierce and Richard Bentley. Each of these men had led or was about to head various Chicago, Illinois and national bar associations or to hold high public office.

It was almost amusing, if not startling, that the committee was organized only one month before the November 5, 1946 general election at which the proposal was to appear on the ballot. In the interval, Austin Wyman and Witwer, aided by Robert McDonald, then chairman of the Younger Members Committee, and other Bar Association stalwarts, worked continuously, contacting newspapers, political leaders, billboard owners, and others in a belated but spirited attempt to develop the much needed public interest. Adlai Stevenson, it should be noted, was on the committee only nominally. At that time he was at Lake Success, NY, working on matters pertaining to the charter of the United Nations. On one occasion, Witwer recalls saying to Austin Wyman that if Adlai could save the world, certainly he and Wyman could do something to save the state of Illinois from the "dead hand of the dead past."

This was the fourth unsuccessful "Gateway" effort up to that time since adoption of the 1870 Constitution. In a report which Wyman and Witwer prepared in January 1945, they explained the difficulties encountered and attempted to lay a foundation for future activity on the part of the Chicago Bar Association and others in waging more successful constitutional revision efforts. It was then that many of the ideas and techniques subsequently pursued by Witwer in campaigns from 1950 through 1968 found their genesis. During this all too brief one-month campaign, Witwer became acquainted with people like Werner Schroeder, a prominent Chicago lawyer close to Governor Dwight H. Green, and other Republican leaders, with Jacob M. Arvey and Barnet Hodes of the Democratic organization, with political writers for all Chicago newspapers, and, of course, with leading civic personalities who led various labor, business, fraternal and community organizations. Perhaps the most important contact that he made during the campaign was with Professor Kenneth C. Sears of the University of Chicago Law School who was greatly interested in all efforts for constitutional reform. Sears corresponded with Wyman and Witwer for a substantial period after the November election, discussing the shortcomings of the campaign and what must be done in the future. Witwer was greatly influenced by the total commitment of Sears and saw how unyielding he was in constantly battling with the *Chicago Tribune,* the Illinois Manufacturers' Association, Ruben Soderstrom of the Illinois State Federation of Labor, and others who were relentless in opposition to constitutional reform by the convention method. Most of them were not less opposed to other methods of reform, even the limited Gateway approach. They were committed wholeheartedly to the status quo and viewed the opposition as upstarts. Their own positions were too cozy for them to relish change.

The Gateway Amendment campaign of 1946 was the first of a series of campaigns in which Witwer participated either as chairman, co-chairman, or as general counsel of statewide committees organized to promote public support. These included campaigns for a constitutional convention in 1948, the successful Gateway Amendment of 1950, the successful Banking Amendment of 1952, the successful Reapportionment Amendment of 1954, the unsuccessful Judicial Amendment of 1958, the successful Judicial Amendment of 1962, and the successful campaign for the call of the constitutional convention in 1968. Interspersed between these campaigns were a number of ongoing committees and commissions organized to increase interest in the general subject of constitutional revision. Witwer was continuously involved in all constitutional revision efforts, which came to be known as the "Blue Ballot" campaigns, for a period of approximately twenty-five years, commencing in 1946 and running well into 1971, with the adoption and implementation of the new 1970 Constitution. The effort required a vast amount of his time and energy; it was his life work, stimulating and enjoyable and deadly serious at the same time. His reputation is based upon these activities. Newspapers dubbed him "Mr. Blue Ballot."

The Gateway Amendment of 1946 won a majority from those who voted on it; however, it failed adoption due to the overwhelming percentage of those voting in the general election who failed to vote on the specific issue. Thirty-five point two percent (35.2%) voted "for" the Gateway Amendment, 10.2% voted "against," and 54.6% failed to vote on the issue which, in effect, were counted as "no" votes. This was the continuing tragedy, as Witwer saw it. His aim was to break the lethargy and towards that end he struggled like a man possessed.

Early in March 1947, Witwer received three visitors in his law office in the Continental Bank building. They were Mrs. Walter T. Fisher, president of the Illinois League of Women Voters; Marion Farley, state chairman of the League's Constitutional Revision Committee; and Professor Walter V. Schaefer. They told him that the president of the Chicago Bar Association, James Oates, was prepared to appoint him as chairman of a new standing committee on constitutional revision. They expressed the hope that he would undertake the work, since proposals were then pending in Springfield for the calling of a Constitutional Convention, and that a group of civic organizations, headed by the League of Women Voters and the Union League Club, already was planning a statewide effort to secure passage of the joint resolutions.

Witwer's visitors were in his office as a direct result of a previous meeting Schaefer had with Leon Green, dean of the Northwestern University Law School. The dean felt strongly and impressed upon Schaefer, then on the Northwestern University Law Faculty, that Illinois would never break out of its constitutional straightjacket unless an individual were found who would take the lead and personalize the sought after constitutional reform. Green understood that constitutional revision is not a sport for the shortwinded. He emphasized the need to seek out and appoint an individual who would be objective, who had no definite position on issues that would offend either liberal or conservative, and who had the prominence, ability and persistence to persuade and inspire confidence. The Committee pointed to Witwer's services in the 1946 Gateway drive as a valuable start, clearly establishing his qualifications for leadership. He was not yet forty years of age, yet so early in his career he was looked upon as a leader and, indeed, was a man with the mark of destiny upon him.

Witwer told his callers that he knew very little about the Illinois Constitution, and that they should secure a constitutional expert for the job, one who would not have to school himself. Witwer assumed that experts were in abundance, men like Professor Sears. Schaefer smiled and replied, "Sam, if a client walked in your office with an important piece of law business in a branch of law that you had not heretofore practiced, I'm sure that your reaction would be to go to work and learn all about it rather than turn down the engagement. This is important public law and if you feel you need to know more about the Illinois Constitution, I'm sure you will learn in a hurry."

Schaefer's argument was compelling and challenging. Witwer did not want to be found running from a vital assignment, perhaps the most important that had come his way. After studying the matter for a few days, he contacted the committee and agreed to serve upon certain conditions. One was that the president of the Chicago Bar Association would appoint to the new committee lawyers who in the future were likely to enjoy political influence in their respective parties; another that he would assist him through other Association committees in ascertaining the extent to which Illinois had been hobbled by the old 1870 Constitution. Mr. Oates gave Witwer those assurances and Witwer, in his usual dedicated fashion, commenced work. He was given a top-flight committee made up of lawyers of substantial influence in the community, as well as a number of younger men who were success oriented and had a capacity for hard work. The committee Witwer enlisted to serve in the late 1940s included one man who thereafter twice ran for the Presidency of the United States, Adlai E. Stevenson; a man who during the Stevenson campaigns was the National Chairman of the Democratic Party, Stephen A. Mitchell; a man who became governor of Illinois, Otto Kerner; a man who became solicitor general and then went on the U.S. Circuit Court of Appeals, Walter Cummings, Jr.; a man who became law partner to the most powerful democratic leader in Cook County at the time, Barnet Hodes; and Walter V. Schaefer who was later elected to the Illinois Supreme Court.

Time was short and the Committee set about their task immediately, getting ready to present a convincing case for a constitutional convention before the Illinois legislature. In a sense, it was naive to believe that logic alone would win the day. Witwer was surprised to find little, if any, literature about the need for constitutional revision and the shortcomings of the 1870 document. Throughout April he devoted many hours of study to the substantive problems, so that if he had to appear before legislative committees on behalf of the Chicago Bar Association, he would possess some knowledge.

The first meeting with the Executive Committee of the State Senate was scheduled for May 7, 1947. Several days before that hearing, Schaefer and Witwer spent most of one night drafting a statement captioned "A Constitutional Convention for Illinois —

The Need for a Convention." This was reproduced for distribution in Springfield. Among others who joined Witwer on the trip to Springfield were Mrs. Farley, Professor Kenneth Sears, Laura Hughes Lundy, representing the Women's City Club of Chicago, and William James, vice president of the Illinois State Bar Association.

The meeting in Springfield was a shocking revelation of legislative disdain for constitutional reform. In the first place, Senator Charles Carpentier, chairman of the Executive Committee, later Secretary of State, had no real desire to hear from the Witwer committee. It was only upon the insistence of the more public-spirited Senator Abraham Lincoln Marovitz that they were permitted an appearance before the committee late in the day after being forced by Senator Carpentier to wait throughout the forenoon as the Executive Committee planned for so important a public matter as a softball game with the House that afternoon. Even as the committee session finally proceeded, Chairman Carpentier and others showed great disdain by continuing to chat about other matters, pretending to ignore all that was being said about constitutional problems.

The effect of that treatment was to make Witwer more determined than ever to fight for a constitutional convention. The Bar Association committee resolved that they would provide an adequate "literature of reform," so that the next time they were called to Springfield to testify, they would place on the desks of every senator and House member a detailed and convincing showing of the shortcomings of the 1870 Constitution. They soon made headway in preparing the reform literature through assistance from Professor Kenneth Sears, the successive presidents of the Chicago Bar Association, and the leading editorial writers of the major newspapers of the state.

At the time of the aborted hearing, Erwin W. Roemer of the law firm of Gardner, Carton & Douglas, was the president-elect of the Chicago Bar Association. Like his predecessor, James Oates, Roemer was totally committed to constitutional reform. With Witwer's concurrence, he sent a copy of the material which Schaefer and Witwer had prepared to Governor Dwight H. Green and requested a meeting to discuss the Governor's position on the joint resolution for calling a convention. The Governor replied that he had long recognized the need for constitutional revision and would continue to support carefully considered proposals, noting, "I am sure you are aware, however, of the considerable opposition that exists both in and out of the legislature to the constitutional convention plan." Green was then closely allied with the *Chicago Tribune,* which opposed the call for a constitutional convention.

A month or so later, Roemer, Witwer and one or two others from the Association committee called on Governor Green in his Chicago office. He maintained a gubernatorial suite on the 19th floor of the Union League Club instead of an office in a state building. Witwer recalls that the Governor sat between the American and State flags and conducted public business. Green was cold and withdrawn and it became quite clear that he would not throw his support behind the joint resolution for a convention call. After leaving that conference, Witwer knew he could not support Green for re-election, though Green would be the candidate of his own Republican Party. Soon after, Witwer started to think of the possibility of the election of Adlai E. Stevenson as governor. Witwer knew Stevenson was committed to the call of the convention and to the cause of needed reform generally. This was the time when others began to look upon Stevenson as an ideal public servant. Stevenson seemed the epitome of patrician class. His voice and bearing suggested rectitude. Already a legend, a mystique was being created about him, and Witwer, like many other deeply earnest citizens, were in its thrall.

On June 17, Governor Green wrote to Oates, responding to his telegram for support of the joint resolution, stating that he would "support the measure fully and cooperate in every way possible toward its enactment." By this time Green, possibly before others, was beginning to see that his re-election was not certain. He was facing a tough campaign in 1948 and could not treat with indifference state issues of prime importance. But there was no sincere commitment on his part, Witwer felt, and his response to

Oates was merely expedient.

In the months that followed, Witwer had close working relationships on the Association committee with a number of well-regarded lawyers, including Walter J. Cummings, Jr., a partner in Sidley, Austin (Stevenson's firm); Kurt J. Salomon, attorney for the Hearst *Herald-Examiner;* Judge Julius H. Miner, who managed to be close to the competing Colonels of the *Tribune* and the *News;* and Leon Stoltz of the Editorial Department of the *Chicago Tribune* (who basically had an interest in the reform, being as liberal as anyone could be and remain on his newspaper). On June 28, 1947, Witwer received a letter from Stephen E. Hurley, next in line as president of the Chicago Bar Association, and currently chairman of the City's Civil Service Commission, containing words which Witwer long treasured:

> It has pleased me no end to hear so many fine things as I have about your excellent and well-directed efforts toward a constitutional convention. I know that you will look back on these efforts with a deep sense of personal satisfaction and that through efforts such as yours the desired solution of the most difficult problems will be proudly achieved sooner or later.

As time went on, Witwer was to receive an increasing number of such letters. They gave him personal satisfaction and inspired him to continue in his endeavors, despite great personal sacrifice.

On July 2, Witwer received a note from Adlai E. Stevenson thanking him for material which he promised to read. Stevenson, in his elegant way, expressed hope that he could be "of some service in connection with this important work." Stevenson always managed to suggest more than he said and to create the impression of great intellectual ferment. This delighted his more dedicated and less eloquent friends.

After July 1, Roemer became president of the Chicago Bar Association and continued to give Witwer the same high measure of support which Witwer had received from his predecessor. On one occasion he and Witwer went downstate to address a bar group concerning the need for constitutional reform. They could not get anyone to argue the negative and so Roemer acted as "Devil's Advocate" and presented the usual arguments against constitutional reform, while Witwer presented those in favor.

At this time the committee included such additional stalwarts as George B. McKibbin, Ruben G. Cohn, Walter F. Dodd, and Louis A. Kohn, who fit the description of scholars and gentlemen, a tag that always appealed to Witwer.

As part of the program to develop a literature of reform, and with the encouragement of Professor Sears, Witwer himself undertook to write a paper on the relationship of the Illinois Constitution and the courts, which the *University of Chicago Law Review* requested for publication. When Witwer accepted the undertaking, he assumed the existence of a great deal of law review material on the constitutional problems of the courts. Once again, he was disappointed. Relatively few things had been written which, in any degree, focused on the matter; most prior material dealt with legislation and rules of court impacting on the administration of justice. Important in its own context, this was not too useful in the more basic constitutional situation. Thus, it became necessary for Witwer to dig more deeply than he had contemplated. He was aided, of course, by Sears, Judge Harry M. Fisher, a rare judicial scholar and innovator, and others who gave him valuable suggestions. In the last analysis, as he recognized, the job was his alone to do. Because of the impending publication deadline, Witwer found it necessary to use his entire three-week vacation in August 1947 to research and write the article. He was to make even greater sacrifices as time went on, and he began to expect them. After the article was published in the Autumn issue, Roemer was so pleased with it that he arranged for the Chicago Bar Association to purchase 6,000 reprints for distribution to its membership and to outstanding editorial writers and other formulators of public opinion throughout the state who might influence the much-needed improvement of the court system.

The same issue of the *University of Chicago Law Review* carried other constitutional articles, one by Barnet Hodes on the need for home-rule, and others focusing on the shortcomings of the Illinois Constitution. This matter of home-rule was a favorite subject for the politically ambitious and astute Hodes, as of that time the youngest corporate counsel the city had ever had. He could speak in a practical way of the special problems faced by cities like Chicago.

No paper Witwer had written was more influential in terms of his leadership position. Soon after its wide distribution, Witwer heard from A.T. Birch, chief editorial writer of the *Chicago Daily News*, that he would be quoting him in several editorials in which he called for a stronger Illinois judiciary. Witwer thereafter received scores of letters from members of the bar and other interested citizens who commended him and indicated a desire to help in the ongoing convention campaign.

About the same time, articles by Walter Cummings on revenue reform, Wayland B. Cedarquist on methods of securing "party circle" legislation, others on home-rule and reapportionment were prepared, published, reprinted and distributed widely. In short, there was considerable intellectual ferment in support of the revision effort late in 1947 and into 1948 and, in addition, the crucial involvement of Stevenson was strengthened in the public campaign for the call of the constitutional convention.

At about this time the Chicago Bar Association launched a public effort for a revised judicial article, either as part of a new constitution or as a separate amendment. The renewed effort in Illinois drew national attention with inquiries from the National Municipal League and officials of the legislatures in Hawaii and in other states starting constitutional reform programs. Editorials dealing with such problems and quoting generously from Witwer's court article began appearing. On December 5, 1947, Otto Kerner, Jr., then United States Attorney and later governor of Illinois, accepted appointment to the Chicago Bar Association Committee. The new names were symptomatic of the gaining impetus. Senator Charles Carpentier, chairman of the Senate Executive Committee, might continue to be more interested in playing softball, but there were some who preferred the hardball of constitutional reform. No one would remember the score in the softball game, but they would remember Witwer and his cohorts.

There were some ancient leaders of the bar who were not sympathetic to Witwer's efforts. John D. Black, who was the senior partner of the prominent law firm of Winston, Strawn & Shaw, and a former president of the Chicago Bar Association, objected to the distribution of Witwer's court article and said that the procedure for amending the 1870 Constitution was already too liberal. This was the same gentleman who had earlier opposed the admission of Black lawyers to membership in the Association on the ground that it was a social club. In writing to President Roemer, Witwer commented, "If the present amending procedures are too liberal, as Mr. Black asserts, then I am at a loss to know what could be done to make the amending procedure more difficult, short of providing that the Constitution shall never be amended or revised. Seemingly, some people would approve of that course."

Subsequently, when Governor Alfred E. Driscoll of New Jersey came as the invited guest of Witwer's committee to address a bar membership meeting designed to stimulate interest in the constitutional convention proposal, Black, as director of the Association chorus, famous for its Christmas Spirits show, unexpectedly worked into the program a song to the effect, "you do things your way, Governor Driscoll, and we'll do things our way." It was, of course, rude, but Driscoll smiled, and subsequently in his speech said that with such musical talent he was sure that Illinois would find its way out of any dilemma. He and Witwer may privately have hoped that Black and his reactionary cohorts would lull themselves into oblivion.

Witwer began to find that his role was not a particularly popular one in other quarters. The Driscoll dinner occurred on February 19, 1948, and several days before that the *Chicago Tribune* carried a characteristic editorial, describing Driscoll as an "internationalist," throwing doubt upon his Republican credentials, and winding up with the statement, "It would seem that the Chicago Bar Association could easily find speakers more worthy of being honored by its membership than Driscoll, unless, that is, it admires the type." This was a typical *Tribune* utterance in the era of Colonel McCormick. However, the *Tribune* began to change, as the Colonel left the scene. Twenty-one years later, Governor Driscoll spoke at the orientation session of the Sixth Illinois Constitutional Convention without the slightest controversy.

An important role was played by the little dynamo, Louis A. Kohn, one of Witwer's closest friends and a distinguished Chicago attorney. Early in 1948 Kohn indicated to Witwer his interest in the constitutional reform movement. He joined the committee and proved to be indefatigable. Here was a man who was interested in results, and never concerned about whether he would get the credit. It always bothered Witwer that Kohn did so much for good causes, and received little appreciation. Kohn's contacts with Adlai Stevenson had commenced during World War II, when, in military service, he corresponded with Stevenson from Manila, in the Philippines, seeking to interest him in political life. He had known Stevenson as a lawyer in Chicago prior to the war and was impressed. As Kohn put it to Witwer: "Here I was in the midst of the war wondering what kind of a society we would have when we returned home. It seemed to me that we had a duty to make our democratic system work if we were to pay such a fearful price as we were paying in the Pacific; also that people like Stevenson were needed."

Early in 1948, Kohn asked Witwer to write to Stevenson, then at Lake Success on United Nations duties, and urge him to run for the governorship in Illinois. Stevenson replied politely that if he had any talents they would be in the United States Senate — the only political avenue that would interest him. At the time, Kohn was vigorously assisting Witwer with the Bar Association committee. It was he who had made most of the arrangements to bring Governor Driscoll to Chicago for the already mentioned meeting. As mentioned, too, he was constantly advancing the name of Adlai Stevenson and imploring Witwer and others to urge Stevenson to enter politics. Witwer was not partisan in such endeavor. He was concerned more with revision efforts through Stevenson and others. Witwer would place this cause ahead of his own political future and such loyalty as he had for the Republican Party.

In January and February 1948, Kohn and Stephen A. Mitchell, then also active in the Chicago Bar Association committee, asked Witwer to join with them and Herman Dunlop Smith, a business-man, in calling on Colonel Jacob M. Arvey, chairman of the Democratic Party Central Committee of Cook County, to urge Arvey to consider Stevenson as the nominee of the party. Witwer assumed that the others knew of his Republican leanings, although he did not flaunt them. They asked only that he speak with respect to the senatorial race and not reiterate his view that Stevenson should run for governor. Arvey might lend an interested ear. He had been a bright organization man when he entered military service during the war. He returned with the same concern that Kohn had for the public good but he had become the Chairman of his party organization and was victory oriented.

On the appointed day, they met at the Arvey office and had a most interesting conversation, as Witwer said, in typical under-statement. Each person was called upon to express himself about Stevenson. When Witwer's turn came, faithful to his commitment, he urgd Arvey to consider Stevenson for the Senate seat. Much to his delight, Arvey said that there was little likelihood that the Democratic Party would endorse Stevenson for that seat; that if Stevenson was going any place, it would have to be the governor-ship. Arvey said, "a man named Paul Douglas was going up and down the state in a jeep with his wife, Emily," and he already had a strong claim to the nomination for the Senate seat. Like the incumbent, C. Wayland Brooks, the *Tribune's* darling, Douglas had a good military record. He had enlisted when over-age and had fought in bitter battles and suffered permanent injuries.

In the course of Witwer's remarks, he said to Arvey, "As a Republican, I can assure you that there will be many Republicans and Independents giving their support to Adlai Stevenson."

At the time Witwer's colleagues appeared shocked and Stephen Mitchell seemed angered as well. Later, outside the Arvey office, Mitchell castigated Witwer for having the temerity to suggest to the Democratic leader what a Republican thought would be wise for the Democratic Party. The next morning Mitchell telephoned Witwer to apologize and said that he had had a further talk with Arvey, who was quite pleased with the fact that Witwer had spoken as he did, saying that if Stevenson was to win, he had to draw heavily on disenchanted Republicans and on Independents.

As a result of that meeting, Witwer became a close friend of Arvey's and thereafter Arvey was always supportive in all of the Blue Ballot and constitutional reform efforts in which Witwer became involved. Many times Witwer called on him at his headquarters and asked for advice in getting out the vote in various uncertain wards and townships. One time, shortly before Arvey's death, Witwer encountered him at the Standard Club in Chicago and he said to Witwer that he thought Witwer had more good friends in the Democratic Party than he had in his own Republican Party. Witwer sometimes was persuaded of this, too, rather ruefully. But, generally, he would remain faithful to his party except when greater issues were involved, transcending partisanship. Constitutional reform was one such issue.

With the nomination of Adlai E. Stevenson for governor, Witwer began communicating with him increasingly about his stand on constitutional revision, and meeting with him and his advisers, including Louis Kohn. On April 9, 1948, Witwer discussed with Stevenson the possibility of an open letter to Governor Green calling specifically for a constitutional convention. While sympathetic to the general revision effort, Stevenson preferred not to make any specific suggestion as to the legislative procedure to be followed or to refer to particular constitutional needs. Stevenson believed that something should be said in the open letter, in "laymen's language," assuring downstate that revision could occur without opening the door to domination of the legislature by Cook County. He was then considering the possibility of a restricted or limited convention, which he asked Witwer to research. He also wanted to be certain that he was on safe ground in asserting, as Witwer suggested, that both parties in their past platforms had favored constitutional revision.

At this time he preferred not to be involved in promoting a "party circle" bill to implement any joint resolution which might come out of the legislature for a constitutional convention or amendment. Soon Stevenson submitted the question to his advisers and, throughout his campaign, his position started to gel and he came around ultimately to the point of calling for a constitutional convention. Among those advisers were, significantly, Walter Schaefer and Richard J. Daley, who were soon to play prominent roles in the judicial and political areas, largely because of their association with Stevenson. It was Stevenson who later placed Schaefer on the State Supreme Court against the wishes of the organization politicians, who had one of their own in mind.

In May, the Chicago Bar Association Committee sent a questionnaire to numerous state officials, including Governor Green. Green wrote a lengthy letter, requesting further study of the problem, and stating that in order to achieve meaningful constitutional reform, it would be necessary to remove the fears of downstate Illinois that it might lose under reapportionment — this was before the U.S. Supreme Court handed down the historic *Baker* v. *Carr* decision, making proper representation, "one man, one vote," a constitutional necessity. Green said, further, that a reapportionment of the state should take place in advance of a convention in order to correct grievous inequalities between Cook County and downstate, and also between the wards and townships within Cook County. Nevertheless, after all this, he stated that he would support a consitutional convention referendum, and would urge the General Assembly to adopt a joint resolution for such call. It was clear from his letter that those commitments were made without enthusiasm or strong belief. They were exacted by political necessity and could change readily. To those who were anxious to get on with revision, there was little doubt that Governor Green did not offer an avenue of hope, and Stevenson did. There were other reasons, too, for supporting the latter man. He was a refreshing contrast to the stale politicians around him.

Stevenson, on April 26, 1948, had answered the Chicago Bar Association inquiry, also with some necessary ambiguity about the specific steps proposed, while expressing a fundamental concern to do something about our "unamendable" Constitution. Stevenson insinuated faith on the part of people like Witwer, while Green did not.

The committee continued a vigorous program throughout the spring, and at the annual meeting held on June 29 when the guest speaker was Philip B. Pearlman, then Solicitor General of the United States, a good deal of attention was paid to constitutional reform. As the summer and fall progressed, the Stevenson gubernatorial campaign became more and more explicit in terms of supporting constitutional reform, but, so far as possible, Stevenson still avoided too much specification, obviously a wise position for him at that time. After all, Stevenson was a diplomat, who left lines of retreat open. By September 1948, the League of Women Voters had scheduled a joint appearance for Green and Stevenson at an October 8 meeting, at which time both candidates were asked to give their views concerning constitutional reform. The Republicans had failed to adopt a resolution in support of a constitutional convention call while the Democratic State Convention had adopted one. The lines were now drawn on the issue. One could rely upon commitment, rather than faith alone.

By the end of September, Witwer was working on speech material for Stevenson and occasionally going with him to attend meetings. Green was essentially talking for a compromise solution. He could not be too forthright or he would antagonize some of his more backward supporters. Stevenson made his historic statement about public and private subterfuge, evasion, and easy virtue, which characterized Illinois' efforts to "get along" under the Constitution of 1870, a quote which Witwer used many times thereafter. Witwer sat at the speaker's table and became totally convinced that Stevenson was the only hope for constitutional reform. Barnet Hodes, law partner of Arvey, obtained from the Chicago City Council a resolution calling for a constitutional convention referendum. Witwer began cultivating Hodes again. He surely could be influential for the cause in the right places. He was a politician, but something of an intellectual as well. Hodes had both expediency and principle as his guide posts. His services for Chicago indicated many constitutional limitations for the city.

These had to be overcome by constitutional reform, including home-rule.

During this period, Witwer was kept busy with speaking appearances throughout the Chicago area, largely initiated by the League of Women Voters. As the election approached, his contacts with Walter Schaefer increased and, of course, after the overwhelming and largely unexpected victory of Stevenson in the November 1948 election, all of Witwer's thoughts turned toward Springfield and what could be accomplished in the coming months in securing favorable action on the constitutional convention call and the supporting "party circle" bill. The Joint Committee for a Constitutional Convention, which was organized late in 1948, now gave a broader base to the effort than that which it had had simply with the leadership of the Chicago Bar Association and Illinois League of Women Voters. At that time, Professor Kenneth Sears was state chairman and, when the legislature became involved in the convention call battle, Witwer had become the Committee's spokesman for the issue, with the approval and encouragement of Stevenson himself. The Republican Witwer's support for his party's gubernatorial opponent appeared to be paying off. Witwer could scarcely imagine at the time that he would become the candidate of the Republican Party for United States Senate. He knew that he would have much explaining to do if that ever happened.

Shortly after Stevenson's election, Witwer received a phone call from Schaefer, who had become Stevenson's top administrative assistant. Schaefer asked Witwer to work on a statement concerning the constitutional convention, for use in Stevenson's Inaugural Address and, also, to work on a legislative program consisting of a joint resolution for a call of the constitutional convention and a "party circle" bill. Witwer heard repeatedly from Louis Kohn during November and December. Kohn had, likewise, become a close aide of Governor Stevenson. The new governor was drawing to his side some of the best men in the state, and some, like Witwer, from the opposing party. Stevenson was never a hardcore party stalwart.

In his inaugural address, Stevenson called for a constitutional convention, using some of the material which Witwer had submitted. Soon afterwards the work of the Bar Association Committee and the State Joint Committee, consisting of the League of Women Voters, Chicago and Illinois State Bar Associations, Illinois Agricultural Association, the Union League Club of Chicago and numerous other groups, was well under way. The effort was to encourage legislators to come out publicly, and the decision of the Governor, following his inauguration on January 2, 1949, was to go first to the House of Representatives in the belief that the Senate votes would be forthcoming readily if the proponents could get past obstacles in the House. Witwer visited in the Governor's mansion with Stevenson, his aides and legislative leaders, one of whom was Richard J. Daley, who had become the director of the Department of Revenue. Witwer had known Daley in committee work at the Chicago Bar Association and their relationship was a friendly one. During the next two or three months, they were to become even better acquainted. This doubtless was of great importance in a number of the Blue Ballot campaigns, which were to follow the unsuccessful constitutional convention effort in 1948. Looking further ahead, the association with Daley was to become vital in Witwer's election as president of the Sixth Illinois Constitutional Convention; but no one could foresee it at that time.

During the first two and a half months of the Governor's term, while the convention call resolution and party circle bills were filed in January by their legislative sponsors in both houses, no particular legislative progress on the Stevenson program was noted. On one occasion, Witwer was told by Kohn that Governor Stevenson had inquired of Senator "Botchy" Connors, a non-intellectual leader of the Democrats, concerning the reasons his legislative program was not going forward. It is said that Connors indicated to Stevenson that an appointment of a "lodging house inspector" in Chicago was still dragging and that he thought it possible to "get on" with the program once that appointment was made, as requested. The office of "lodging house inspector" was then very important in getting out the vote in certain West Side wards, where the lame and the halt and even the dead cast ballots. It was under this pressure that Stevenson in time found it necessary to make the appointment in question, which he would have preferred to delay.

This was an education in Illinois politics, not only for the new governor, but for many of his idealistic friends. Stevenson continued to talk elegantly, but he had to court those whose knowledge of the refinements of speech were meager and whose idealism was scarcely visible. One of them, Alderman Paddy Bauler, had said, "Chicago ain't ready for reform." Nor, perhaps, was the State. What was an essentially idealistic governor to do in such circumstances?

Early in January, the *Chicago Tribune* carried an editorial, *"What's Wrong With the Illinois Constitution?"*, asserting that there was nothing seriously wrong in Illinois government. Witwer took it upon himself to reply by a letter to the Voice of the People. In due course it was printed in full with accompanying note from the editor, seeking to answer the points Witwer made in his letter. The exchange triggered a series of editorials and articles in other newspapers concerning the inadequacy of the 1870 Constitution. In general, most agreed with Witwer's position. This did not persuade the *Tribune,* of course, firm, as always, in its policies.

In February, Governor Stevenson presented his legislative package for a constitutional convention, including the so-called "Party Responsibility Bill." House Speaker Paul Powell then announced that he was going to ask the appropriate committees of the House to schedule hearings promptly. A few days later on February 10, Witwer received a telegram from Charles H. Webber, chairman of the Illinois House Executive Committee, inviting him to address that committee in the House chambers at 2:30 p.m. on Tuesday, February 15, 1949. Work on the drafting and redrafting of the so-called "Party Responsibility Bill" before its introduction had been undertaken by attorneys Owen Rall and Rubin Cohn.

Witwer sought to prepare himself for his appearance in the House of Representatives after the Chicago Bar Association officers had decided that he should make the presentation on behalf of the Association. The members of the Joint Committee were equally desirous that Witwer would be their spokesman. Professor Sears could not attend because of an academic conflict. Because Witwer was relatively young and not too well known, it was felt in bar circles that an officer of the Chicago Bar Association, George Woods, in line for the Association presidency, would introduce him to the legislators. In the meantime, people like Kohn, Daley and others discussed with him the legislative and political procedures likely to be encountered in addressing the Executive Committee. Witwer scarcely realized that it would be the kind of meeting that it turned out to be.

Because of the great interest in the subject, the House chambers could barely accommodate the full attendance. As it happened, it was treated as a session of the House, meeting as a committee of the whole. In addition, numerous senators were on hand and representatives from the League of Women Voters, the bar associations and other civic groups packed the galleries.

When the matter was called up by Chairman Webber, George Woods stood up and announced that he was an officer of the Chicago Bar Association and was there to introduce Witwer. However, he did not confine his remarks solely to such introduction, but offered the gratuitous comment that the Illinois Constitution of 1870 was unworkable, was causing numerous problems, and that it was necessary to revise and alter it. Having done that briefly, he sought to return to his chair and to have Witwer commence presentation. However, Reed F. Cutler, minority leader of the State House of Representatives, took the floor and demanded that Mr. Woods remain for cross-examination. Woods protested that he was there only to introduce Witwer. Cutler reminded him that, as a lawyer, he had "opened the door" by his comments on the existing constitution and Cutler wished now to test him. For a least fifteen or twenty minutes, Cutler literally humiliated Woods, who knew little, if anything, about the constitution and simply could not respond to the vitriolic cross-examination. In time, Woods became very nervous and emotional, and actually was tearful. Finally, the sadistic Cutler released him, with a sneer and a tic of his huge ungainly body.

It was with this background that Witwer proceeded to answer questions, most of which were hostile, presented by members of the Chicago West Side bloc, Cutler and other opponents of constitutional revision. One of the representatives, John Lewis, took the floor and virtually characterized Witwer as a Communist or fellow traveler, a remark which was printed, substantially unchanged in the *Chicago Tribune* the following day. The challenge of the occasion, the shambles which Cutler sought to make of the proceeding, and Witwer's own preparation, made it possible for him to respond in a rather convincing way; at least, it was subsequently said by the *Chicago Daily News* that he had done so with skill.

Witwer's appearance before the legislators consumed the better part of two-and-a-half hours, mostly in bitter debate. He stood at the podium at the lower level in the House chambers, where twenty years later he would be passing on his way to the upper podium to be inducted as president of the Sixth Illinois Constitutional Convention. The thought of such an eventuality did come to his mind. It was his greatest hope at the time that the legislature would pass the resolution, and he even then felt that he had a background qualifying him to chair the convention which he hoped would be held in 1950 in response to the effort then being made.

Witwer returned from Springfield and, for the better part of several days, he was emotionally exhausted in consequence of that unusual, if not shattering, confrontation. Then he had to prepare for a repeat performance the following week when he was to appear again as the spokesman of the Chicago Bar Association and the Joint Committee in support of the Party Responsibility Bill. He was heartened when Richard J. Daley applauded his work the preceding week and urged him to do a similar job with respect to the bill. He then said, "Sam, one of these times you ought to plan to be a judge." Witwer made light of the comment at the time; but had he sought a judgeship during the early period of Daley's tenure as mayor of Chicago, there is little doubt that he would have been slated as a judge. When Witwer emerged as a Republican candidate for the

United States Senate, it was the end of his securing judicial appointment from the partisan Daley. However, they remained on friendly terms.

Witwer's performance on February 22, 1949, was not as successful in substance as the earlier one. He could not get geared up to make a strenuous argument for the Party Responsibility Bill. In the first place, he did not believe in leaving to party "bosses" or organizations the decision of whether to call or not to call a constitutional convention. While the method of the party circle was historically justified (for it was in this manner that the 1870 Constitution and the first five constitutional amendments were submitted prior to adoption of the "Australian Ballot Act" by Illinois), nevertheless, it ran counter to his views to vest controlling authority in political bosses in this all-important popular function of government. As a result of this lack of conviction regarding party circle voting, Witwer did not come away from the session with the enthusiasm that he had the previous week. One could understand the let-down, and there would be more ups and downs in the unpredictably long struggle of two decades to follow.

Following the two sessions in Springfield, he received a telephone call from A.T. Birch, associate editor of the *Chicago Daily News,* who applauded him for his work on the resolution for a constitutional convention and said he thought that his newspaper could support him if he had ambitions for political life. He hinted about Witwer's aspiring to the lieutenant-governorship. Again, Witwer made light of the suggestion. Soon Birch arranged for Witwer to meet John S. Knight, the ebullient publisher who had succeeded Colonel Knox. Birch and Knight continued to be unusually supportive of his efforts both in constitutional revision and in Republican politics in the years that were to follow.

After the hearings before the legislative committee, the Governor and his leadership people made every effort to get out the legislative vote. On April 15 the joint resolution came before the full House. The night before the critical roll call, word came to the Governor from the West Side bloc legislators, the river wards contingent, that unless he would scuttle the then pending Chicago

Crime Commission bills, they would not support his joint resolution for a convention. The Governor, naturally, declined the gross bargain. Witwer walked the streets of Springfield with Daley and Schaefer that evening, trying to count noses and to figure out where they stood. It was a matter of great disappointment when they missed by some five votes in getting the necessary constitutional majority required to pass the joint resolution in the House. Following that defeat, Witwer returned to the governor's mansion with Kohn where Stevenson put his arm around Witwer's shoulder and said, "Sam, we live to fight again another day." And so it was.

It was a tremendous disappointment to Witwer when they failed to get the necessary votes for a convention call in the House, particularly because they believed that the Senate approval was in sight. Had they succeeded, it would have saved eighteen years of unsuccessful effort by the piecemeal method of revision under the Gateway system that was to occur between 1950 and 1968, until the Witwer forces finally succeeded in calling a constitutional convention. Witwer's involvement continued unabated in those eighteen years, for at the time it seemed plausible that constitutional reform could be accomplished by amendment, and that a convention was an impossible dream.

Soon after the defeat of the convention proposal, the Republican leadership headed by Senator Wallace Thompson of Galesburg (whose son subsequently served in the Sixth Illinois Constitutional Convention), introduced in the General Assembly a resolution for a Gateway Amendment (the fifth such effort since 1870) as well as amendments to the Election Code providing for the separate Blue Ballot. This latter proposal, using a ballot of distinctive color and helpful instructions, as it turned out, may have been more significant in the long run than the Gateway Amendment itself. The amending process was to be eased somewhat by requiring a two-thirds vote of those making a choice on the issue as an alternative to a majority vote of those participating in the election, which had proven an insurmountable obstacle in the past; the resolution, also, provided that three, rather than a single amendment, could be presented at each election.

While the constitutional reformers hoped that the "Gateway" measure had potential, Witwer felt, as he looked back later, that most of the proponents of that measure in the legislature and in the forces of labor and manufacture really believed that they were remaining in control of the process of constitutional change, notwithstanding the lip service given Gateway by such dubious persons as former Governor Green, sadistic Representative Cutler, the hardbitten labor leader Soderstrom, and many other constitutional recalcitrants.

Just before the joint resolution was to be voted on, Kohn and Witwer met briefly with Stevenson. They urged him to hold out for a Gateway amendment that would provide a simple majority vote on the issue presented, rather than a two-thirds vote called for by the Thompson Gateway proposal, pointing out the great difficulty in securing a two-thirds vote on any really substantive or controversial constitutional change. Of course, Stevenson was sympathetic, but he rejected the thinking of his two friends, saying that he had battled for the matter long and hard enough at the expense of his other legislative goals and that for him to insist upon a simple majority, rather than an extraordinary vote, would appear to be mere petulance and afford his opponents further excuses for obstruction. Stevenson was not only the diplomat, but also the realist.

Soon afterwards, the joint resolution for a Gateway amendment and the Blue Ballot legislation were approved overwhelmingly. It was then that Stevenson, through Kohn, asked Witwer to become state chairman of the campaign to secure voter ratification. A few Republicans also urged him to do so. He could feel again that his efforts transcended politics. The Joint Committee, which had worked for the convention resolution, was now reorganized under the name, "Illinois Committee for Constitutional Revision." Witwer was elected state chairman. His cochairman was Charles B. Shuman, president of the Illinois Agricultural Association, whose son and namesake was later to serve in the Sixth Illinois Constitutional Convention and act, at times, as a rather gentle gadfly to Witwer.

Much of the ensuing battle for ratification of the Gateway amendment is told elsewhere and need not be repeated here. Historians have not given enough attention to the role which was played by Nathan E. Jacobs and Alan Jacobs of the public relations firm of Bozell & Jacobs, Inc. during the years 1950 through 1970. Nathan Jacobs, then manager of the Agency's Chicago office, had become personally interested in Stevenson's crusade for a new constitution and he had volunteered his assistance and that of his colleague and nephew, Alan Jacobs, to the Joint Committee. Thus, when the Gateway campaign was launched, Witwer as a matter of course, turned to Bozell & Jacobs and secured substantial assistance in charting the public relations program. Nathan and Alan Jacobs became involved with Witwer in almost everything he did in public affairs for a period of twenty years. While Witwer had learned many lessons in the 1946 abortive Gateway campaign and a good deal in the '48 and '49 efforts for a constitutional convention, his public relations experience and any skill he acquired in that field really stemmed from the Gateway campaign of 1950. While it has been said that the 1968 campaign for the convention call was the most comprehensive effort in the long, hard history, Witwer believes that it was equalled by the scope and dynamic quality of the 1950 campaign. Certainly, many of the things that were learned at that time were adopted later. It was Witwer's testing time and the learning period for the constitutional reformers.

This was probably the first "good government" campaign in the history of the state in which an all-out, professionally directed and carefully thought through campaign was launched to secure, not only bi-partisan support, but also the involvement of civic, business, labor, political, church and other organizations. The campaign was all-inclusive, at least in intent. It was in this campaign that Witwer was introduced by banker Guy Reed and George McKibbin to the leaders of the Commercial Club of Chicago, believed to be the most influential group in the city. Witwer then commenced a series of addresses before that powerful organization on constitutional reform. While the Club at no time openly sponsored any campaign, the finance committee of each successive

Blue Ballot campaign henceforth consisted largely of leading members of the Club who solicited substantial contributions from corporations, individuals and foundations to aid in what they deemed increasingly a worthy cause. The ultimate conversion of the *Chicago Tribune* to the side of constitutional reform was not without some relationship to the respect that Witwer and his associates commenced winning from the leadership people of the state and, particularly, from the so-called "Chicago establishment." Gateway afforded a means of educating people to a recognition that the state Constitution was restricting all people and that it was no longer a conservative or sensible course to insist upon living under the strictures and rigidities of the 1870 document, refusing to adjust laws and institutions to the needs of a much changed and still changing society. Standing still in a rapidly moving world meant that you were going backwards.

A second substantial advantage of the Gateway effort was the sense of involvement by many people in a great public cause. The Blue Ballot in and of itself came to be a symbol for what was right. It focused attention on the need of the citizenry to participate in the decision-making process. In some respects, it is possible that without this indoctrination and the identification with the Blue Ballot, the referendum of December 15, 1970 would not have been successful and Illinois might not today have its new Constitution. The importance of the Blue Ballot device is emphasized by the fights pursued to maintain the integrity of that method. There were always those who would weaken or dilute it.

And, certainly, the widespread acquaintance with political, governmental, business, labor, agricultural, and other leadership throughout Illinois which Witwer maintained uninterruptedly for three decades started in the Gateway campaign. To it, also, he owed a growing self-confidence and skill and public exposure.

The adoption of the Gateway Amendment in 1950 was acclaimed by the press as an unprecedented and epochal achievement. While all prior Gateway proposals, over the period of 58 years, failed by wide margins, the 1950 effort was successful and secured the largest favorable plurality in the history of Illinois at that time. The vote required to adopt was 1,865,810, while 2,512,323 votes were cast in favor of the amendment and only 735,903 against — a 2 to 1 triumph. It was the first amendment to the 1870 Constitution in half a century.

Following the successful effort, the committee sought to remain in service to assist in determining the three priority proposals which would be submitted to the electorate in the 1952 general election. Because of the special and at times conflicting interests of the various constituent groups, it became evident that the Illinois Committee for Constitutional Revision could not fulfill that role. In consequence, the Committee became inactive and took no official position in or out of the legislature concerning the selection of the first three amendments to be proposed under the new system.

There was a good deal of maneuvering by others as soon as it became known on November 7, 1950, that Illinois would have a new method of revising its Constitution. Floyd Thompson, a noted lawyer and former justice of the Supreme Court of Illinois and candidate for high office, who had headed one or more unsuccessful revision efforts in years past and had been relatively inactive and silent in the 1950 campaign, called a press conference and announced that he and several of his colleagues would be taking over the direction of the ongoing constitutional revision movement. This was rather surprising to Witwer at the time, but, later learning of the aggressive qualities of Judge Thompson, it was understandable. It was not in Thompson's nature to say, "By your leave." He would brusquely assume it and barge in. As time went on and Thompson had to face the actual hard work of effectuating constitutional reform, he and other latecomers to the movement dropped by the wayside. Thereafter, the same group, led by Witwer, which had been carrying the battle for years continued to be the "voices in the wilderness" of ongoing constitutional revision under Gateway. The historical verdict has been in their favor, and not only because of their persistence.

When the General Assembly convened on January 3, 1951, Governor Stevenson made no particular effort to sponsor any single substantive constitutional amendment under the new Gateway procedure. He left it largely to the legislature to make the choice of the three articles to be amended. One of those selected by the General Assembly provided a new Revenue Article, permitting classification of property but prohibiting graduated income tax. Another related to the Counties Article, giving sheriffs and treasurers the right to succession in office, and lifting salary limitations on certain county officers. The last was an amendment to remove the double liability provision for state bank stock owners.

Neither Witwer nor the Committee which had fought for the Gateway Amendment had much to do with the selection of the amendments. In fact, the general reaction on the part of many constitutional reformers was one of considerable disappointment. While it was recognized that the Revenue Article was badly in need of revision, the form in which the proposal came from the legislature was not overly attractive. As to the other amendments, they seemed to be of relatively little public importance as compared to the needs to revise the Legislative Article, the Judicial Article and many other provisions of the Constitution which had been emphasized during the debates on the 1949 Constitutional Convention effort. Witwer was most disappointed and irate when he learned that the bankers had managed to achieve the submission of an amendment removing the double liability on state bank stockholders; for he felt that that was essentially a private matter which could have waited while more basic matters were resolved.

This had an ironic twist. Early in 1951, Witwer was contacted by an officer of a major Chicago bank and a friend of years standing, who inquired as to Witwer's availability to lead a campaign to secure adoption of the very Banking Amendment which Witwer deplored. At the time, Witwer responded that in all other instances he had served purely as an uncompensated volunteer in constitutional revision work and that he could not very well take another year out of his law practice to campaign for an amendment that seemed to have more private interest than public concern as its motivating purpose. Obviously, the double liability provision was a harsh one which could not be justified in principle and which had not worked particularly well to the advantage of anyone, other than litigants who pursued bank stockholders at times of economic chaos and breakdown such as followed the disastrous 1929 stock market crash. The banker's response to Witwer was that there was no expectation that he would serve as a volunteer chairman, but that he would be compensated for any legal services he would render. After considerable thought, Witwer undertook the assignment, feeling that it was an entirely proper and responsible work for a lawyer possessing his experience and that the Banking Amendment would, at least, be a forward step in cleaning up one aspect of the obsolete constitution of 1870, albeit not a major one. He was then retained by the Illinois Bankers Association as a special counsel.

At that time, Witwer requested his banker clients to make a public announcement that in this instance, unlike all prior campaigns, he was not serving as a volunteer chairman but was being professionally engaged and compensated as counsel. Witwer felt that it was important to make the distinction, lest, at some future point, he would be accused of misrepresentation. As it turned out, that was precisely what occurred in 1960 when he was a candidate for the Republican nomination for the United States Senate. In the course of the primary campaign, one of his leading and more aggressive opponents attempted to make it appear that Witwer's services in the Blue Ballot campaigns were not voluntary but had been paid for handsomely by "sinister interest," such as "the syndicate." Happily, at that time, Witwer was able to direct inquiring newspaper investigators to articles which appeared in the financial pages in February 1952 in every major Chicago and downstate newspaper, disclosing what Witwer had required as a condition of his employment. The rumor was dissipated immediately.

Basing his services on experience as chairman gained in prior campaigns, he planned and programmed a statewide campaign of public information involving widespread distribution of carefully prepared literature explaining the history of the double liability provision, its arbitrary nature, and how it could function to hamper efficient banking services in Illinois state banks as distinguished from national banks which did not have such double liability. Witwer presented the issue as a fight to sustain the dual banking system, rather than to have all the banks in Illinois, sooner or later, nationalized and brought under the domination of the federal system.

Of course, the interested banking institutions, through the Illinois State Bankers Association, provided adequate funds for a carefully prepared public relations campaign. The firm of Bozell & Jacobs, once again, became involved in this, like Witwer, on a strictly professional basis. Witwer worked virtually full-time in helping to organize local committees throughout the state, meeting with newspaper and political leaders, as well as greatly interested state bankers. At the outset, it was realistically recognized that there was little reason to assume marked public interest in any measure relieving holders of state bank stock from a potential augmented liability. A second problem Witwer faced was in conducting the campaign somewhat in isolation from the simultaneous campaigns for the Revenue Article Amendment and the two amendments to the Counties Article, which he felt could drag down the Banking Amendment to defeat. Aside from efforts of certain political leaders, there was little concerted activity in the other concurrent campaigns, although numerous civic groups sought to get together under the leadership of Robert S. Cushman, a distinguished tax lawyer, in the Revenue Amendment campaign.

In 1952, and again in 1966, Witwer was not overly supportive of the proposed Revenue Article Amendments submitted in those years. Perhaps the reason he·was not supportive in 1952 was his professional commitment to the adoption of the Banking Amendment, if it was at all possible. In addition, Witwer was not pleased with the substance of the Revenue Amendment, as written. Subsequently, in the Revenue Article effort in 1966, he found little to commend to the public. And while it was a maze of compromise and ambiguity, he did not publicly oppose it. He let his silence speak for him. Revenue changes, he was to learn constantly, are the most difficult to sustain, because of popular suspicion of the taxing power. It was apparent to many that revenue reform could come only in the context of a new constitution, overhauling all of the rigidities of the past.

As the 1952 campaigns progressed toward the November 1952 decision, it became quite evident that the vote would be close for the adoption of the Banking Amendment.

But the opportunity to direct the campaign was a fortunate one for Witwer, for it once more brought him into contact with business leadership throughout the state in addition to well-known bankers in every community. These were contacts which proved of substantial benefit in subsequent constitutional reform efforts when Witwer was seeking to enlist broadened support from business, which, in the past, had been withheld from constitutional convention call efforts as well as the several Gateway campaigns. Witwer did not realize then that less than two decades later he would have to contend with the bankers in a difficult and less desirable fashion in the constitutional convention. The past could not always be a guide to the future.

As matters turned out, the Revenue Amendment failed by a substantial margin, the Counties Article Amendments dealing with succession of county sheriffs and treasurers failed, while the other two minor amendments passed, each by a very narrow margin under the two-thirds test. Witwer long recalled the uncertainty concerning the Banking Amendment, which existed on the night of the election and for days thereafter. In the case of general elections for state officials or presidential races, the media maintains a system of continuing the reporting of the ballot counts in all counties throughout the night following the elections, relying on what are known as "police reports," as distinguished from the formal and official vote tallies which necessarily await filings with the county clerks and election officials. However, on matters such as the constitutional amendments, there is generally not sufficient public interest warranting the newspapers in maintaining that kind of costly service. In consequence, when the wire services shut down about midnight, the fate of the Banking Amendment was uncertain. On the basis of projecting the then known vote, Witwer was of the opinion that it had probably passed and he so advised his clients.

However, it became necessary throughout the following two days to make literally hundreds of telephone calls throughout the state to newspapers, election officials, local bankers and politicians to ascertain what, in fact, had occurred in many of the downstate counties, some of them sparsely populated. As these informal reports came in piecemeal and he made further projections, the outcome became more doubtful — at one hour it would appear that by projection the Banking Amendment was adopted by a small margin and by the next hour that it was under the required two-thirds vote by a small amount. In the final outcome, the amendment prevailed on a statewide basis by slightly less than one-third of one percent of the required vote on the issue. It was adopted by just slightly in excess of the necessary two-thirds vote, as was the successful Counties Article Amendment. Witwer was delighted to have led the successful effort, even if the margin was slender, and the bankers were quite pleased. They were rid of double liability and potential future claims of hundreds of millions of dollars. Now, Witwer and they could turn their attention to other more important matters.

For many years thereafter, Solomon A. Smith, the blueblood chairman of the Board of the Northern Trust Company whom Witwer had first met as a young man soon after arriving in Chicago, invited Witwer to address the Northern Trust officers and administration group every year in which there was a Blue Ballot proposal before the voters. Smith would then ask Witwer to bring appropriate literature and he would assemble the entire group, consisting of several hundred people, to hear Witwer's Blue Ballot lecture and to receive the materials. Smith always initiated the matter by a few humorous words about their earliest contacts and, of course, with a reminder that under Witwer's leadership, state bank stockholders had been rid of the burden of double liability.

Aside from his salary as a delegate and president of the Sixth Illinois Constitutional Convention in 1969-70, the Banking Amendment campaign was the only instance in the more than three decades of Witwer's involvement in constitutional reform efforts in which he was compensated for his services. In that long period Witwer turned down opportunities to become a paid lobbyist and to obtain other financial advantage out of what has been his vocation and dream. It was the kind of integrity and dedication not often exhibited in this sometimes crass world.

In view of the close margin by which the Banking Amendment passed, "double liability" would not have been removed from the stockholders of state banks had Witwer not afforded the right kind of leadership in that particular campaign. It was a victory scarcely to be predicted and was principally related to the association with the good government symbolized by the Blue Ballot. Not only did the new ballot format and color help make possible that victory, but its successful utilization in the banking campaign provided a further identification with good government which would serve well subsequent efforts such as the 1954 Reapportionment Amendment, the 1958 and 1962 Judicial Article Amendments, and the 1968 Call of the Constitutional Convention in all of which Witwer was involved. These earlier Blue Ballot efforts had their cumulative effects, and the movement for constitutional reform in Illinois must be viewed as an historic continuum which started decades ago.

Governor Stevenson sought unsuccessfully for a call to a new constitutional convention for Illinois. Unsought, the Democratic nomination for president of the United States was thrust upon him in 1952, but that quest was unsuccessful, too, although Stevenson delivered some of the greatest political speeches in American history during the course of the campaign. His eloquence and wisdom made him one of the superlative failures of our national life.

Witwer, too, sought a new Constitution for his state and, in time, much time, he won his tireless struggle. Meanwhile, he sought and won the Republican nomination for the United States Senate, but no senatorial laurels came to him. It was only a detour in the road to constitutional reform, as we shall see.

It was not until 1953, and the administration of William G. Stratton, Stevenson's successor as Governor, that the first attempt was made under the new Gateway method to reapportion the legislature, a problem which had troubled state government in

Illinois for decades. Downstate was vastly over-represented in the General Assembly in contrast with Chicago and Cook County, which had grown disproportionately since the enactment of the 1870 Constitution. Like most state charters, that document mandated reapportionment, but that required legislative action, which was not forthcoming when the result would be a loss of power in some entrenched areas of the state. Stratton, who enjoyed a fine political instinct, not only by inheritance from his father, a popular holder of high office, but also through specialized training as a political science major at the University of Arizona, was determined to develop a compromise plan that would permit Illinois to be redistricted more fairly by analogy to the federal system. And Stratton was reputed to be a mathematical whiz kid, who could solve all sorts of problems.

Accordingly, he proposed an amendment which would have had the Illinois House of Representatives redistricted on the basis of population — "one man, one vote," as it began to be called — while leaving the Senate to a geographical type of representation, as is the case of the United States Senate. In effect, this would have given the populous Chicago area control of the House and the less populous downstate control of the Senate. At the time, this seemed to be a reasonable compromise, supported by historic and federal constitutional precedent. Remember, this was before the historic case of *Baker* v. *Carr* and subsequent decisions required representation based upon population in both houses of the legislature, and not merely in one. While there was a good deal of legislative opposition in both parties, Stratton used the power of his office effectively to bring about the adoption of the joint resolution in the 1953 session shortly before adjournment on June 30. Stratton did not hesitate to enjoy political muscle where a more idealistic, less practical man like Stevenson might be hesitant.

Early in August, Witwer was contacted by friends of the Governor concerning the possibility of his giving leadership again in the campaign for the proposed amendment. Witwer was asked to provide the Governor with an outline of what he thought was required for a successful campaign. After some consideration, he agreed to help and serve as state chairman. It will be recalled that the Illinois Committee for Constitutional Revision had been quite active in the successful campaign for the Gateway Amendment, but had not participated in the 1952 referenda campaigns involving the Counties Article, Revenue and Banking. Now once more, there was a good deal of interest within the Committee. Before long it was back in business, ready to do an effective job. Just as was the case with the Gateway Amendment, the Committee was able to secure the assistance of Charles Shuman as state co-chairman. Shuman had been successful in swinging the downstate vote in favor of the Gateway Amendment and it was correctly believed that he would do as well on the Reapportionment Amendment, although downstate was suspicious of reapportionment as a surrender of its unequal power.

The campaign followed the procedures which had been used so successfully in the Gateway effort. All public relations activities were under the leadership of Bozell & Jacobs, with Alan Jacobs virtually in full-time activity. Once again, the effort was placed upon a bi-partisan foundation and the committee was able to secure not only the support of Edward F. Moore, Republican County Chairman (through the influence, of course, of Governor Stratton), but also that of Richard J. Daley, who was the Democratic Chairman of Cook County in succession to Colonel Arvey, and who, in time, took an active role as a leader of his county organization in urging ward and township committeemen to get behind the issue.

During this period, Witwer, accustomed to dealing with Arvey, called on him to ask whether the Committee indeed was going to get all-out support, as pledged, on election day. Witwer asked Arvey whether it would be possible for the organization vote to be "pulled" or withheld even though commitments had been made publicly. Arvey smiled and said, "Yes, indeed, Sam, it could be, but that is not going to happen." He stated that there were several Chicago wards which were uncertain in their loyalty and as to these he could give no guarantee of performance, although he would do his best with them. One was the second ward, predominately Black and under the dictatorial leadership of Congressman William

Dawson, once a Republican, now a big man in the Democratic party. He recommended strongly that Witwer see Dawson, and Witwer journeyed to Dawson's dark and forbidding basement office on the South Side one Saturday morning. While waiting for Dawson to call him in, Witwer was amazed when the door to Dawson's office opened and there emerged one of the leading United States Court Judges, once a power in Democratic politics. He had been closeted in conference with Dawson. Witwer wondered what conceivable judicial work was afoot. Dawson said he would do what he could to uphold the Democratic endorsement, but he showed no great enthusiasm. His reticence may have been due to the unanswered question, "What's in it for me and my people?"

When the actual tallies were known a few days later at the November 2 election, the amendment did very well in the Dawson ward, thanks, probably, to a call which Arvey made to Dawson to supplement Witwer's visit. The outcome of the election was immensely gratifying, with one of the largest pluralities given an amendment in the history of the state. Of the 3.5 million voting in the election, 2.6 million voted on the proposition and 2 million voted affirmatively, a tremendously favorable margin. Accordingly, the measure passed under both counting methods, and in Cook County the favorable vote was a miraculous 92%. This left little doubt that Richard J. Daley and his Democratic organization had fulfilled, and more than fulfilled, their commitment. Similarly, the Republican leadership had done its part. Witwer would remember this during the course of the Sixth Illinois Constitutional Convention, even if others forgot, that politicians sometimes count. The press viewed the adoption of the Reapportionment Amendment by so large a margin as to call it a landmark accomplishment. More laurels were added to Witwer's sometimes furrowed brow. It was such triumphs in the midst of defeats that encouraged him to continue despite personal sacrifices. But it was now time, more than time, for him to think of his personal life. He had done more than his share in uncompensated public endeavor.

Several months after the success of the amendment, a banquet was held in the Red Laquer Room of the Palmer House in Chicago, attended by most of the political leadership of the state. It was sponsored by the Reapportionment Committee, and Witwer himself delivered the principal address. He viewed it as his "swan song," and somewhat later he formally announced his retirement as chairman of the Committee. At that time all Chicago newspapers carried editorials thanking him for his years of leadership. Most people recognized that he needed to return to his law practice, which had suffered somewhat from the recurrent interruptions as he had campaigned continuously over the preceding ten years. Little did Witwer then realize that it was actually just a brief interlude of rest, hardly enough to refresh him to engage in another two decades of effort.

The success of the Reapportionment Amendment added to his growing list of powerful acquaintances and contacts throughout the state and doubtless had much to do with setting the stage for his subsequent political activities as he became candidate of the Republican Party for the United States Senate, and earlier when he served as Illinois Chairman for Eisenhower and Nixon in the national presidential campaign of 1956. Doubtless, his contacts with Governor Stratton in 1954 were of such a nature as to have influenced greatly those partisan political developments. To this day, Witwer enjoys a warm, personal relationship with Stratton, whom he regards as one of the state's outstanding governors. He did not desert the governor in his time of trouble, just as he later stood by the unfortunate Attorney General William Scott. Both men were charged with tax offenses, Stratton being vindicated by jury verdict.

In 1954, possibly in consequence of his success in securing the adoption of the Reapportionment Amendment, Witwer was elected a member of the prestigious Commercial Club of Chicago. As matters developed in subsequent years, this too assisted Witwer in relaying the importance of unfinished constitutional reform to the business, financial and educational leadership of the city. While the Club never officially adopted constitutional reform as a stated program (its practice being to deal only informally in all such matters), the Club has since proudly viewed its role in the Blue Ballot efforts as being fundamental. In its history the Club lists its involvement in the Illinois constitutional revision movement with the Burnham Plan and other great civic undertakings.

At the testimonial banquet, Witwer was seated at the speaker's table and immediately to his left, in order, were Mayor Richard J. Daley, Mrs. William G. Stratton and Adlai E. Stevenson. Before the dinner commenced, a newspaper photographer approached Stevenson and said, "Will the three of you [referring to Stevenson, Mrs. Stratton and Daley] please squeeze together so that I can get you in a picture?" At that point Stevenson quipped, "My man, I am sure that the Mayor of Chicago and I would be very pleased to squeeze together with Mrs. Stratton, but she may feel that that would be carrying the bi-partisan spirit just a step too far tonight!" Witwer sometimes missed the intellectual and moral verve of Stratton's predecessor. He was not always at ease himself in light touches.

A few months later, it became evident that it would be difficult to continue to keep the Committee operating in an active posture, although it was formally kept alive to protect its favorable income tax rulings, which, up to that time, had permitted substantial contributions to be received on a tax-deductible basis. After the adoption of the 1954 amendments (one relating to the old Illinois/Michigan canal and the other to extend the term of state treasurer from two to four years), there was a general feeling by proponents of constitutional reform that successful efforts could be made to secure, at last, an amendment to the Judicial Article.

The Illinois State and Chicago Bar Associations had commenced work once more. The draft prepared by those organizations proposed a unified court and an appointed judiciary under the so-called merit selection plan. This feature resulted in strong opposition in the legislature and in the total defeat of the program in 1953.

Thereafter, there were no constitutional amendments proposed until 1957 when the legislature, under the bi-partisan leadership of Governor Stratton and Mayor Daley, adopted a compromise judicial reorganization proposal. It made unprecedented changes in the structure and administration of the court systems, while leaving substantially unchanged the judicial elective system.

Witwer was not a member of the Joint Committee which worked on the 1957-58 proposal, although he acted, of course, as a consultant and labored closely with the Committee and later with the campaign committee known as the Committee for Modern Courts, which provided the formal leadership in the public campaign of 1958. Witwer's friend, Louis Kohn, as usual, was extremely active in pressing for adoption of the amendment and he kept Witwer in close contact with the leaders. Perhaps Witwer's most important involvement in 1958 came after the November election when the Judicial Amendment was defeated in a close vote. A review of the votes in various townships and wards suggested that had the ballots — which were marked with a checkmark, or on which the word "yes" was written — been counted, the required 66 and two-thirds percent vote would have been secured. As it was, without those markings being counted, the vote was only 64 percent in favor of the amendment. This circumstance led to a vigorous effort to obtain a recount and to submit to the courts the argument that on constitutional issues the legislatively required "x" was unconstitutional, the issue being whether the voter intended an affirmative vote so long as it was clearly expressed.

A lawsuit was filed in the Circuit Court of Lake County. Gerald Snyder, then soon to be president of the Illinois State Bar Association, joined Witwer in presenting the arguments for a recount and for a declaratory ruling. The lower court disagreed with them and they took an appeal to the Illinois Supreme Court. The matter came before that court in November 1959 when Witwer was seeking the nomination of the Republican Party for the United States Senate seat. Witwer and Abraham Brussells, then a practicing lawyer and later a judge of the Circuit Court of Cook County, argued the case. The Supreme Court rejected their claim on January 20, 1960, in *Scribner* v. *Sachs,* 18 Ill.2d 400. Witwer recalled distinctly his appearance before the Court for more than one reason. Not only was it an interesting case in which he made his first arguments concerning the Illinois Constitution to the state's highest court (he has argued numerous constitutional issues since then), but also on the same day after leaving the courthouse, he walked over to the Executive Mansion where he visited with Governor and Mrs. Stratton and spent the night as house guest. At that time, Stratton was seriously considering endorsing Witwer in the primary campaign for the U.S. Senate seat, which he subsequently chose to do. The newspapers at the time were interested not only in Witwer's appearance before the Supreme Court on a major constitutional issue, but also keenly concerned in following developments in the race for the Senate seat.

As it turned out, it was fortunate that Witwer was unsuccessful in the court proceeding. A recount would have required a substantial amount of time and money, and the Amendment of 1958 was not as well drafted as the Judicial Amendment, subsequently adopted by the General Assembly in 1961 and approved by the voters in 1962. The failure of 1958 was thus a blessing in disguise, as it helped set the course for the much better later effort.

The 1962 amendment again was sponsored by the Committee for Modern Courts, which was led by James Rutherford, a retired Chicago insurance executive. He did an excellent, if not inspired, job. Both parties gave their support to the effort, Otto Kerner, Jr., then being the incumbent governor and, of course, Richard J. Daley was the perennial Mayor of Chicago. Witwer's role, again, was largely advisory. He held the title of legal counsel to the Committee. The amendment campaign, once again, was conducted by Bozell & Jacobs on the public relations front. The Committee followed many of the same techniques and strategies pursued in earlier Blue Ballot campaigns. The amendment passed by a comparably large margin at the November 1962 general election, being approved by a majority, 57%, of those voting in the election, although falling short of the two-thirds approval vote on the issue, receiving only 65%. This was the approximate percentage which the 1958 amendment had attained. Mathematical rigidity in constitutional revision was tantalizing. A little more or a little less was the implacable difference between victory and defeat, delirium and heartache.

Unquestionably, the 1962 Judicial Amendment made a vast favorable change in the administration of justice in Illinois. The unified court and administrative provisions are viewed throughout the country as models. The only disappointment, of course, has been with respect to the method of selecting judges. Again, the 1962 amendment failed to deal with that problem. To have insisted upon merit selection provisions being written into the amendment would have defeated it entirely. Of course, it would never have emerged from the General Assembly, let alone have been adopted by the electorate who still wanted to hold on to the illusion of popular choice. It was on these great advances of the 1962 amendment that the Sixth Constitutional Convention later built and continued to work for the improvement of the judiciary. Unquestionably, the 1962 amendment was a major forward step in constitutional reform in Illinois and, while it disappointed many in failing to deal with the problem of selection, no one who thoughtfully and fairly studies the situation would have the state return to the old method of 1870 vintage in the administering of justice with the plethora of independent and separate courts, or the lack of unified administration, the absence of a disciplinary system and numerous other ancient handicaps.

While Witwer did not occupy a chairman's role in either of the Judicial Amendment campaigns of 1958 and 1962, it was generally recognized that he had indeed emerged from retirement to become a significant leader in those efforts. Of course, recognition of the need for judicial reform was his major motivation at the outset, as evidenced by his 1947 article in the *University of Chicago Law Review*, "The Illinois Constitution and the Courts." Following his retirement as chairman of the Committee in 1955, he never thereafter became chairman of any other Joint Committee, notwithstanding his active role as a consultant and leader in many of the subsequent Blue Ballot campaigns.

The story of the work of the legislative constitutional commissions has been well told in the Janet Cornelius history as well as in the book by Gertz and Pisciotte, *Charter for a New Age.* Witwer served on the three General Assembly constitutional study commissions as a public member. Again, he held no titular office in any of those commissions, but was an active and influential member. Perhaps his most important service on the commissions occurred on the last of them when the state was getting ready to hold the Sixth Illinois Constitutional Convention. Since he was being considered generally as a likely president of the Convention, his views were given substantial weight by the other members of the Commission and by most staff personnel. Witwer was especially glad to have been involved in the sub-committee which drafted the proposed rules for the Convention. It was on that sub-committee that he worked closely with Louis Ancel and Joe P. Pisciotte. The rules which came before the Convention from that committee were adopted without major change. Witwer has often felt that one of the reasons that he was able to keep the Convention from defeating itself by interminable delays and wrangling was that there was a structure of openness but which permitted the Convention president to lead with a strong hand. For that he gave Ancel and Pisciotte great credit.

At last in 1968, the General Assembly submitted a proposal to the electorate as to whether or not to call a Constitutional Convention. The voters approved the call overwhelmingly, and an enabling act was passed by the legislature to govern the selection of delegates to the convention and other basic procedural and substantive aspects. The Supreme Court found the enabling act to be constitutional.

In 1969, the 116 delegates were elected, fortunately on a non-partisan basis. It was only proper that Samuel Witwer, the long-time leader of the fight for constitutional reform, led all other delegates throughout the state in the number of votes cast for him. He was the best known and most favorably regarded.

A man is fortunate, indeed, if early in life he finds a great cause, or one is thrust upon him, and he doggedly pursues it until the cause and he, as its leader, triumph. In any event, Witwer would have been a successful lawyer, a good citizen, a fine family man and a devotee of his religion. With this great constitutional cause, Witwer had more than mundane matters with which to concern himself. He had the joys and sorrows of a good fight, the occasional failures and ultimate success, to gladden his heart and make his life a truly useful one. He could say that the victories that had been won in the struggle had been his, the first such in more than fifty years. The major constitutional achievement was yet to come.

We return now to a time in Witwer's career when Illinois constitutional reform took a secondary role to his effort to lead a presidential campaign of his party in Illinois and later to become a United States Senator.

GOING FOR
THE ROSES
Part 1

*There were five or six of us running for the Senate
nomination. They would line us up at the so-called
candidates' nights, and we'd get up and tell where
we stood. I don't think there was anything
particularly edifying about the ritual. We were like
a bunch of trained seals.*

— Samuel W. Witwer

The year 1960 was signaling the end of the Eisenhower era and
was about to usher in what later became romanticized as
Camelot. In Illinois, as elsewhere in the nation, attention was
focused on the race for the White House. The public, then no less
than today, was so dazzled by the glamor of presidential politics that
scant attention was paid to issues in contests for Senatorial or
House seats. The big headline-grabbing issues — Quemoy and
Matsu, the alleged missile gap between the United States and the
Soviet Union, federally funded health care for the aged, a newly
Communized Cuba under Fidel Castro — these were the subjects
with which Dwight D. Eisenhower, Richard M. Nixon, Nelson L.
Rockefeller and John F. Kennedy dominated the front pages and
electronic air for most of one year. Across the nation, hundreds of
candidates for the United States Senate or the House of Representatives either had to latch onto these issues, or invent their own
issues, to give their own campaigns substance. These contests had a

way of taking on a life of their own, often divorced from the larger reality of grave foreign and domestic problems. In Illinois, the major statewide office to be contested in 1960 was the United States Senate seat held for two terms by Democrat Paul H. Douglas, white-thatched patriarch of the Illinois Democratic Party. Douglas, a former professor of economics from the University of Chicago, was preparing to seek a third six-year term despite his age (68) and despite the vague sense among political observers that Douglas represented a tired, old face. If 1960 was to open the age of Kennedy and youth, surely Paul Douglas did not fit that image. Samuel W. Witwer, at 51, did not exactly fit that mold, either, but his was a younger, fresher face than Douglas', and Sam Witwer determined he would be the instrument that deprived the venerable Douglas of extending his lease on one of Illinois' two Senate seats. Witwer did not appreciate until well into 1960 that running against Douglas would be only half the battle. Witwer first had to confront a bruising primary fight to win his party's nomination for the Senate. It was a time-consuming, bloody battle that had virtually nothing to do with national issues of the time. It was a slugfest that plunged Witwer into the most interneccine partisan wars, skirmishes for which he had no relish yet could not avoid. It was, all told, a toughening experience, one that well-equipped Witwer for a major political fight a decade later to determine whether Illinois would replace its 1870 Constitution. If details of Witwer's campaign for the Republican Senate nomination in 1960 appear picayune from the perspective of later generations, it merely confirms the ephemera that enmesh candidates regardless of the broader tapestry of their time.

For most of his 30's and 40's, Witwer enjoyed the best of both political worlds. As recounted earlier, Witwer through a law partner enjoyed a casual acquaintance with the "Mr. Republican" of his era, Senator Robert A. Taft of Ohio. He also developed a cordial relationship with Adlai E. Stevenson, the Democratic governor who, after his election in 1948, worked closely with Witwer on state constitutional revision, as did four other governors. Because of his leadership of Blue Ballot campaigns, Witwer needed to maintain bi-partisan ties, both personal and professional. In that effort, he was so immensely successful that in 1956, when Witwer accepted a White House appointment as chairman of Illinois Citizens for Eisenhower-Nixon (a role outside the formal Republican Party structure), a few of Witwer's associates were mildly surprised to learn of his Republican leanings.

But Witwer was a Republican. Of that he had no doubt. He was not a straight-ticket voter, however, and as an early if modest contributor to the first Stevenson for Governor campaign, Witwer can be presumed to have voted for the democratic candidate for governor in 1948 (a presumption that was to become an issue to haunt him).

As 1959 drew to a close, Witwer was ready to become a full-fledged Republican as the party's candidate against Douglas, whose foreign policy views Witwer respected while disdaining the Senator's support for government control of the economy. Despite these differences with Douglas, there really existed no emnity between them which gives rise to the intriguing question: At what point did Witwer decide to try to oust Douglas?

It is altogether too simplistic to suggest that Witwer was succumbing to the narcotic of power. Or that, having achieved that level of success in private life that he needed new challenges, he was about to embark on an ego trip. Witwer's entry into elective politics appears to have been a logical outgrowth of several influences throughout his life.

"I don't know at what precise time I made the decision to 'go for the roses'," Witwer said nearly 20 years later. "It must have been three or four years after John S. Knight, A.T. Birch and those fellows started working on me."

Knight, the crusty, eagle-eyed publisher of the *Chicago Daily News,* and Birch, chief editorial writer and top thinkpiece writer for that newspaper, became admirers of Witwer in the late 1940s, when Witwer began attracting attention in the Blue Ballot campaigns. Birch had suggested to Witwer that he aspire to high office as early as 1949, after Witwer returned from a tumultuous legislative session in Springfield where he had testified on behalf of constitutional reform in the presence of hostile legislators.

Two other forces had been working on Witwer even earlier. One was the memory of a childhood experience when his father had taken him to hear a speech by the great populist, Senator William E. Borah of Idaho, in Gary shortly after World War I.

"I was thrilled by Borah's oratory," Witwer recalled. "Borah just — oh, he fascinated me. I might have been indoctrinated to get into politics that very night." Witwer recalls also that he held in high esteem an Indiana state senator who belonged to the Gary Methodist Church, the church the Witwers attended. When one church-goer asked young Sam Witwer if he planned to become a Methodist minister, Witwer remembers startling himself with the vehemence of this reply, "The country needs good senators, too!"

"So there's no question that some seed pertaining to the Senate was planted when I was still a boy," Witwer said.

There was a second, perhaps more persuasive influence that pushed Witwer in the same direction. His long-time Hyde Park neighbor, fellow Methodist and Republican, George McKibbin, wrote Witwer an unsolicited letter urging Witwer, still a young man, to get into politics. "George was sort of my political father," Witwer said. "His letter outlined for me all the reasons a person should seek office, and he counseled me that if you don't get elected, that's somebody else's fault, not yours, if you've made an honest race. That letter had a profound impact on me. I kept it for years and shared it on a few occasions with young men I wanted to encourage to get active in politics."

Whatever the convergence of influences, 1960 was to be Witwer's year to strike. His first step was to secure the support of Governor William G. Stratton, leader of the Illinois Republican Party.

On November 10, 1959, Witwer met with the Governor in Springfield to explore the possibilities for 1960. Witwer's memory of that first meeting blurs with recollections of subsequent conversations, but Stratton recalls that on that day, he resolved to support Witwer once he (Stratton) had smoothed the sensitivities of other party leaders who might be aggrieved at being overlooked.

Stratton referred principally to former Congressman Timothy P. Sheehan, at that time chairman of the Cook County Central Republican Committee. Sheehan had been the GOP's "sacrificial lamb" against Mayor Richard J. Daley in the Chicago municipal election of 1959, and Sheehan believed the party owed him first consideration for the Senate spot.

Later that same day the Governor met with William H. Rentschler, 34, of Lake Forest, a wealthy candy manufacturer who also entertained designs on the Douglas seat. After that meeting, Stratton instructed his press secretary, Johnson Kanady, to spread the word among political writers that Stratton tried to discourage Rentschler from running (unsuccessfully, as it turned out), and that Stratton leaned toward Witwer as a "blue ribbon" entry on the 1960 state ticket.

Witwer and Stratton huddled again on November 17, and afterwards, confronting reporters outside the Governor's office, they went through the charade of saying nothing final had been decided upon. Each man praised the other effusively. That was the only signal the press needed. Witwer was going to run and Stratton would support him. (Stratton at that time told associates the party needed a good-government candidate like Witwer to prevent the young, attractive and articulate Rentschler — whom Stratton called "still wet behind the ears" — from snatching important newspaper endorsements in the primary.)

Witwer began making plans to announce his candidacy in early January 1960. As the 1959 Christmas holiday season drew to a close, it became apparent that Witwer would have a lot of company other than Rentschler to compete against in the April primary.

There were to be six candidates in all. The lineup was, in some ways, bizarre. One of the candidates who secured a spot on the ballot, John R. Harrell of Louisville, Ill., said he was running because God urged him to run on April 20, 1959, and the Almighty had communicated the message that He "wants America released from all foreign entanglements and obligations." Another candidate was John A. Riker, a Chicago lawyer who was a consultant on drainage and flood control for the Metropolitan Sanitary District of

Greater Chicago. Neither Harrell nor Riker had any base of political support and consequently were treated by the press as curiosities.

Two other candidates were to be taken very seriously, indeed. They were former State Treasurer Warren E. Wright of Murrayville, and State Sen. John W. Lewis of Marshall, a leader among forces opposing state constitutional reform. Wright, a former banker and real estate broker, had defeated a Stratton-backed candidate in the 1958 primary for state treasurer, although he lost the subsequent election to his Democratic opponent. Lewis, a farmer and popular auctioneer on the county fair circuit, had been a member of the General Assembly for 20 years with a 100 percent attendance record. Both Wright and Lewis were far better known among the Springfield press corps than Witwer, which meant that their campaigns would get good coverage on the state wire services operating out of Springfield.

Those were the contestants. Witwer. Rentschler. Wright. Lewis. Harrell. Riker. As the campaign progressed, only two became serious threats to Witwer. Rentschler emerged as the most nettlesome, vexing opponent on the campaign trail, occupying much of Witwer's time answering charges both spurious and childish. But Wright emerged as the most unexpectedly strong vote-getter.

The day after New Year's Day 1960, Witwer resigned as a vice president of the United Republican Fund. So did Rentschler. This was a necessary preamble to launching an intraparty fight. On January 5, Witwer called a press conference to announce his candidacy. He announced plans to carry his campaign into all 102 Illinois counties. He attacked Senator Douglas' "fuzzy thinking" on economic affairs. He told of visiting Vice President Nixon's home the previous week to discuss the 1960 campaign, when Nixon would be running for president. Witwer was pleased, he said, to affirm that his political views and those of Nixon "coincide on virtually every issue. We both believe that sound fiscal management will enable America to enjoy continued economic growth and prosperity in peace — without inflation."

Reporters insisted that Witwer comment on recent statements by Adlai Stevenson critical of President Eisenhower's most recent Summit trip abroad. They also wanted Witwer's reaction to Stevenson's frequent criticism of the Nixon record. These were difficult questions for Witwer to field, considering his past association with Stevenson, but Witwer had steeled himself in the 1956 campaign, when Witwer headed Illinois Citizens for Eisenhower-Nixon, for occasional shots at Stevenson, and his replies to these questions were more spasmodic than reflective.

"Stevenson is so anxious for publicity to keep alive his hopes for a Democratic convention draft, he is willing to undercut the influence for peace that millions of people throughout the world see in President Eisenhower's recent trip abroad," Witwer said.

He added that Stevenson's attempts to label Nixon as reactionary were "completely contrary to the Vice President's dynamic, progressive record on civil rights, labor, foreign relations, economic policy and every major issue."

Experienced politicians of the opposition party shrugged off such remarks as rhetoric. It was difficult for Witwer to treat any type of political criticism against a personal friend in a cavalier fashion. He needed to be genuinely angry to criticize someone with conviction. Witwer was a loyal Republican and a sincere supporter of Nixon, but he could not summon up anger at Stevenson, whose political career he had had a small role in launching.

"I don't know if it's possible to be in politics without being inclined to go for the jugular," Witwer said while being interviewed for this biography. "I've often reflected on the fact that I never had that instinct." He broke into a broad smile and added, "Might have gone a lot farther if I had it."

There was one period early in the 1960 primary campaign when Witwer admits to being genuinely angry. Shortly before his formal announcement, Witwer sought the endorsement of the Cook County Central Republican Committee. The endorsement was to have been a routine affirmation of Stratton's expressed preference for Witwer. Furthermore, none of the other major rivals for the Senate nomination resided in Cook County, and Stratton had made a point of stressing that Witwer would be the only representative of Cook County on the entire state ticket. It was unthinkable that the Cook County GOP *not* endorse Witwer.

But the unthinkable almost happened.

On cue, Witwer strolled over to the Bismarck Hotel, where the county's Republican slatemakers were meeting. They were scheduled to hear Witwer, simply as a matter of ritual, at 2:00 p.m., when he was to thank them for their endorsement. His friends, Alan Jacobs and lawyer Albert E. Jenner, Jr., waited with Witwer in a hotel room. They waited for the summons to Witwer. At 2:30 p.m. there had been no call. Nor at 3:00 p.m. At 3:30 p.m., nothing.

Behind the closed doors, a fight had broken out over whether to endorse Witwer. It was fueled by Siñoñ Murray, a West Side legislator who detested Witwer's "suspiciously pinko" schemes for reforming the state constitution. Murray and several other legislators who sat on the committee as elected Republican ward committeemen disliked Witwer's past advocacy of legislative reapportionment. Then there was the "*Tribune* crowd" within the committee, a band of arch-conservatives who viewed Witwer (correctly, it should be noted) as a moderate or slightly progressive type of Republican, the type more likely to be championed by the *Chicago Daily News* than by the *Chicago Tribune,* at that time the Midwest citadel of rock-ribbed Republicanism. And, not the least significant was opposition from a few slatemakers with known ties to organized crime. Witwer was a "reformer," and no worse recommendation existed for defenders of gangland's ties to the inner circles of both political parties.

Witwer, finally made aware of the controversy his proposed endorsement had stirred, grew livid. He jumped out of the chair and yelled at Jacobs and Jenner, "The hell with them! I don't want it!"

Jenner tried to calm Witwer, who grabbed his hat and headed for the door. "I'm leaving," Witwer shouted. "I'm getting out of here, and tell them for me they can give the endorsement to someone else. This is demeaning."

Jacobs agreed with Witwer, but Jenner prevailed. He kept Witwer in tow for a few more minutes, and by 4:15 p.m. the slatemakers' rebellion had subsided, due partly to the insistence of County Chairman Sheehan. They sent word to the upstairs room where Witwer waited.

"I went downstairs with a sense of irritation," Witwer said. "It was all I could do to rise above it and express my gratitude for their endorsement. But all the pleasure had been taken out of it."

Witwer later learned that Governor Stratton had telephoned a few of the more fractious slatemakers and threatened political reprisals unless they dropped their opposition to Witwer. What Stratton wanted, he usually got. He wanted Witwer on the ticket.

From the mellowing distance of 20 years, Witwer could see that some of the opposition to him was neither personal nor sinister. "To some of the ward and township committeemen, I had not been a 'regular' Republican. I had been an Eisenhower Republican. I was suspect for my independence. I was viewed as a moderate. I can understand how they felt. Some of them would have felt more comfortable with a candidate closer to their own views.

"I have oftentimes thought, 'I wonder what would have happened if I had walked out of there in a huff?'

"I suspect that would have ended my candidacy. It would have made the newspapers, because the press had been alerted at noon to be ready for an imminent announcement of the endorsement of Witwer.

"Yes, it's interesting to speculate what would have happened if Bert Jenner hadn't stopped me from walking out of that hotel. It was one of the few times I can remember being so damn angry I was ready to explode through the roof," said Witwer.

In mid-January, the battle began for endorsements outside the formal party structure. Charles H. Percy, chairman of Bell & Howell and head of the National Republican Committee for Programs and Progress, endorsed Witwer as "an able administrator . . . a conservative in his economics, but dynamic and progressive when it comes to the well-being of individuals." The same day, Percy himself had been sought after to run for the Senate. James C. Worthy, head of the United Republican Fund, had urged Witwer to withdraw in favor of Percy and accept the role of state manager for the presidential campaign. The same day, industrialist R. Douglas Stuart announced he was chairing a committee of 1,000 prominent Illinoisans who backed Rentschler as "the one candidate who can retire Senator Douglas to private life next November."

These endorsements constitute the psychological warfare of any campaign. Their chief value is publicity for a day. Their value as a vote-getting device is dubious. Just as dubious were the press releases in which candidates sought to distinguish themselves from each other on the issues.

Among the major candidates — Witwer, Rentschler and Wright — some differences on issues did exist. Decades later, most of the differences seem unimportant. Witwer clearly was the most liberal, although there was little in his philosophy to the left of a Taft or a Nixon. Wright was cantankerously conservative and an isolationist. Rentschler was conservative, although his youth gave him an image of being more progressive than he was.

Rentschler's campaign had a pronounced effect on Witwer's meager fund-raising. Many leaders among Chicago's North Shore establishment — industrialist Harold Byron Smith, Sr., Quaker Oats executive Robert Stuart and Gen. Robert E. Woods (ret.), one-time top executive of Sears, Roebuck & Co. — raised large sums for Rentschler and declined to support Witwer. Rentschler's Lake Forest connections paid off handsomely for Rentschler. It cost Witwer dearly when he needed that same support for the general election, and it was denied him.

Those issues that made the headlines or filled air time had absolutely nothing to do with war, peace, inflation or unemployment. And almost all of these headline-grabbers were generated by Rentschler against Witwer.

One such tempest arose in early February, when Rentschler addressed a luncheon in Danville. He attacked the "shabby and shoddy alliance between a big-city Democratic machine (Chicago), a handful of crooked labor bosses and organized crime" and said it was this same alliance that wanted to nominate the weakest possible candidate (Witwer) against Douglas.

In case that message was too subtle, Rentschler referred to a current scandal in the Chicago Summerdale Police Department in which a number of policemen were accused as members of a burglary ring. Rentschler said this scandal would "create a general revulsion with Illinois political machines. The people are weary of political bossism and dictation. I am convinced that any hand-picked candidate will bear the brunt of that widespread disgust."

"Hand-picked candidate" had become the widely known euphemism for Witwer. Another was "Stratton's puppet candidate." Thus did Witwer find himself linked, however thinly and ingenuously, with the Chicago police scandal. The press could have ignored Rentschler's linkage as patently absurd, but instead reporters clamored for a response from Witwer. All Witwer would do was issue a statement that said, simply, "I had hoped I would not have to waste valuable time refuting scurrilous and irresponsible babblings of an opponent." Rentschler, however, kept the story alive, responding to Witwer saying, "The Governor's man appears overly sensitive."

Rentschler repeated this attack a score of times. It was picked up by one downstate newspaper after another. Finally, the *Chicago Tribune* demanded that Rentschler explain his charges, and only then did Rentschler drop that line of attack.

Witwer spent most of February and March traveling the state, attacking Senator Douglas, and defending President Eisenhower's economic policies against criticism by Douglas. The Senator had been blasting Ike for "ruinous inflation." Witwer accused Douglas of "playing a numbers game in shaping statistics to meet his political purposes." The rise in inflation during Eisenhower's eight years in the White House had averaged 1.3 percent a year. That this figure should have been the subject of heated debate would seem ludicrous during periods of double-digit inflation 15 and 20 years later.

Try as he would, Witwer could not keep the focus of his attacks on the Democratic incumbent. Rentschler kept getting in the way. If not Rentschler, then Wright, the former state treasurer. Wright practiced a folksy, homespun style of politicking. He rode from county to county with a hefty supply of dimes in his car. At each county seat, he'd park himself inside a public phone booth and spend his dimes calling everyone he knew who lived in the county. It was effective. Wright was wooing away some important downstate party leaders, such as Secretary of State, Charles F. Carpentier, and Witwer suddenly was glad he had vowed to campaign each of the state's 102 counties. Speaking on the so-called "rubber chicken" circuit kept Witwer away from home most of the time.

There were many times when all six of the Republican rivals appeared on the same platform, usually before a ward or Cook County suburban township party organization, seeking that party unit's endorsement. Witwer referred to himself and the others as acting "like a bunch of trained seals" at these joint appearances. Each would expound on domestic or foreign issues; none would electrify his listeners with startling charges; the partisan audiences would respond with polite applause; and the evening usually ended with a routine endorsement of Witwer.

These appearances generated negative reactions in some of the press. The *Wheeling Herald* bemoaned the level of political rhetoric in the GOP primary. The *Herald* said Witwer "comes closest to possessing the ability and record needed to fill the post of U.S. Senator" but withheld an endorsement of him. It said Wright, Lewis and Harrell "would have made excellent running mates on a Medieval ticket. They have extraordinary 13th Century minds." And the newspaper ridiculed Rentschler's youth and ambition as "no substitutes for an appreciation of the problems facing our country."

All four Chicago newspapers were content to endorse Witwer over his opponents, citing Witwer's civic record as overwhelming evidence of his superior qualifications. Rentschler succeeded in picking up the endorsement of several downstate newspapers that opposed Stratton's bid for an unprecedented third term in the Executive Mansion. Stratton was being opposed by State Senator Hayes Robertson of Flossmoor, a wealthy conservative manufac-turer, in the gubernatorial primary. Many Republicans, linking

Stratton and Witwer, automatically went for Rentschler or Wright merely because they opposed Stratton. This was reflected in newspaper editorials and columns around the state. It was common to read of Witwer as the "Governor's hand-picked choice" even in columns that were not otherwise critical of Witwer.

It is ironic that Witwer probably would not have run for the Senate nomination had he not been assured of the Governor's support for party endorsement. Yet the price Witwer paid for this support, which was vital to any chance Witwer had of winning, was the automatic inheritance of all of Stratton's critics. (Well, not all. The *Chicago Daily News* was almost rabidly anti-Stratton in 1960, yet it was the most staunchly pro-Witwer newspaper in the state.)

Witwer acknowledged trouble enlisting the most conservative Republicans to his side. "They weren't at all happy with me that I didn't assail Douglas as a Socialist or a Communist. Some were very hostile because I didn't attack Douglas personally and try to beat the drums and create a lot of public excitement. But, I'm just not that way and I wasn't about to do it."

However, Witwer did try to spice his rhetoric with zippy phrases attacking Douglas on various issues, usually economic. Addressing 225 Party faithful at Smorak's Restaurant in Bloomington, Witwer called Douglas "a dangerous man, a menace to our way of life . . . a political witch doctor whose only nostrums are bigger government and higher taxes." However, Bloomington Mayor Robert McGraw consistently mispronounced the speaker's name as "Witmer" that night, and the press paid more attention to McGraw's gaff than to Witwer's excessive rhetoric.

In a rally at the Grundy County Courthouse, Witwer lambasted Douglas as a "political mortician . . . shrewd and cunning in doing things that are destructive . . . his solution to all problems is to run to Washington and inject big government into all our lives and appropriate millions of dollars."

This second attempt to appease the conservatives in his party was upstaged by Wright's leaking word that Earl Eisenhower, brother of the president and public relations man for a suburban newspaper chain west of Chicago, was endorsing Wright for the

Senate. The report was accurate and newsworthy. Witwer commented that he doubted it would have any effect on the primary race. It probably didn't.

In a speech before Quad City business leaders at a luncheon in the LeClaire Hotel in Moline, along the Mississippi River border of western Illinois, Witwer outlined a four-point program that became the blueprint for his issues-war against Douglas. The points, briefly, called for (1) holding the line on federal spending; (2) holding the line on wages and prices; (3) continuing "sound management" (i.e., restrictive interest rates) on the money and credit in circulation to inhibit the growth of inflation; and (4) adopting tax and depreciation policies to encourage expansion of business. In short, sound Republican orthodoxy.

But Rentschler, the tall, handsome and earnest-looking candidate against "party bossism," never gave Witwer much chance to coast along on orthodoxy. Flamboyance was the Rentschler style.

On March 30, in a speech at Galesburg, Rentschler made his first direct attack using Witwer's name. He produced a copy of a 1947 University of Chicago Law Review article in which Witwer had written an attack on party "bosses" dictating nominations for public office. (In reality, the article criticized Cook County judicial selection, in which judgeships were filled by party leaders, not voters.) Rentschler quoted the article out of context in an attempt to demonstrate that as early as 1947, Witwer was indifferent about "bossism." The article actually demonstrated just the opposite. But, Rentschler seized on any pretext to link the phrase "bossism" with Witwer. "The voters I have talked with don't relish the idea of someone ramming a candidate like Witwer down their throats," Rentschler said, rather inelegantly.

The most amazing thing about Rentschler's attack was that it attracted publicity in newspapers all over the state, a testament to Rentschler's prowess as a publicist and self-promoter. The *Chicago Tribune,* in a lead editorial, scolded Rentschler for quoting the Witwer article out of context and twisting its actual meaning.

Witwer, for his part, was getting fed up with Rentschler. He reminded voters that Rentschler had sought Governor Stratton's support the previous November, just as Witwer had done. "Why I am blameworthy for having won what he sought, I do not know," Witwer said. "His attacks are deliberately false, deceitful and disgusting."

One day, Witwer began getting calls from the political editors of all four Chicago newspapers, each asking the identical set of questions. Since the questions dealt with libelous charges that had been fed to the newsmen, they won't be repeated here. In general, the charges sought to link Witwer to the Mafia, accused him of having a cash hoard of $300,000 in tainted money, and similarly outlandish things.

Shaken by the slander, Witwer successfully refuted each charge point by point, but he was unable to learn the perpetrator of the falsehoods. He was alternatingly angry and depressed at the depths of political skullduggery to which he was being exposed. No publicity ensued.

The final bombshell exploded on Witwer a few days before the April primary, and this time Witwer was less successful in avoiding flak. The detonator was Rentschler.

Rentschler called a press conference to accuse Witwer of having contributed $65 to Stevenson's 1948 campaign for governor. Rentschler said Witwer's "credentials as a Republican are seriously open to question."

This time, there was more substance to Rentschler's charge, however valid his conclusion. This time he was not quoting Witwer out of context. Indeed, Witwer *had* contributed seed money to help foster the fledgling career of his friend, Adlai Stevenson. How was Witwer to answer this one?

Witwer answered truthfully, although he fudged the issue somewhat by de-emphasizing the personal aspect of his relationship with Stevenson. In a Rockford hotel room, Witwer wrote out his response and had it distributed to the press. He said he had "solicited and secured the cooperation of the leaders of both parties in supporting constitutional reform. In that connection, I developed close associations with Adlai E. Stevenson and the late Governor Dwight Green in the hope of interesting both in working for constitutional revision. I did not support Stevenson in the 1948 race. I recall making small contributions to the campaigns of both Stevenson and his opponent, Green."

It worried Witwer and his wife, Ethyl, as they sat there in the Hotel Faust in Rockford, that there was no easy way they could prove hurriedly having contributed to both Stevenson *and* Green. It didn't matter, because Rentschler the next day accepted the explanation at face value and invited Witwer to explain, in his capacity as bi-partisan leader for constitutional reform, how much money he gave to the Republican *and* Democratic candidates for governor in 1952 and 1956. Also, perhaps Witwer would like to explain how it came to pass that Witwer helped draft Governor Stevenson's inaugural message of January 1949.

Reporters were doing Rentschler's bidding, carrying these questions to Witwer, almost sensing the distress they were causing. Witwer adamantly denied donating funds to any Democrats in 1952 and 1956, and he downplayed his role in Stevenson's inaugural address. He said he had furnished both Stevenson and Governor Green information on constitutional revision during their campaign against each other, and some of this material found its way into Stevenson's inaugural speech. Actually, Witwer's connection had been much more substantive than that. After Stevenson's defeat of Governor Green in November 1948, Witwer had worked with Stevenson's top administrative aide, Walter Schaefer, on the language of the new governor's inaugural speech calling for a constitutional convention. Witwer had met numerous times with Stevenson at the Executive Mansion to discuss strategy for constitutional reform. Present at some of these meetings was Stevenson's revenue director, Richard J. Daley, later to become mayor of Chicago. These were not ties Witwer wanted to exploit on the eve of a Republican primary election. He sat tight and waited for the primary election to come and pass.

Nearly two million Illinois voters went to the polls April 12. More than half took Democratic ballots (there was a heated three-way contest for the Democratic gubernatorial nomination). Those who took Republican ballots were marking for Witwer, Wright or

Rentschler. The other three contenders were not conceded any chance of an upset. None was expected to get enough votes to play the spoiler's role in determining the difference between the top vote-getter and his runner-up.

Witwer, his wife, their daughter and their three sons gathered at the "Witwer-for-Senator" headquarters at 69 West Washington to await the results. Witwer glanced hurriedly at the large chalkboard mounted on one wall of the suite's main room. Returns would be posted here as they were relayed by phone takers in a small room off to the side. Witwer smiled optimistically and expressed confidence victory would be theirs. Ethyl held her husband's arm and smiled even more radiantly. The Witwer children, particularly Carole and David, to whom this type of activity was all new and strange, just looked puzzled and studied with keen interest the electronic gadgetry being installed by the first radio and television newsmen to arrive.

The first returns from downstate were not encouraging. Wright, the former State Treasurer, was beating Witwer in more than half the counties, and in many counties, Wright's vote was exceeding the combined total of Witwer and Rentschler. An incredible showing for Rentschler was chalked up in the University of Illinois stronghold of Champaign County, where the candy-maker candidate got nearly 7,500 votes to less than 4,000 for Wright and only 2,500 for Witwer.

Witwer was saved by the vote from Chicago and its suburbs. The party-endorsed candidate, Witwer carried every ward in the city. He swept the 30 suburban townships. His Cook County total reflected the strong support by regular party organizations and the solid backing of the metropolitan dailies. In Cook County, Witwer got 119,305 votes to 59,459 for Rentschler and 46,173 for Wright. (The three also-rans won a cumulative total of less than 46,000 votes.)

The cumulative totals from downstate told the story in reverse order. Wright led with more than 175,000 votes, followed by Rentschler with 138,000 and Witwer third with 129,000. The statewide totals, in the official canvass that followed, showed

Witwer with some 250,000 votes, or 21,000 votes more than Wright and about 50,000 more than Rentschler. It was close.

Governor Stratton, who defeated his primary opponent by 59 to 41 percent, recalls talking to Witwer repeatedly from his home in Morris, about 50 miles southwest of Chicago. Shirley Stratton, answering the telephone at the desk in her husband's office-library, would signal him that Witwer was on the line. Stratton would hold up an arm, get silence from his aides in the crowded room, and exchange voting returns with Witwer.

"I never heard Sam more nervous than he was that night," Stratton said. "He kept saying after every new set of figures came across, 'But I'm only leading by 20,000 votes!' I'd tell him, 'Let Warren Wright worry about those 20,000 votes. As long as you're ahead, stop worrying!'"

Witwer did not claim victory until after 4:00 a.m., after the polls closed. He quietly credited his victory to three factors: the reputation and name recognition he had built up leading statewide Blue Ballot campaigns; his "solid, solid support" by Governor Stratton," and his endorsement by all of the metropolitan dailies.

There was one set of statistics that gave Witwer special delight. His hometown of Riverside had given him 2,000 votes, to only 324 for Rentschler and 90 for Wright.

Regardless of the statements he put out after his primary victory, Sam Witwer was not overjoyed at the results. He would have preferred a convincing majority, rather than a thin plurality, in winning a mandate from the Republican voters to carry the fight against Senator Douglas. Witwer was not a supreme egoist, but he recognized with a healthy self-respect that he offered creditable qualifications as a blue ribbon candidate. He also recognized that as the party-endorsed candidate, his share of the total vote should have been much larger. He wondered whether he was personally responsible for the weaker than expected showing.

Sam Witwer, maker of hundreds of speeches as lawyer, churchman and champion of civic reform, was not his own best advocate as a campaigner. "I started almost as a neophyte," he said. "I didn't have that outgoing, campaigning zeal that is pretty important in catching publc attention. I was a little too philo-sophical, I think, to interest the average voter."

Whatever their affection for Sam personally, his closest friends admitted that Witwer found it easier to expound on an abstraction or a cause than to trumpet his own virtues without embarrassment. (This was not a handicap from which Rentschler suffered.) Since his days at Harvard Law School, when Witwer consciously began to develop a more inhibited personality, he had become a basically private man. It ran contrary to his nature to intrude himsef upon strangers (as would Warren Wright), to beam at them and affect an aura of good will, to thrust out his arm and grasp their palms in the ritualistic handshake. The same man in pin-striped suit and vest who could rise with dignity and aplomb when his name was called during some august proceeding of a church group or in a courtroom, could not with the same ease stop pedestrians in a shopping mall and tell them, "Hi, I'm Sam Witwer. Running for the United States Senate."

Both Stratton and Senator Everett M. Dirksen had tried to loosen up Witwer. Stratton reminded him, "He who tooteth not his own horn, hath a horn which remaineth untooteth." Dirksen, ever the glad-hander, encouraged Witwer to do more cozying up with women, giving them an affectionate pat or chuck on the chin.

Yes, Witwer had problems adjusting to the personal demands of campaign life. The grueling primary campaign was a rough testing ground for his more important race against Senator Douglas in November. But, Witwer's campaigning style improved, as did the quality of his opposition. He and Douglas were to maintain a genuine respect for each other's sincerity and integrity.

Given the quality of his opposition in the primary, there is probably very little Witwer could have done differently to affect the results. His personal campaign style had to be far less important to the outcome than the virulence of Rentschler's slashing attacks and the anti-Stratton tide in some parts of the state.

As Witwer said the morning after his primary win, puffing slowly on a congratulatory cigar, "What a way to start a political career. After this, anything will be anti-climactic."

Considering the uphill fight that awaited him, it might have been tempting for Witwer to quit right then, while he was ahead. But, Witwer was a man who wouldn't quit.

GOING FOR
THE ROSES
Part 2

There's something, frankly, about organized partisan political work that just leaves me cold. I cannot develop that sense of my party right or wrong, and I can't get myself revved up to be an advocate of an all-out party position at all costs. I just can't do it.

— Samuel W. Witwer,
February 20, 1979

T he second and final phase of Sam Witwer's attempt to become a United States Senator marked his emergence as an "equal among equals" in big league politics. Until this point, Witwer had been a supporting player in great historic scenes dominated by other actors. Yes, he was important to the Eisenhower campaign in Illinois in 1956, but the glamor did not attach permanently to Witwer, it remained with the hero of Normandy. That was as it should be. Yes, Witwer was crucial to the ongoing battle for constitutional reform in Illinois, but in these situations it was the cause, not its advocates, that commanded star billing. That, too, was as it should be. There is a mystical annointing process in the winning of an election, and it was only after winning the rock-'em, sock-'em Republican senatorial primary of 1960 that Witwer had earned, in the eyes of political colleagues, star status in his own right. Witwer himself must have felt some of the "magic" that is

135

conferred by an electorate. His friends during this period say that Witwer showed enormous growth as a campaigner on the stump, as well as new sensitivity to his "rights" as a major figure at the head of his party's ticket. With this role came new responsibilities, and the one that Witwer probably found most vexing to deal with was the need for displaying "party regularity." He was running not only against an entrenched two-term incumbent in Democrat Paul Douglas, but he also was called upon to be the Party's spokesman on national issues affecting Republican chances for retaining the White House. It was not an easy and, as Witwer later was to admit, he did not relish the role.

In any controversy involving Richard M. Nixon, who was to become the GOP candidate for president in the summer of 1960, or involving Henry Cabot Lodge, the nominee for vice president, it mattered not at all whether Witwer agreed with Nixon or Lodge. What mattered was that Witwer was expected to back the Nixon-Lodge position. This, he did. Not at the sacrifice of principle, but at the sacrifice, perhaps, of careful study on his own part of the issue at dispute, and at the sacrifice, surely, of the energies he was trying to devote to the drive against Douglas. Witwer never complained about this. Yet, this role had to be alien to his nature.

History resists categorization into neat little sections each with its own clear label. There is no way to recreate the Witwer-Douglas campaign of 1960 without the distortion such categories inevitably create. A chronological approach would take readers through an incredibly burdensome maze of meetings, rallies, picnics, speeches, issues, cities, villages, sunny days and rainstorms — a mish-mash of events that really tell no story at all.

The Witwer campaign through the summer and fall of 1960 can be understood best as a series of changing relationships. First, Witwer's relationship with Governor Stratton. His relationship with the Nixon-Lodge campaign. His relationships with Ethyl and the rest of his family, with a few close friends, with himself. There was no real relationship with Senator Douglas. The front-running incumbent saw no advantage in acceding to Witwer's relentless challenges for face-to-face debates, so the two contestants met but rarely in the campaign. Their exchanges were the stuff of political rhetoric, not the substance of a personal relationship.

The 1960 primary campaign ended with Witwer overflowing with gratitude for Governor Stratton's role in Witwer's victory. As the euphoria wore off and Witwer took a closer look at what was happening, their friendship cooled.

This stemmed from Witwer's gradual realization, as he studied his showing in the primary in various regions, that he had received, at best, luke-warm support from the regular Republican organizations downstate. In one of his first meetings with the Governor after the primary, Witwer told Stratton, "It would appear to me that you probably have more payrollers and wives and husbands and sweethearts of payrollers than the number of votes that showed up in my column." Stratton shrugged this off. "Sam," he said, "you got your certificate of nomination, didn't you?" Witwer replied, "Yes, but I don't know that it portends very much in the fall." Witwer appreciated the tremendous odds against his upsetting Douglas. But he also intended to fight for every vote he could get. It was important to establish his credibility as a candidate for a later election, should he fail (as most observers expected) to beat Douglas.

For that reason, Witwer's feelings toward Stratton exploded in rage in mid-June. Witwer had been invited to deliver the keynote address at the Illinois State Republican Convention in Decatur on June 18, and the night before the convention, as he prepared to leave for the trip to Decatur, Witwer learned that Stratton had not slated him among the eight at-large delegates whom the convention would choose to attend the party's national convention in Chicago the following month.

For both major political parties, tradition dictated that in a presidential election year, the nominee for the U.S. Senate be given a showcase role at the national convention. Witwer had had no warning that he would be denied status as a full delegate, nor even as an *alternate* at-large delegate. As he and Alan Jacobs, who was handling Witwer's public relations and writing most of his speeches, headed toward Decatur, rehashing the slight to Witwer, attempting to fathom Stratton's motive for such a gross humiliation of his party's Senate nominee, Witwer's anger mounted.

Witwer confronted Stratton shortly before the convention opened in a hotel in downtown Decatur. Witwer began shouting at Stratton, and the Governor shouted back. Many reporters were within earshot of the exchange, but press accounts on the remarks vary so widely it's best to rely on the memory of the participants for what was actually said.

"I hit the ceiling. I told Stratton I was outraged," Witwer recalled.

"It was my responsibility as leader of my party to attempt to accommodate many conflicting interests," Stratton recalled, adding, with a sly smile, "but I don't think I explained things to Sam in terms that polite. I wasn't too pleased at having Sam challenge my leadership."

"If you don't put me into that (national) convention, it would be the most demeaning thing that could happen to a candidate," Witwer told Stratton. "I'm not at all sure I'll take it." Stratton could interpret the last remark only as a threat to quit the ticket. Stratton did not think Witwer would actually do that, but the Governor sought to sooth Witwer by slating him as an alternate delegate, in place of Lt. Gov. John Chapman, whose name Stratton simply scratched from his list.

Similarly, State Auditor Elbert S. Smith, who had gotten an advance peek at the list, was angry that his name was omitted. Stratton admitted to an oversight on this. He added Smith's name to the list of alternate delegates, substituting him for Richard L. Wattling, president of the Illinois Young Republicans.

In all of the back-room debate and confusion that accompanied these alterations, no one told the lieutenant governor that he had been bounced from the delegation. So, during that part of the state convention when the list of recommended candidates for delegate and alternate was read to the convention, Chapman jolted upright at not hearing his own name. He stomped off the convention stage, taking his wife with him. He later publicly berated Stratton.

Witwer had been denied a full delegate's spot so that the honor could be given to Julius Klein, a Chicago public relations man, a Republican Party gadfly, who had raised money for the GOP in past years. Other non-candidates given full delegate spots were Charles H. Percy, then president of Bell & Howell Co.; Sears Roebuck executive James C. Worthy, and Edward L. Ryerson, a retired steel company executive. Of these, only Percy, who had been named in advance as chairman of the national convention's platform committee, needed a full portfolio as delegate. The others were being rewarded for service to the party.

The Witwer-Stratton rift was the talk of the day-long state convention. It overshadowed Witwer's keynote address, and it fed the ravenous demands of reporters looking for conflict. Long after they had patched up their fight, Witwer and Stratton found themselves denying that any feud existed. Witwer grew so irritated at press accounts of the rift many weeks later that he denied that any harsh words had been exchanged between him and the Governor, that stories of the feud sprang from fertile imaginations of the media. Witwer explained his feelings:

> The insidious thing about it was the intimation to me that my own party really didn't think I had a fireman's chance. They already were treating me like a stepchild, this early in the game. I was mad as hell, and I told them (the Governor and his advisors) off, as I could do. And so they decided they better not play with me on this thing, and they gave me an alternate's spot.

Events of the day mocked the opening words of Witwer's keynote address; "This is a VICTORY convention...of a UNITED Republican Party! We are united! We are determined! We are confident!"

The speech was sprinkled with alliterative phrases that sounded not at all like Witwer. He referred to Democratic presidential candidate John F. Kennedy as "millionaire Joe Kennedy's hair-clipped boy who wants us to apologize to Khrushchev." He poked fun at "Hubert Humphrey's favorite candidate, Hubert Humphrey," ridiculed leading national Democratic figures, Chicago Mayor Richard J. Daley, Senator Douglas ("Daley's doleful Douglas — the chief tear-jerker and statistic dispenser of the Democratic gloom and doom claque").

Most surprising in Witwer's speech was an uncharacteristic slap at his friend, Adlai E. Stevenson. Republicans nationally had been furious at Stevenson for accusing President Eisenhower of responsibility for the failure of Summit peace talks in Paris the previous spring. The Soviets, led by Premier Khrushchev, broke up the Summit in a rage over the downing of a U-2 spy plane over Russia; they refused to take part in the talks unless Eisenhower apologized for the aerial surveillance. Eisenhower returned to the United States as a dignified leader who had refused to knuckle under to Khrushchev's demands. Stevenson, in a widely publicized speech, said Eisenhower handed the Soviets "the sledgehammer" with which to disrupt the Summit.

Witwer no doubt expressed the popular sentiment of the season when he attacked "indecisive Adlai, who, at a time of crisis, uses crude tools like the sledgehammer and crow-bar to build himself a lightning rod." This was Witwer's way of saying Stevenson had attacked the administration in hope of fanning support for a Stevenson draft for the 1960 Democratic nomination for president. Witwer's heart was not in those remarks.

"I had the worst time giving that speech," Witwer said 20 years later. "Of all the speeches I've given, I look back on that one as the worst. Not only because it had been a day of travail over the delegate thing, which was very demeaning. I literally had difficulty giving that kind of speech. And yet it was expected by the troops. I take the responsibility for saying it. I really had to almost get up and read it, and I can't read a speech worth a hoot, but the troops had to have it. The troops weren't very responsive that day . . . ."

Witwer found it extremely difficult to be partisan. "I wasn't a very good partisan candidate," Witwer said. "I think I did my best when I would address people without set remarks, and just try to talk about basic issues, and even then it was difficult because Douglas didn't have too many points of vulnerability. He was a committed man, he was a liberal, but shucks — that in itself wasn't grounds for damning a man. I had to be what I was, which was not an all-out conservative. I was a moderate Republican."

Witwer's reputation as a moderate was, of course, one of the reasons Stratton recruited him for the ticket. The main reason had been Witwer's prestige as a long-time spokesman for good-government causes, a role that guaranteed Witwer support of a certain constituency and access to the board rooms of the Chicago power elite. But it was also important that the Senate nominee not be an extremist identified with the political fringe. Witwer's moderate political views strengthened the ticket almost as much as his personal prestige. Yet, it was these same convictions that prevented Witwer from being able to cater to die-hard partisans. They wanted "raw meat." On those occasions when Witwer attempted to serve it to them, he was not in top form.

Nonetheless, once the Decatur ruckus subsided, Witwer and Stratton resumed their relationship as allies, and they remained warm friends ever after. On July 15, when he addressed an organization of party workers in Streator, Witwer told a press conference, "Any political grapevine reports that the governor and I are at loggerheads is pure hogwash." A few days later, in Springfield, Witwer grew testy when reporters pressed him on the rift with Stratton. "We have had no harsh words on this matter," Witwer said, skirting the edges of fiction. "I am a team player and I plan to attend the convention as an alternate. This is a little bit like a record. The more it is played, the worse it gets."

Witwer's assertion of his rights did earn him new status. Stratton saw to it that party leaders took advantage of every opportunity to spotlight Witwer. At platform hearings the week preceding the GOP convention in Chicago, Witwer testified on the need for a plank calling for a Department of Justice office to coordinate efforts against organized crime. "It is a startling fact that nowhere in government does there exist a permanent force capable of unifying the action of the thousands of federal, state, local and special law enforcement units all over the nation," Witwer testified. His appearance won wide-spread coverage and favorable editorial comment.

Witwer also was worked into the Republican National Convention program. He appeared on the dais and spoke during opening-night ceremonies. While his segment was not aimed at the prime-time market, Witwer had the distinction of appearing immediately before an address by former President Herbert Hoover. On the last day of the convention, Witwer flew to the Champaign County Fairgrounds, addressed a crowd of some 5,000 attending a GOP county convention, then flew back to Chicago in time to be present for Nixon's and Lodge's acceptance speeches, which closed the national convention in the International Amphitheatre.

At this time the various organizers and planners who staff political campaigns began meshing the Witwer effort with the national Republican drive. Plans were laid for United Nations Ambassador Lodge to be the principal speaker at Witwer's fund-raising dinner in mid-September. Lodge's schedule called for his coming into Illinois for a statewide blitz with Witwer the week before the November election. At the same time, it was agreed that Witwer join Stratton as the party representatives to greet and accompany Nixon whenever the Presidential nominee came into the state, which usually meant into Chicago.

Thus, it was on that night of Sunday, September 25, 1960, Witwer greeted Nixon at Midway Airport after the vice president had flown here to take part in his first televised debate with democratic nominee John F. Kennedy. Nixon had been out of the hospital only two weeks and was still suffering from a knee injury that had caused him to be hospitalized. He lost weight in the hospital, and dropped another five pounds during the intensive campaigning he conducted before coming to Chicago. Witwer was stunned at his first sight of Nixon coming into the terminal from the landing field.

"He looked terrible," Witwer said. "He looked ghastly."

Witwer helped Nixon disentangle himself from well-wishers and the usual crush of photographers. As the two slid into Witwer's open car, Nixon said, "Sam, if you can get me right to the hotel, I'd appreciate it."

"Well," Witwer replied, hesitantly, "there are a number of cars out here that have formed a procession of a sort, and they're expecting you in several of the wards as we go through."

Nixon shook his head. "Well, I guess we have to do it, but do what you can to get me to the hotel. I don't feel well."

So, the car with Nixon and Witwer wended its way at the head of a procession through several Southwest Side wards, including a few which at that time were still reliably Republican, and Nixon endured these encounters with street crowds who were cheering him but his smile masked what Witwer knew was intense pain.

It was midnight when Witwer got Nixon to the Pick-Congress Hotel, facing Grant Park across Michigan Avenue in downtown Chicago. The two, accompanied by Nixon's Secret Service guards, rode the elevator to Nixon's floor. As the door opened, Witwer said, "Mr. President, I hope you get some sleep. You don't look very well."

Nixon smiled grimly looking over his shoulder as he entered his hotel room. "For that matter, Sam, you don't look so well, either. You better get on home to Riverside."

"He looked like approaching death," Witwer recalled. "I always had the feeling that people never took the health factor enough into consideration when they evaluated his performance in that first debate with John Kennedy the next night."

An estimated audience of between 65 and 70 million Americans watched the debate the night of September 26 as it was televised live from the CBS studios at 630 N. McClurg Court, on Chicago's Near North Side. The consensus was that Nixon came off second-best to his opponent Kennedy among television viewers, although those who heard the debate only on radio rated Nixon the winner. Witwer had anticipated Nixon's haggard appearance on the tube. It deeply disturbed him that the Vice President's advisers were not doing enough to watch out for his health. What Witwer did not learn until much later was the Nixon's television advisers, aware of his slow recovery after leaving the hospital, had tried to get Nixon to come into Chicago the preceding Saturday so that he could benefit from one full day's rest before the Monday night encounter.

Through a mix-up in phone messages, they had been unable to get through to Nixon. For that reason, his advisers really had no time to brief Nixon on the scope of the ordeal that faced him. Nixon walked into the debate well versed on substance but inadequately prepared on style. Witwer shared the view of many observers that his performance in the first debate probably caused Nixon's defeat by the narrowest of margins in the general election six weeks later.

The session with Nixon had been the second most emotional experience for Witwer during September. The most traumatic had occurred eleven days earlier. It was September 14, the date of Witwer's all-important $100-a-plate fund-raising dinner featuring Lodge. The previous night Witwer, Ethyl, their children and Jacobs, the candidate's public relations aide, sat around the living room of the Witwer's Riverside home sharpening the points Witwer should make in his dinner speech. It had been a happy session, giving the whole Witwer family the chance to be a part of planning for Witwer's "big night." Sam, Jr. described it as a "big bull session. We just sat around and talked the whole thing over. Dad said we really helped to sharpen it all up."

Witwer awoke the morning of September 14 exuding energy and a brimful of goodwill. He was confident his speech would be a success, that the dinner would give a boost to his campaign and raise badly needed funds. He was eager to get downtown, to get the day's work done, to get to the ballroom of the Conrad Hilton Hotel for that night's main event. The adrenalin was flowing in Witwer as it does in an athlete before a big game. Then came a phone call that jolted him. The caller informed him that his long-time friend, mentor and ally, George B. McKibbin, died of a heart attack that morning. He keeled over shortly after arriving in his law offices. It was McKibbin's custom to arrive to work earlier than anyone else. He died alone at the age of 73.

Witwer was shaken. The least of his concern was the loss of McKibbin as treasurer of his campaign committee. "He was like a father to me," Witwer said. McKibbin, who ran a close race as the GOP candidate for mayor of Chicago in 1943 — when Witwer was just starting to get active in political and church affairs in the Hyde

Park community where he and McKibbin then lived — more than anyone else was responsible for Witwer's entry into political life. His death on what should have been a festive day in Witwer's political career, cast a pall over the whole proceeding.

Lenora Brand, Witwer's secretary, described her employer as "extremely shocked" when he finally showed up at his LaSalle Street office, in the same building where McKibbin had died hours earlier. Witwer was preoccupied by grief, but he knew the dinner had to go on. His family and friends marveled at how he pulled himself together and went through the motions of getting ready for the fund-raiser.

The dinner opened with a bang. Literally. Just as the speeches were to begin, a light bulb exploded at the rear of the ballroom. The crowd of several hundred supporters gasped, then quickly discerned what had happened. Lodge spoke into the microphone: "That reminds me of the United Nations." A big laugh. Witwer gave the appearance of amusement, too, but to him there was no humor in the evening.

Witwer's speech, into which he, his family and Jacobs had poured so much attention, spelled out an eight-point program of issues which Witwer used as the intellectual blueprint of his fall campaign. The points were, in brief: (1) National security, world peace and a foreign policy that encouraged less-developed nations to contribute to American resistance to the spread of Soviet Communism; (2) Acceptance of the need for updated technology in weaponry for defense, along with patient pursuit of world disarmament; (3) Prosperity and full employment without dependence on government pump-priming; (4) Individual freedom of opportunity without regard to race, religion or creed; (5) Less government interference with society; (6) A tax system based on ability to pay and one not stifling of individual initiative; (7) Exhortation against monopoly; and (8) Commitments to fight inflation.

These points were non-controversial. They were safe, moderately conservative and assured of offending neither the conservative nor liberal wing of the Republican Party. It is also true that these points, and the growing expertise with which Witwer discussed them as the campaign unfolded, neither lost nor gained Witwer any votes.

Witwer raised the largest single portion of his 1960 campaign revenue at the September 16 dinner, which netted at least $35,000, even assuming that some of the tables were so-called "freebies" to help "paper the house." And this raises an intriguing question about campaign finance, 1960 style.

In early November, both Witwer and Douglas complied with a federal deadline for reporting campaign revenues and expenses to the Clerk of the U.S. Senate. The same law, which had not been changed in decades, set a spending limit so unrealistically low that no contested candidate for the Senate or the U.S. House had been able to obey it in decades. However, to keep within the law so far as the public records went, Douglas reported getting $26,356 in contributions and spending $21,037. Witwer reported raising $23,094 (with the largest contributors identified as McKibbin and his wife, Helen, who gave $1,000 each) and spending $21,454. Both Douglas' and Witwer's reports bore little relation to reality. Most of these expenses were earmarked for accounts not required to be reported. Both raised and spent far more than they could allow themselves to report. There is no public record of what Douglas actually spent (it was estimated around $750,000), but Witwer acknowledges his total expenses for the year including costs of running in the primary as well as mounting the challenge against Douglas approximated $220,000, and the campaign ended with Witwer $36,000 in debt. The Witwer campaign was inexpensive even by 1960 standards. As a point of comparison, that same year, the Democratic candidate for lieutenant governor spent $250,000 to get elected, and he had not faced a primary contest. It was not until 14 years later that Congress got around to reforming campaign finance laws in the wake of Watergate, and a U.S. Supreme Court decision in 1976 outlawed any legislative limits on total campaign spending, while legitimizing limits on individual contributions.

It is a commentary on that era that the most honorable of candidates were forced to engage in legalistic fiction, that leaders of virtually every established institution — business, labor, the press, religion — were aware of the need for such deceptive practices, yet did not consider the practices to be anything requiring immediate reform. Surely, Douglas and Witwer deserve no retroactive censure for following the practice of their times. It is merely unfortunate that it required a national scandal, a constitutional crisis, many years later to bring about a change in the law.

Ethyl Witwer emerged as a full-time campaigner between the September 14 dinner and the election. She had been drafted as a stump speaker very reluctantly during the primary campaign when she acceptd an invitation to "say a few words" at a dinner of Black Republicans in Chicago's 2nd Ward, only to find on her arrival that her name was printed on the dinner program book identifying her as the principal speaker. From that surprise baptism in speech-making, she allowed her schedule of engagements to grow slowly. By November, she was giving speeches at the rate of 20 a week, a pace that qualified her beyond question as an "old pro" at campaigning.

Two questions kept popping up every time Ethyl appeared before a group or was interviewed by a reporter. Was Mrs. Witwer aware that she bore a striking resemblance to Pat Nixon, wife of the Vice President? ("I am very flattered that some people seem to think we look alike.") And, does Mrs. Witwer believe her husband will win in November? ("Yes, I am sure Sam will win. I have terrific faith in that man.")

Her new responsibilities put no strain on the Witwers' marriage. Even though there might be two or three days in sequence when Sam and Ethyl were unable to converse for more than a few minutes, each adapted to the hectic pace and the couple felt as close as they had throughout their marriage. Ethyl's mother had made it possible for her to become a more public figure; Mrs. Wilkins lost her husband, Ethyl's father, the previous year and so was free to leave their Gary home and move into the Witwer's large house in Riverside to take charge of the cleaning and cooking. At this time, two of the Witwer children, Carole, 14, and David, 11, were living at home, while the 19-year-old twins, Michael and Sam, Jr., were away at Dickinson College in Carlisle. The twins had spent summer vacation campaigning with their dad on the county-fair and fish-fry circuits. The Witwers traveled the state in a 40-foot campaign trailer decorated in patriotic colors and emblazoned with a block-letter appeal to "Vote for Samuel W. Witwer/Republican for United States Senator/He Gets Things Done!" This way, Witwer probably spent more time with his sons that summer than he would have if the boys had spent most afternoons at a swimming pool or a sandlot ball game.

Witwer's most frequent complaint against Douglas, as noted earlier, concerned the Senator's refusal to debate. Actually, Douglas tried to ignore most of Witwer's blasts. But a couple of times his opponent scored a bull's eye, nettling Douglas into coming into the open to answer a Witwer salvo.

In early August, Witwer surfaced with an issue that cut to the very heart of Douglas' reputation as a public servant who put principle and integrity above loyalty to party. Witwer learned that the Senator had been holding up confirmation of 59 nominees for Illinois postmasterships. It was obvious that Douglas hoped the Republicans would lose the White House in November, allowing a Democratic administration to substitute deserving Democrats for the Republican-sponsored nominations that Douglas refused to let the Senate approve. Witwer issued a public denunciation of Douglas' stalling act, noting that all of the pending nominees had been certified as qualified by the Civil Service Commission; of those awaiting confirmation, Witwer pointed out, 43 were war veterans.

Douglas was wounded by the attack. After a few days during which his staff gathered some statistics, Douglas issued a statement insisting that of nearly 80 nominations he had received since January 1960, he had approved 24. Many of those from which he had withheld approval, Douglas said, involved postmasterships that had been vacant for a long time. "I question the sincerity of Republicans in getting them filled so fast before the election," said Douglas. Arguments could be made on both sides of this issue, of course. Yet, the net effect was to hurt Douglas; the exchange portrayed him as a patronage-grubbing politician just as interested in the spoils of office for his Party as any other politician would be. (At a more serious level of government — the federal judiciary —Douglas was to build a record that was not apparent in 1960. Once the Democrats had recaptured the White House, Douglas dogmatically refused to allow any Republicans to be appointed to any federal bench in Douglas' geographic control, which included Illinois and the two adjoining states that comprised a federal circuit. But this die-hard partisanship was not part of Douglas' public image during the Witwer campaign. The Douglas camp therefore felt doubly compelled to discredit the Witwer criticism on the postmasterships and to nurture Douglas' reputation as fiercely independent of partisan pressures.)

Witwer also scored in accusing Douglas of keeping Lyndon Johnson, the Democratic vice presidential nominee, out of Illinois so that Douglas' constituents would not be so easily reminded of Johnson's Southern-oriented record on civil rights and oil regulation. "I challenge Senator Douglas to tell the people what he thinks of Johnson, including Johnson's attitude toward civil rights," Witwer thundered in a press release hammered out by Jacobs on a typewriter in the back seat of their campaign car. The press release and five carbons of it were grabbed by local reporters as Witwer and Jacobs arrived at a gathering of Knox County Republicans. Witwer may have been surprised at the big play his statement got in newspapers around the state (the LBJ attack had not been conceived as a major policy matter), but the answer rested in the fact that both major wire services were represented at Knox County the day Witwer spoke there, and the Johnson angle made fresh copy for overnight leads the reporters had to file with their bureaus in Springfield.

Spurred by press reception to his initial remarks about LBJ, Witwer let loose another blast at the Texan a few days later when Johnson got the Texas Legislature to enact a law allowing him to run for re-election to the Senate as a hedge against his possible defeat for vice president in November.

Witwer was genuinely appalled at Johnson's gall in pulling such a stunt, and he wasn't going to let Douglas off the hook about it. "If Douglas wants to be associated with the Johnson record of expedience, prejudice and naked ambition, it's all right with me," Witwer said, and again his remarks were widely quoted.

From Washington, where Congress was in special session (a short and fruitless post-convention session), Douglas was impelled to issue some type of response. He finally released a terse statement saying, "Senator Johnson has pledged support to the Democratic platform, and I believe he has done so in good faith." Douglas didn't try to defend Johnson's simultaneous campaigns for the Senate and Vice President. Two points should be noted. (1) Douglas had nothing to do with the Democrats' national strategy of confining LBJ to Southern states in the campaign, but it is clear that Douglas was happy with that strategy; and (2) Douglas did not like Senator Johnson and was embarrassed whenever his colleague's Senate record was trotted out for liberals to dissect. In 1966, campaigning (unsuccessfully) for a fourth Senate term, Douglas confided to a Chicago journalist, "I always thought Johnson was a captive of the oil industry when he was in the Senate. To some extent (as President) he still is."

Witwer continued to have fun needling Douglas whenever an opportunity would unexpectedly offer itself. Such an occasion arose the night of August 5 at a Peoria shopping center. Douglas was addressing a crowd of shoppers in the plaza over a loudspeaker in the Senator's sound truck when Witwer's car drove into the plaza. Witwer emerged from his car and conveyed word to Douglas that the amplifier in Witwer's own sound truck was broken. Douglas did the courteous thing. He informed the crowd he was going to let his opponent, Witwer, address them over Douglas' own sound system for five minutes. Witwer wasted little time on amenities, digging right in, "Senator," his voice boomed, "I have been chasing you the length and breadth of this state trying to get you to agree to debate me, and I have not to this date heard from you that you are willing to do so. I ask you here and now, will you meet me in a series of debates? Specifically, how about a formal debate right here in Peoria?" Douglas squirmed in discomfort. He responded with remarks inaudible to local reporters, who asked him to repeat his answer. Douglas testily repeated that yes, of course, he would debate with Witwer at some future time — "if it can be worked into my schedule." Witwer drove off content that he chiseled another little niche in Douglas' armor.

Debate challenges are a cliche of political campaigning; their impact on the public is negligible. But the press helped Witwer keep alive the image of Douglas ducking his challenge. *Chicago Sun-Times* political columnist John Drieske devoted a column to recollections of Douglas' pique in 1948, when challenger Douglas could not get the Republican Senate incumbent to debate with him. But now that Douglas was the incumbent, Drieske suggested, the need for debates did not seem as urgent to Douglas. Drieske wrote, "Douglas isn't going for the Witwer proposals that they campaign together, as a sort of troop of strolling players, hitting the hamlets as a two-man show."

Finally, there came a time when Douglas could duck no longer. In mid-October the two debated at the annual meeting of the Illinois State Chamber of Commerce in the Conrad Hilton Hotel. There was to be 10 minutes for opening remarks by each, followed by three rebuttal periods of five, three, and two minutes each. The chamber had recruited a Northwestern University baseball coach to act as timekeeper, to blow the whistle on the candidates when their answers got too wordy. Douglas won a coin toss and opted to go first.

What followed was a no-holds-barred exchange that held the rapt attention of the 1,250 businessmen at the meeting for most of one hour. M.W. Newman, a reporter for the *Chicago Daily News,* described it this way in his coverage of the event: "The Witwer-Douglas debate never will replace the Lincoln-Douglas debate in Illinois history. But, in one short set-to, it has torn up the pea patch real good, juiced up the Illinois Senate campaign and passed up the Nixon-Kennedy debating style in favor of snort, snap 'n' snarl." Newman described Witwer as "flushed and trembling with excitement at finally cornering his adroit rival."

Douglas took the traditional route in responding to the charge that he had been avoiding debates. He denied it. "He (Witwer) is trying to build up an imaginary grievance," Douglas insisted. Douglas assailed the Eisenhower administration for "a miserable record of veto, obstruction and objection." He tried to keep the debate centered on economic issues and what he called the need for a change in domestic and foreign policies. But Douglas bristled at Witwer's charge that the Senator, during eight years in office, had succeeded in getting only nine bills that he sponsored or co-sponsored through the committee process on Capitol Hill.

Douglas noted that Witwer had overlooked all the resolutions and private bills (usually, those conferring a grant of citizenship) that Douglas had successfully sponsored. Douglas claimed credit for raising the minimum wage from 75 cents to $1 an hour, and for getting union welfare and pension fund disclosure laws enacted. "I am sending down to my opponent a detailed list of my accomplishments so he can become informed on my record," Douglas said, then indulged the theatrical gesture of requiring others at the dais to pass, hand to hand, sheets of paper itemizing his accomplishments to Witwer, seated on the opposite side of the lectern. It was good "show biz."

Douglas touched a Witwer nerve just once, when he accused the Republican of taking one stand on aid to distressed areas while campaigning in Northern Illinois, and advocating the opposite position in Southern Illinois. He said Witwer railed against "wild government spending" in the affluent northern part of the state, while calling for increased federal aid in the economically depressed southern part. Witwer confronted the microphone and "cate-gorically" denied being such a hypocrite. "I don't want the job that badly," he said in a deep voice that pounced on each word for a staccato effect. "I want the job, but not that badly." His rebuttal attracted a burst of enthusiastic applause.

Their single debate won Witwer some of the best publicity of the entire campaign. Did anyone win? Who knows? Douglas was philosophical about it. "I'm resigned to win and I'm resigned to lose," he said. "But I'm more resigned to win." Witwer definitely felt a psychological lift from the encounter.

But Witwer's euphoria was short-lived. It was deflated four days later when the *Chicago Sun-Times* published the first returns from its famous straw poll on key races. It showed Douglas garnering 60.38% of the vote to 39.62% for Witwer. Such a spread, translated into popular votes, would mean Witwer losing the election by more than 1,000,000 votes. The straw poll devastated morale among Republicans. It showed Governor Stratton losing by an even larger margin than Witwer. It showed Kennedy topping Nixon by a projected margin of some 90,000 votes.

Witwer refused to act discouraged. He plunged into the arena with new gusto, adding new stops on his schedule, squeezing in every radio and television appearance where he was invited to appear. He said later the final two weeks of the campaign were tough on him because he felt obliged to buoy the morale of his staff and supporters (and not least of all, his family), yet he appreciated the likelihood of his defeat.

Witwer's campaign trailer had been converted, in a neat publicity stunt, into a "pollmobile." It was outfitted with a voting machine that allowed visitors to indicate which of a dozen issues most troubled them. After 12,000 people had "voted," the not-so-surprising result showed foreign policy, specifically the Cold War, dominating their concerns. Witwer and Henry Cabot Lodge cited this "survey" as evidence that voters ultimately would choose the Nixon-Lodge ticket over the Kennedy-Johnson ticket, because of the GOP candidates' edge in foreign policy experience. Lodge came into the state and barnstormed through a dozen downstate cities with Witwer. On the weekend before the election, Witwer staged a "Victory Flight" to 18 cities starting at Ottawa and ending 48 hours later in Chicago. He was accompanied by Ethyl and by President Eisenhower's brother, Earl. The pace was grueling. Witwer found himself anxious for the ordeal to end.

Ironically, during the final weeks, Witwer, aware of the imminent demise of his effort, won the war of newspaper endorsements against Douglas. George M. Burditt, a surburban Chicago legislator who headed Volunteers for Witwer, and who subsequently ran for the United States Senate, claimed Witwer had won support of every major daily paper in the state, along with more than 100 weeklies. Of most significance were endorsements by papers that previously supported Douglas. These included the *Chicago Sun-Times, Chicago Daily News,* the *St. Louis Globe-Democrat,* the *Moline Dispatch,* the *Decatur Herald-Review,* the *Champaign Courier,* the *Carbondale Southern Illinoisan* and *Chicago's American.*

An important holdout for Douglas was the *Illinois State Register* in Springfield, the state capitol. In reiterating its support for Douglas, the newspaper felt obliged to discredit Witwer, and the only way it could do this was by resurrecting the familiar linkage with Governor Stratton. "Mr. Witwer, the hand-picked candidate of Governor Stratton, is attempting to belittle the battles for righteousness fought so gallantly by Senator Douglas," the newspaper stated. "Mr. Stratton's candidate, Mr. Witwer, is charging..." was the drift.

The pro-Witwer editorials generally followed the line that the Republican offered a fresh voice on the national scene. Typical was the *Waukegan News-Sun,* which headlined its endorsement editorial, "We're Ready for Witwer!" "Win or lose, Witwer has waged a great fight," the *News-Sun* said. "Working against great odds, Witwer has stumped the whole state over and over again, battling for what he believes is right . . . The people of Illinois deserve a man like Witwer as their Senator." The editorial decried Douglas as a relic of the past, applying the solutions of the 1930s to problems of the 1960s. That was almost a literal pickup of the Witwer line.

Witwer spent election eve with Nixon, who came to Chicago as part of a last-minute blitzkreig to tilt key states into the Republican column. The two joined Governor Stratton for an impromptu rally in front of the CBS-TV studios on N. McClurg Court. Everyone was groggy by this point. Saying lines by rote. Answering questions like robots. Waving at crowds like disembodied puppets. Glassy-eyed.

The night of the election, November 8, was almost an anticlimax for Witwer. He went to his campaign headquarters toting newspapers that had given prominent display to stories of an appearance in which Witwer was flanked, in a hands-held-high victory stance, by baseball great Jackie Robinson and John Roosevelt, son of the late Democratic President.

"A candidate can tell if he's winning or losing by what happens in his headquarters," Witwer told friends many years later. "As soon as the polls close, your supporters set up camp with you and your family. Then the media boys come in, setting up their own press telephones. Then, just before you start answering phones, for the first returns, there are a few minutes of great frenzy, great excitement, when everyone is talking at once and you can't hear yourself think."

Witwer paused, shook his head with am embarrassed grin, then continued, "The first ones to leave are the press. They fold up their equipment and slink out, undermining whatever attempt you and your staff are engaged in trying to keep spirits up among your supporters until the returns are more definitive. Then, singly or in groups of two or three, your supporters begin to disappear. Until all of a sudden, maybe it's midnight, and you look up and all you're left with is your family. It's a tremendously lonely experience, but you're never more grateful for your family than at that moment."

For Witwer, election night was not the Night of the Long Count. The returns indicated fairly early that he would lose, although not by the massive margin initially projected by the *Sun-Times* straw poll. The final vote was 2,093,846 for Witwer, to 2,530,943 for Douglas, giving the incumbent a margin of 437,097 or a percentage breakdown of 55-45. Stratton lost by a much greater margin, while Nixon lost the state by a measly 8,000 votes — a margin that Republicans forever would attribute to vote fraud in Chicago. Oddly enough, Republicans retained control of the state Legislature, testimony to the power of incumbency on the local level.

Witwer philosophized for months about how people avoided a defeated candidate. He concluded their behavior reflected nothing negative about him personally, that it simply mirrored "a strong mood in American life whereby we honor victory. We do not have any place in our book for those who honorably are defeated."

It amused Witwer that many associates who put distance between themselves and him after his Senate loss hurriedly returned to try to win his favor 10 years later, when Witwer emerged victorious in the fight to ratify a new state constitution. "In America, everything is winning," he said. "It should not be that way. It discourages people whose motivations are good, whose talents are sound, from coming back into politics. I made up my mind I was going to continue doing what I believed in. My discouragement at losing one election would not get in the way of my continuing work for constitutional reform. So it wasn't long before I was back in the thick of things."

During this post-election period, Witwer often mulled over the advice of his dear friend, George McKibbin, who had told him, "Never expect too much of your friends. Accept with pleasure and surprise anything they really do for you."

Witwer believes the treatment accorded him in defeat caused him to be more compassionate and understanding of others with problems. "But the campaign toughened me up and got me ready for the Constitutional Convention," he said.

Was Witwer tempted to stage a political comeback and run for another elective office? He was tempted, yes. Did he carry it very far? No. He made a few speeches around the state at his own expense and tested a few close friends with the idea of running for governor in 1964. "Nobody was very enthusiastic about seeing me come back," he said. "I got no signals of support from the regular party organization or from financial groups. So I felt, no, I am not interested. That was the end of it."

Witwer remembers sage advice from a distinguished legal colleague, Kenneth F. Burgess, who told him, "Sam, you ran with distinction. You came out with respect. Never allow yourself to be shopworn." That advice influenced Witwer's decision not to run again.

"I pondered that many times," Witwer said. "I thought, 'I guess he's right. I don't have to have my whole future in the political field.' And always in the background, I had this basic dream, about one day being able to preside over a Constitutional Convention . . . My run for the roses was a happy experience. It was an enriching experience. I had my disappointments, but they never left me soured. My basic dream was still viable."

Witwer took offense at one post-election description of him as a "crushed man." "I have never been crushed in my life!" said the man who wouldn't quit, the man whose dream finally would be realized after another decade of an unrelenting quest.

1.

2.

3.

4.

5.

7.

1. Former Governor Otto Kerner and Witwer meet in Springfield to plan 1968 campaign for the call of the Convention.

2. 1979 Commencement speaker Hannah H. Gray, President of the University of Chicago, congratulates Witwer for services to Illinois and Dickinson College.

3. Governor Richard Ogilvie presents Witwer as newly elected President of the 6th Illinois Constitutional Convention on December 8, 1969. In background, former Governor Otto Kerner.

4. Convention opening day greetings from Adlai E. Stevenson III, State Treasurer and former Governor Samual Shapiro (center).

5. The Convention moves to its new chambers in the House of Representatives of the Old State Capitol in March, 1970.

6. The Convention delegates sign the new Constitution on September 3, 1970, each in turn at the original desk of Abraham Lincoln who had served as a legislator and delivered his "House Divided" speech in the same room.

7. Witwer receives the medal of the Chicago Press Club as its 1970 Man of the Year.

CREATING
A NEW
CONSTITUTION

*That which we now undertake is the most solemn
function of government a state can perform.
Constitution making is the fundamental and organic
act of a free society, a task unequalled in importance
in the life of a democracy.*
— Inaugural Address of Samuel W. Witwer
President, Sixth Illinois Constitutional Convention

The Sixth Illinois Constitutional Convention, in gestation for decades, was born into a climate hostile to change. America was about to enter its seventh year of active combat in Vietnam. Student riots were disrupting campuses across the country. There were jitters in the business community as the national economy, for the first time in the history of the republic, reeled from inflation and recession at the same time. The country's soul suffered from societal divisions — hard-hat versus hippie, old-style patriots versus draft resisters, proponents of the new sexual freedom versus defenders of traditional morality, newly emerging feminists versus those fearful of change in the role of families, civil libertarians versus a vigilante mentality bent on preserving law and order.

That was the national backdrop against which Sam and Ethyl Witwer arrived in Springfield on December 5, 1969, a few days before the official convening of the Convention. The raw, wintry wind bit Witwer's face as he stood in front of the State Capitol, an ornate, majestic structure dating from the era of Illinois' century-

158

old constitution, and contemplated the challenge confronting him and the other 115 delegates arriving in the capital for pre-inaugural huddles. No constitutional convention had been successful in Illinois in a century. The only convention held in the period — fifty years earlier — had been a dismal failure.

Experience in other states was no more encouraging. The previous year, Maryland voters had rejected a new state charter that legal scholars had acclaimed as an ideal document. The year before that, a constitutional convention in New York had foundered on politics and a controversy over separation of church and state. During the previous decade, Michigan stood alone among major states that had succeeded in the arduous task of constitutional revision, and Wolverine State voters had ratified that project by the narrowest of margins. By what right did Witwer believe Illinois could succeed where more liberal states, states traditionally more accommodating to change, had faltered? There must have been a touch of messianic fervor in Witwer's dogged optimism.

Another thought intruded on Witwer as he gazed at the Capitol. He recalled a day in 1949, just 20 years previously, when he accepted Governor Adlai E. Stevenson's invitation to address the Illinois House of Representatives to explain the need for a constitutional convention. That day he had been subjected to outrageous abuse by a big and sneering politico, Reed Cutler, a member of his own party, filled with tricks and tics, who openly equated proponents of constitutional reform with agents of a Communist conspiracy. Despite Cutler's harangues that day, Witwer inhaled the glory of leadership as he spoke on the rostrum in the well of the House chamber, and he envisioned a day when he would be standing on the identical rostrum presiding over a successful constitutional convention. That vision nourished Witwer's efforts for a score more years, and now, on the eve of the state's Sixth Constitutional Convention, he was imbued with that lofty sense of purpose one feels when he is about to fulfill a rendezvous with destiny. For that is what it was — a rendezvous that Witwer had staked out with steadfast determination. The opening of "Con-Con" marked the convergence of all the roads

Witwer had taken — in law, in politics, in education, in religion —
and this convention provided the opportunity for Witwer to call
upon the strengths he had derived from these other avenues of
experience to surmount hurdle after hurdle.

The first path Witwer had to retread was that of political
leader.

Witwer wanted to be the convention's president. There was
nothing presumptuous about the desire, and he was not coy about it.
By background, by experience, by dint of his long labors to achieve
the calling of the convention, Witwer felt superbly qualified to be its
president. And yet, intuitive caution pevented him from becoming
an avowed candidate for the job. "You could let this whole thing slip
away if you don't stand up and let everyone know you're willing to
fight for it," one delegate warned him. Witwer didn't agree. He had
fought too long for non-partisan election of delegates, he was too
committed to the ideal of offering non-partisan leadership, to
indulge overtly in grubbing for votes, in the style of a legislative
wheeler and dealer. This did not mean Witwer abstained from
political (as opposed to partisan) activity. As delegates arrived and
settled into their rooms at the Leland Hotel, the St. Nicholas Hotel
or the Statehouse Inn, Witwer met with them on their own
temporary turf, singly or in groups, to let them assess him while he
sought to measure their priorities. Before coming to Springfield,
Witwer had touched base with the editorial chiefs of the major
metropolitan newspapers, and the press was a unified chorus
urging Witwer's election as president.

Witwer's unwillingness to trumpet his ambition may have
encouraged other delegates to launch trial balloons for their own
candidacies. There emerged a young lawyer from Chicago's North
Side lakefront, Peter A. Tomei, brilliant and brash, who saw himself
as more qualified than Witwer. Tomei was an independent Democrat,
meaning he had been elected against a candidate supported by
Daley's Democratic organization, and Tomei wanted to establish
himself as leader of about a dozen delegates similarly elected. There
emerged several downstate Republicans with vast legislative
experience — John C. Parkhurst of Peoria, a former member of the

Illinois House Republican leadership; former State Auditor Elbert S. Smith of Decatur, also a one-time legislator; and former State Senator Thomas G. Lyons, Democratic committeeman of a Chicago North Side ward, who was quickly identified as leader of Mayor Daley's loyalists in the convention.

Lyons approached Witwer with what seemed like a reasonable request that Lyons be elected as temporary president in return for later supporting Witwer as permanent president. Witwer was tempted to agree, then perceived the plan as a ploy for delaying selection of a permanent president until rules could be established that would have sharply limited the powers of the president. Witwer spurned the entreaty.

At an orientation session for delegates, Witwer pursued his low-key approach in conversations during recesses. He avoided taking stands on many substantive issues, although he did not try to hide his record of staunch advocacy of merit selection of judges. He did not want his election as president to be snagged on any single-issue controversy. His campaign was subdued, yet persistent.

On the morning of December 8, 1969, the day the convention was to be gaveled into session by Governor Richard B. Ogilvie, Witwer learned his election was assured. Mayor Daley arrived from Chicago (to watch his son, Richard M., sworn in as a delegate) and met briefly with Witwer, promising him full support by Daley's legions. On the key roll call, Witwer was elected with 88 votes, with 15 cast for David Davis and 10 for a maverick Democrat from Chicago, Leonard Foster.

It is interesting to speculate as to who would have been a successful president of the Convention if Witwer had not been elected to that post or had he stepped down as a result of the Gardner imbroglio (described later) or for any other reason. Several men had been nominated originally or talked about, either by themselves or others — David Davis, Thomas Hunter, Leonard Foster, John Knuppel, Peter Tomei, John Parkhurst and Elbert Smith. All of them, except possibly Smith and Parkhurst, had too narrow a base of support, or were too conservative, temperamental, inexperienced or otherwise disqualified. Selection of anyone other than Smith might have been disastrous, except possibly for Davis or Parkhurst. Smith certainly knew how to run meetings. He had poise, humor, and amiable personal qualities. He was admired and liked, if not loved, by all of the delegates. But even a friend must ask the hard question as to how he would have fared in a crunch. One might wonder, too, if he had the long-term dedication and commitment to constitutional reform that might have made it possible for him to persevere in every rough contingency. With afterthought given to the matter, it is clear that, despite any assumed failings of personality, Witwer was not only the best choice for the office, but the only choice. It is doubtful that the Convention could have succeeded under any other auspices.

It was one of the proudest moments of Witwer's life as he mounted the steps of the rostrum to accept the gavel from Governor Ogilvie. Witwer's hand was grasped and pumped enthusiastically by Chief Justice Robert Underwood of the Illinois Supreme Court. Witwer was greeted similarly by Ogilvie and three former governors with whom he had labored for constitutional reform — William G. Stratton, Otto Kerner and Samuel Shapiro. He glowed in the warmth of the occasion.

Some delegates — particularly Republicans and Independents — felt Witwer had "dealt" with the Daley machine to achieve his post. It was true that Daley delivered his hard-core following of some 40 delegates to Witwer's candidacy, but it was untrue that Witwer had bargained or traded away anything for that support. Daley merely accepted Witwer as the outstanding choice among Republicans because it was apparent that a majority of 59 votes could never be mustered for any Daley Democrat. Daley, who sought to have all Chicago delegates treated fairly by Witwer, did make one specific request of Witwer: "Sam, take care of my boy." Daley was enormously proud of his son, Richard, and wanted him to shine in his first political venture. While Witwer had amassed more votes for delegate than any candidate in any district during the general election for Con-Con, the younger Daley had run a close second. The mayor may have thought he had won from Witwer an understanding to appoint Daley's son to an important committee chairmanship, but Witwer did not perceive that subtlety at the time nor did he make any such appointment.

Before tackling the issue of committee leadership, however, Witwer had to grapple with another problem testing his political prowess. The enabling act under which the convention was convened provided for only two officers — a president and a vice president. In Witwer's view, this was unwise. If he were to be president, the vice president likely would be a Chicago Democrat, saddling the convention with two leaders from Cook County and none from the rest of the state. This would imperil downstate acceptance of the new constitution. Even before the convention started, Witwer began maneuvering to assure the election of at least two vice presidents, and, as events turned out, the rules finally provided for three such positions.* Chosen were two rivals for the number one spot, Thomas Lyons and Elbert Smith, and a teacher in his mid-20s, John Alexander, from Virden. Witwer accepted Alexander reluctantly, but at the time it appeared prudent to do so, because Alexander had campaigned so successfully in his own behalf among the delegates. Odas Nicholson, a Black lawyer from Chicago's Hyde Park neighborhood, was elected convention secretary. Thus, the convention leadership was balanced with two certifiable Republicans (Witwer and Smith), two Chicago organization Democrats (Lyons and Nicholson), and an ostensible Republican who became something of a loose cannon during the proceedings (Alexander).

Witwer knew that, next to the impact of his own leadership, perhaps transcending it, was the necessity for strong committee leadership. This could come only if he had the decisive voice in naming the chairman, vice chairmen and the full composition of

---

*For details of the intrigue in election of the vice presidents, as well as for details of the internal mechanisms and workings of the convention itself, read *Charter for a New Age,* by Elmer Gertz and Joseph P. Pisciotte (University of Illinois Press, 1980). The book is a definitive study of the convention. Its insights into the governmental and civics aspects of the convention offer a worthwhile supplement to any study of Samuel Witwer.

each committee. Of course, he would consult with the vice presidents, as required by the rules, and the Convention as a whole would have the right to ratify or reject his choices, but, just as the president of the United States and the Governor of the State names his own Cabinet, subject to Senate approval, it was necessary that the President of the Convention be in the position to make certain that the right men and women were assigned to the appropriate tasks. Some felt that it was more democratic and practical to name a Committee on Committees and have such an elite group make the assignments. Witwer believed that this would wreck the Convention by creating prolonged delays and unnecessary maneuvering and controversy. Yet, that proposal came near winning the approval of the Committee on Rules. Even a wise and honorable delegate like Bernard Weisberg supported the idea of a Committee on Committees. It took Witwer's own tie-breaking vote to squelch the proposal. Breathing more than one sigh of relief, Witwer embarked upon his delicate task of devising committee assignments.

He had to consider most carefully the composition of the Convention — Republicans, Democrats, Independents; Chicago, Cook County, downstate; men, women; whites, Blacks. He was not oblivious to the personal qualities and qualifications of those whom he might choose. And he had to consult with the vice presidents — Lyons close at hand, Smith not so close at hand but willing, Alexander most distant and less willing. Smith and Lyons recognized the preeminance of Witwer in making the choices; Alexander was less willing to do so. He felt that he ought to have a greater role in who was named or not named. Witwer consulted, also, with some of the convention staff and some outside of the convention ranks, whom he had learned to trust during his many years of agitating for a constitutional convention; men like Louis Ancel and Richard Lockhart, in particular. He solicited the first, second and third choices of each delegate without any commitment to honor them. He heard from delegates in more personal fashion as to their desires, some rather exigently. After clearing all quarters, he selected his choices. But the clamor did not abate. Some of his stormiest sessions came after he had announced his selections.

In this media-conscious society, Witwer had to be exceedingly careful at all times not to affront the press. He realized that he needed their support if the Convention was to proceed smoothly and if its product was to be ratified by the voters nine months to a year down the road. But this did not mean, to Witwer, that he had to be subservient or to sacrifice principle. Early in the Convention, he received a challenge from the *Chicago Tribune,* which many regarded as all-powerful. For years it had fought all efforts to hold a Constitutional Convention. The *Tribune* opposed the pending selections of Elmer Gertz, John M. Karns and George Lewis as committee chairmen. At the earnest behest of Louis Ancel, Witwer met with the top people of the *Tribune* to discuss the matter. Witwer was in no yielding mood, because he had good reason for each of the appointments. Gertz, he felt, was a classicist in the field of civil rights and liberties. The *Tribune* seemed intent upon focusing unfriendly attention upon Gertz and his committee but Witwer stood his ground and declined to withdraw his nominees.

When the Convention was over, the *Tribune's* support for the new Contitution appeared to be uncertain for weeks. Then shortly before the referendum, a front-page editorial appeared in favor of the document. Later, at a banquet given by the Union League Club, in honor of the delegates, the same *Tribune* people who had castigated Gertz publicly apologized and assured him that he was "a great delegate." Witwer's steadfastness and Gertz' performance paid off in relation to that powerful newspaper.

Witwer had to be careful not to favor one newspaper at the expense of another. When there was a leak of his committee chairman choices to one newspaper, another newspaper complained bitterly. Witwer suspected that there were some delegates who had to be advised of his plans, who were courting favor with particular newspapers by giving them scoops. He could do little or nothing about this, but he remained alert.

Normally, there would be no question about Witwer's goodwill towards the Black delegates, all of them Democrats, and toward the Black community generally. For years he had been on the board of directors of the Chicago Urban League and had shown his devotion to increased opportunities for that long deprived minority group. On the floor of the Convention, he later spoke in favor of the provision of the Bill of Rights extending protection against discrimination in the areas of employment and property. But very early in the Convention a controversy arose with respect to Black leadership on the Convention committees.

In the dickering between Witwer and Lyons as to representation by Democrats in the committee leadership, Lyons proposed none of the thirteen Black delegates as chairmen of any of the committees. Witwer appointed James H. Kemp as vice chairman of the Bill of Rights Committee and Charles A. Coleman as vice chairman of the Executive Committee. Then, a delegation of Black delegates —Kemp, Hunter, Patch and Coleman — called upon him, protesting the failure to name even one of them as the chairman of a committee. Witwer told them that, since they were all Democrats, it was up to Lyons to substitute one of them for one of the white chairmen, possibly David E. Stahl. Reluctantly, Lyons and Paul F. Elward were brought into the discussion. Witwer would not budge from the stand he had taken, nor would Lyons agree to substitute one of the Blacks as a committee chairman. Before leaving, he asked Witwer to call him at his ward headquarters that night if Witwer changed his mind and bumped one of the other chairmen, an Independent or Republican, in favor of a Black. Witwer stood firm.

Then, all of the committee chairmen and vice chairmen were invited to attend a press conference the following morning. Kemp and Coleman attended and made no issue of the matter, although that was not the end of it. When Witwer officially announced his choices on the floor of the Convention, Kemp delivered an attack upon him, almost unrestrained in its intensity, ending with Kemp's resignation as vice chairman of the Bill of Rights committee. Kemp was induced to reconsider, but for the rest of the Convention, Witwer could not be sure of Kemp's attitude. As expected, Kemp opposed merit selection of judges with great vigor. As the Convention neared its close, Kemp got his revenge, if such, indeed, was his intention. Arrangements had been made for R.R. Donnelley & Company, a non-union printer, to print the official archive edition of the new Constitution, because it was generally believed to be the only qualified printer for such purpose. Kemp attacked this decision relentlessly and prevailed, because few wanted to affront organized labor. When Donnelley, with great generosity, offered to turn over what it had done to a union printer, Kemp repulsed it again and prevailed. In the end, Kemp was one of the few delegates to oppose the new Constitution, despite its provisions for non-discrimination, home-rule and other sections favorable to minorities and Chicago.

None of Witwer's committee choices was repudiated by the Convention. Would they function as well as Witwer hoped?

The one Convention committee that Witwer actively served on was the Rules Committee, because it would determine the nature, thoroughness, effectiveness and speed of the deliberations. He appointed himself as chairman. If the rules were inadequate or misguided, there would be trouble — the worse the rules, the worse the trouble; the better the rules, the smoother and speedier the functioning of the Convention. The promulgated rules were adequate, if not wholly good. There could well have been further limitation upon the length of each delegate's remarks in debate. Certainly, no one could justly complain that he was not given full opportunity to express himself throughout the Convention, not only because of the rules, but because Witwer's sense of fairness prescribed proper consideration of each matter. Sometimes, as in the cases of the more long-winded or agitated delegates, this meant permission to speak beyond the prescribed limit of ten minutes.

The rules of the Convention, as initially intended and as interpreted by the Rules Committee and the presiding officers, resulted in a method of operation unique to the needs of the Convention at that point in time — openness, with an opportunity for full debate and dissent, but which allowed strong leadership to get the job done. Each member of the Convention could submit written proposals for the new Constitution which were assigned by the President to the appropriate committee for consideration. The committees were free to accept, reject or modify each proposal, and they could originate proposals of their own. When a majority of a committee agreed upon the article of the Constitution assigned to them, or a discrete portion thereof, they would submit it to the whole body of convention delegates with a covering report. Nevertheless, a three-person minority could submit, at the same time, its own proposed article, with an explanatory report. The Convention would then assemble as a Committee of the Whole and receive explanations for the opposing views, followed by a plenary session at which the opposing proposals would be discussed, amended, approved or rejected. After this procedure was completed, the constitutional article, or portion thereof, would be sent to the Committee on Style, Drafting and Submission for editorial refinement. The same process would be followed for each article of the proposed Constitution.

The drafted articles would then come back for second reading which was substantially like first reading. There was then full discussion and an unlimited right of amendment. Upon approval of second reading, the article would again return to the Committee on Style, Drafting and Submission for final editorial refinement.

Ultimately, the whole proposed Constitution was submitted in plenary session for third reading. There could be amendment at this point only if the rules were suspended by a majority vote of the entire membership. Meanwhile, there would be determinations as to what would be submitted as a constitution or package, what articles or section would be submitted separately from the package, the Transition Schedule governing movement from the old constitution to the new, the form of the ballot, and provisions governing when and how the ratifying vote of the people would occur.

At every step, the possibility of delay and complications existed, much to the consternation of Witwer. Schedules were agreed upon, then violated. There was bickering, uncertainty, worrisome considerations. First reading was so protracted that many besides Witwer thought the Convention could not be completed before the assigned space and funding ran out. Witwer continuously faced the specter of running out of time and funds and a breakdown such as occurred in the 1922 Convention. Second reading was somewhat less prolonged than first. Surprisingly third reading was a miracle of dispatch, and, to the amazement of many, the Convention ended within its allotted time and budget.

There were certain ceremonial acts that Witwer found useful, even when they were time-consuming in a convention that had little time to spare. When friends, townsmen and members of families of delegates were present in the visitor's gallery, Witwer would invariably introduce them with graciousness. The same politeness generally was exhibited in his public recognition of delegates, whether from the presiding chair or in the corridors. This kindness was not always reciprocated by the members.

Whatever might have been lacking at times in the relations of Witwer and the members, there was only profound respect, loyalty and good relations between Witwer and the professional staff, from Executive Director Pisciotte down. Witwer had exercised great care in selecting the staff, in this endeavor, he drew upon the skills he had honed as a talent hunter both in his law firm and as president of the Board of Dickinson College. He chose as Con-Con's executive director Dr. Joseph P. Pisciotte, whom Witwer had grown to know and respect when Pisciotte served as staff on the Constitution Study Commission in 1968-69. Together they assembled a staff of some 150 individuals of technical competence and administrative excellence that underwent virtually no turnover for the duration of the convention. Pisciotte and Dorothy A. Nadasdy, his assistant, functioned as if they were born to their multiplicity of tasks. They confided in Witwer and he in them. They worked as a responsible team.

Now and then Pisciotte, a young professor of government on leave from the University of Illinois, was despondent. At times he wondered if it was possible to pull the delegate body together. He abhorred what he described as nitpicking and sharp-shooting. Pisciotte and Witwer offered mutual commiseration and support. They helped each other over the humps, and they consoled those of the staff who were apprehensive.

The Convention opened its sessions in the House of Representatives in relative comfort, if not splendor. But from the outset,

President Witwer and his staff were squeezed for space and whatever else was required to ease the performance of the necessary labors. Only one small room for officers and staff was available at the outset. Office space for the committees was obtained in time, but there was something makeshift in the arrangements. The only ones who seemed completely satisfied with the State House arrangements were the two legislator delegates — Paul Elward and Victor A. Arrigo, and few of the more politically oriented delegates. They were used to the State House surroundings and liked them. If the General Assembly were to convene, as it was scheduled to do, they could accommodate themselves readily. The Convention sessions, to their narrow way of thinking, could be held when and if the House of Representatives was not meeting.

Witwer thought this was unacceptably demeaning, and probably most of the delegates would have agreed with him if it were put to a vote, but it was not. Witwer sought alternative sites with authority he possessed under the rules. The best potential site was, undoubtedly, the Old State Capitol, newly rebuilt and soon to be a tourist attraction. It was scheduled to be the home of the State Historical Society and its archives. Witwer felt that such use could be postponed in the best interests of the state. To him there was no more pressing task than writing a new and excellent Constitution, and no better place than the Old State Capitol. There three earlier Illinois constitutional conventions had been held. There Abraham Lincoln, the patron saint of Illinois politics, had served in the legislature. There he had delivered his epochal "House Divided" speech. There he had officed while preparing to assume his Presidential duties. And, there he was laid in state following the assassination.

Delicate negotiations were carried on by Pisciotte with Governor Ogilvie and his staff. In the end, the decision was reached to transfer the Convention to the historic structure. Witwer announced the decision triumphantly. It seemed to be well received by most delegates. Some sulked because there had been no prior disclosure or discussion with them. But the move was made and it proved to be a good one for practical as well as symbolic reasons.

The debacle of the Illinois Constitutional Convention of 1920-22 was a living presence to Witwer during the years 1946-1968 that he struggled for constitutional reform, and especially during the course of the 1969-70 convention itself. The earlier convention was partisan from first moment to last, and the charter that it produced was a partisan one. It went down to well-deserved ignominious defeat. A half-century later, delegates were selected on a non-partisan basis and, even ignoring the lack of political labels, there was a better balance of delegates. Republicans did not have overwhelming superiority of numbers, nor did the Democrats; there was a delicate balance of forces, with a small group of independents playing a decisive role. Witwer was determined that, despite his Republican roots, he had to conduct the convention in an impartial non-partisan fashion.

In a sense, the convention offered Witwer the liberation he had been denied as a partisan candidate for the U.S. Senate a decade earlier. In 1960, Witwer chaffed under the constraints of party loyalty. He longed to throw off the garb of team player and assert his thoughts, without regard to orthodoxy, but that would have been playing against the rules. Here, in Springfield ten years later, the rules had been rewritten, and Witwer was free to offend his more dogmatic colleagues (if indeed that proved to be necessary). He insisted that everything he did would have to be done with consciousness of the political realities, but in a non-partisan fashion. He believed he had selected the committee membership and leadership in a manner to preclude the charge of political partiality, as he had given his word to do so to Mayor Daley and others at the time of his election. He was determined to preside over the Convention's sessions fairly and impartially. Thus, he would avoid the prime vice of 1920-22.

As he said in his inaugural address:

> This convention was indeed "called" by the people of Illinois, having been mandated by the largest numerical majority ever voted for a candidate or issue in the long history of the state. We come together not as partisans nor as representatives of special interests, but as "citizen-delegates" chosen by the electors of this state in order

to "prepare" such provisions, alterations or amendments of the Constitution as shall be deemed necessary." These, in turn, will be submitted to the people for ratification or rejection. Our role is *to propose*. It is properly for the citizens of Illinois *to dispose*.

The Convention of 1969-70 had a membership on a substantially higher level intellectually than the earlier convention, because the reaches of higher education had been extended. Where there had been only token participation in 1920-22 by Blacks and certain ethnic groups, now there were 13 Blacks, 15 women, six Jews, several Poles, Lithuanians, Ukranians, Germans, Italians, a Filipino and others outside of the dominant national strains. In addition to lawyers galore and professional politicians, there were clergymen, teachers on all educational levels, farmers, businessmen; and Witwer had to cope with the whole assortment.

Throughout the nine months of the convention, months in which there were campus riots and great national turmoil, Witwer was mindful that it was not his job to induce delegates into writing the best possible constitution; it *was* his job to steer them into producing the best possible document *that voters would accept*. It is in this context that Witwer (and ultimately, the public) was served superbly by the middle-of-the-road philosophy that had moderated Witwer's beliefs in politics, in law, in religion and in education. He instinctively shunned whatever he thought would impress the voters as radically conservative or radically liberal.

Thus it was that Witwer could support modest alterations in the structure of Illinois government, such as eliminating the State Superintendent of Public Instruction as an elective office, or providing for the joint election of the Governor and Lieutenant Governor, while he fought attempts to restructure the Illinois House with its complicated system of multi-member districts and cumulative voting to assure minority party representation.

Thus it was that Witwer could argue the liberal view about the sanctity of life in urging the convention to submit to voters the question of abolishing the death penalty, yet align himself with those who fought to keep the issue of abortion out of the main document to be submitted to voters, and to prevent its submission to voters as a separate question (for fear that emotional issue would obscure all other debate about the constitution).

Thus it was that Witwer could support abolition of the state's personal property tax (a source of great revenue for the City of Chicago), yet steered events to delay its abolition for many years to give the General Assembly time to find a replacement for the lost revenue.

Thus it was that Witwer, citing his experience as president of the board of a church-related small colonial-period college, could argue against any change in the constitution's ban against state aid to *private* education, yet fully supported committing the state to a high degree of support for *public* education.

Thus it was that Witwer, while fighting hard to give home rule to local communities (a cause dear to the hearts of Chicago Democrats and anathema to downstate conservatives), fought even harder to remove electoral power from the people in the selection of judges, and advocating the merit selection of such, a process abhorred by Chicago Democrats.

And thus it was that Witwer thought it wise to invite each of the political leaders of the state to address the Convention. It would be a courtesy to those who had won the votes of the electorate, a means, perhaps, of winning their support, and a possible way of provoking thought on the part of the delegates. It was not improbable that some of them would have usable ideas. So Governor Ogilvie, Mayor Daley, U.S. Senators Percy and Smith, Lieutenant-Governor Simon, Attorney General Scott, Secretary of State Powell (not yet soiled by scandal), State Treasurer Stevenson, Auditor of Public Accounts Howlett, Superintendent of Public Instruction Page, Senate Leader Arrington, and Illinois Supreme Court Chief Justice Underwood appeared before the body, and sometimes uttered more than platitudes. There was mutual politeness and nothing was lost in the process. But were there any tangible gains? Witwer sometimes wondered as time went on, especially when the cooperation he sought was not forthcoming.

The truth of the matter is that each public official had his own ax to grind and constitutional revision did not rate the highest priority to them. Some were secretly sure that the Convention's effort was doomed, and they did not want to be scuttled themselves with the failure.

Some of them wanted to make certain that, in the zeal for a short ballot, their own office would not be abolished. Only Adlai Stevenson, the State Treasurer, urged that his office cease to be an elected one. William Scott fought for the retention of the system of electing an Attorney General as a check upon the governor and other elected officials. In the end, the State Superintendent of Public Education ceased to be elective. This was probably because Ray Page, the incumbent, had won few laurels and some of his activities were questioned. Still the office itself remained, but the one to hold it was to be named by a newly constituted educational board. The lieutenant-governor was to be teamed up with the governor, and not elected separately. No one seriously thought of changing the status of the secretary of state, next to the governor the most visible elective office. Paul Powell, the shrewd downstate Democratic leader, was too potent to be picked upon at that time. Would the situation have changed or would he and his office have been more vulnerable, if the famous shoe boxes containing a hoard of cash had been discovered during the Convention while he was yet alive?

Witwer pondered these offices and the individuals occupying them; but they were not always high on his priority list for the new Constitution nor in his constant struggle of moving the business of the convention to a timely conclusion, the success of which would be judged ultimately by acceptance or rejection by the voters.

Witwer's challenge of leadership was a complex one, permitting no easy, single course of action, list of priorities, or reliance on any continuing group, coalition or alliance. Having achieved the presidency of the Convention, he could not be assured of continuous support from his own Party nor, indeed, from anyone else, least of all the Democrats, particularly those from Cook County. Not even the independents, who owed so much to him, could be counted on for general support.

Witwer had his problems, by no means slight ones, with each group and, sometimes, it seemed with the separate delegates. In a very real sense, Witwer was the only one at the Convention who was concerned at all times, and not at rare moments, with the success that might be achieved in the form of a good and acceptable new Constitution for the state. He could not govern himself by partisan considerations if he wanted to produce a charter that could win a majority vote at the polls in all parts of the state as well as at the Convention. He knew the possibility existed that he could get the required number of votes from the delegates for a new charter, even if the Daley Democrats disapproved; but no proposed Constitution could win an electoral majority at the referendum unless it had the support of Daley and his loyal cohorts. They would produce the margin by which the proposed constitution would be voted up or down. Historically, Cook County was the region from which the majority of favoring votes were cast in successful Blue Ballot referenda. Downstate cast fewer votes, and they were generally adverse to constitutional reform efforts.

The Cook County Democrats might be obstreperous, personally abusive and opposed to causes that he favored. They had to be fought, contained, but endured; and they had to prevail on certain issues or all the labors at the Convention would be for nought. The problem was complicated by the fact that the Democrats from Cook County, other than those elected as independents who were a special breed of Democrat, were largely a monolithic bloc. Some might be nicer than others on the personal level, but they generally orated and voted in unison. The downstate Democrats were less monolithic. They were not always in agreement with their Chicago area political brethern. But there were areas where all Democrats were in agreement, despite the geographical diversity.

Witwer's problem of leadership was further complicated by the difficulty of knowing who represented the Democratic leadership and how to cope with it. If the Local Government Article was involved, there was no great personality problem, although the substantive difficulties may have been considerable. Philip Carey was vice chairman of the committee, and he was a true gentleman, low-keyed, respected, never insolent. Witwer did not regard him as one of the crosses he had to bear.

The Judiciary Article was another matter, largely because the Democrats were so unyielding with respect to it. This was the do-or-die issue for them. Harold M. Nudelman, the vice chairman of the committee, an associate of the rugged and cunning Democratic wheelhorse, Thomas Keane, was a stark contrast with the genteel William L. Fay, the Republican chairman of the committee. Nudelman fought tooth and nail for the views of his Party with respect to the judiciary, while Fay, characteristically, was quieter, more suave, sweetly reasonable. Sometimes it seemed as if Fay could not always cope with his strong-willed vice chairman, particularly when Nudelman was aided and abetted by his indomitable associate, Odas Nicholson. It was then that Witwer had to intervene, more than he really wanted to.

Thomas J. McCracken, chairman of the General Government Committee, was a mixed bag. He was a leader — intelligent, informed, persistent, a man of integrity. One could accept his word as Gospel. One could like and respect him, until a purely political power struggle arose; then, he could be ferocious, sarcastic, insolent. It was at such times that Witwer felt his stomach whirl about in anguish. It was difficult to contend with McCracken who, when ganging up with Lyons and Elward, would torment the presiding officer.

Some of McCracken's associates made Witwer welcome another sort of Democrat — John M. Karns, the chairman of the Revenue and Finance Committee. Karns, from downstate, never resorted to frontal attacks; there was no cruelty in his character. He could compromise, cajole, paper over differences. There seemed little of the partisan in his make-up.

George J. Lewis, chairman of the Legislative Committee, was a different sort of Democrat, *sui generis,* one might say. He got under the skin of his Democratic colleagues at times. His general demeanor was that of a nice guy, and he was intelligent and well-spoken. But, if he got an idea in his head, as when he suspected the motives of those who seemed to be in the camp of the bankers, he could be wild and derisive, making irresponsible charges with abandon, and disconcerting Witwer. Fortunately for the president, he did not regard Lewis as a powerhouse and could be as tough with him as he chose to be. Witwer had great confidence in Lucy Reum, vice-chair of the committee.

In the commanding position of the Democrats most of the time was Thomas G. Lyons, one of the vice presidents of the Convention.

It was difficult to determine at times whether it was Lyons or Paul F. Elward who was the actual leader of the Democratic forces. Witwer hoped that it was Lyons, who was generally much easier to deal with than the often trying Elward, but even Elward had his softer and more considerate moments. Elward was possibly the hardest working delegate. He became a part of all that went on. He made speeches; he made motions; he offered amendments. He was forcefully vocal and often tedious or annoying. One wished at times that his great talents and high intelligence were better directed. He was one of the two delegates who still served in the lower house of the General Assembly; the more suave Victor Arrigo was the other incumbent representative. Where others might carouse and then oversleep, Elward never caroused and was always on time. Witwer wondered sometimes as to how his fellow Democrats really reacted to their stern spokesman, Elward. Did they wince, as Witwer did? Did they enjoy his barbs and accusations, because they were not directed at them?

Witwer thus had to learn to cope with Democrats of all kinds, individually, their several leaders, and as a group; and he had to continue to give them certain indispensible concessions — home rule for Chicago and Cook County, the constitutionalizing of classification in taxation, the possibility of securing adequate revenue for the public schools in particular and for the maintenance of other public services. While he could not surrender completely on the method of selecting judges, he had to give them the means of voting merit selection up or down at the constitutional referendum following the Convention, and he could not close completely on the prospect of retaining multi-member districts for the House of Representatives and cumulative voting without antagonizing many independent legislators as well as Democratic leaders.

Witwer also recognized many years before the start of the Convention, that the real Democratic leader, Mayor Richard J. Daley, was a very remarkable man. Witwer knew he was astute, shrewd, determined. He knew exactly where he was going and how to get there. And he was much better informed and wiser than credited. He was a student of government and of its organization, structure, and management. Witwer could count on Daley's awareness of what a new Constitution could do for his beloved Chicago.

Daley had been his ally in the long sustained struggle for constitutional reform, commencing in the '40s — as a state senator, as director of the Department of Revenue under Governor Adlai E. Stevenson, and in other governmental capacities, culminating in his becoming mayor of Chicago and the unquestioned head of the Democratic Party in Cook County. But Daley knew, as did Witwer, that this was simply a marriage of convenience. What Daley needed, what Chicago needed, was home rule, so that they would cease to be dependent upon an often unwilling state government apparatus, which, constitutionally, held the reigns of power. For even the most trivial rights, Chicago had to run to Springfield. Daley knew, as did Witwer, that there were certain other concessions that Chicago could win through a new Constitution. If it could not win these, it would not support the proposed charter. It would turn it down as decisively as it had rejected the Constitution that had been tendered a half-century earlier. Daley knew that Witwer was sympathetic to these basic aims, however much the two might otherwise differ. Witwer repeatedly showed that he favored the merit selection of judges, he was opposed to "the right to life" provision in the due process clause, opposed to capital punishment, opposed to the individual right to possess arms, and various other proposals, despite the strong Democratic support for them. But Daley knew that Witwer could be trusted to do what was right, that he would not be governed by cheap political opposition. Witwer had worked with him for good causes; he had worked with Stevenson, Kerner and Shapiro, the Democratic governors of his time, and with Republicans Stratton and Ogilvie as well.

After Daley had let it be known that he favored Witwer for the presidency of the Convention, this had made it certain that Witwer would achieve an easy election to that office. Then, the convention having gotten under way, Daley lapsed into silence, letting his Democratic lieutenants at the Convention take over for him. Witwer was often troubled by this. He seemed to feel at times that he was being held at arm's length by the powerful mayor. He could not be certain where Daley would be in the end.

Witwer's long-term relationship with Daley and the practical necessities of dealing with the Democrats only served to emphasize Witwer's problems with his own Republican party adherents and to underscore the reality that his Republicanism was both a blessing and curse at the Constitutional Convention. In a deliberative body in which a majority of the members were at least nominally Republicans, being a Republican in good standing meant that one had a better chance of election as president, particularly when one had Witwer's party credentials as a former candidate for United States Senate. But given their own way, the Republicans would have voted down even the minimum demands of the Democrats, even if it meant in the end the defeat of the proposed basic charter. They would have blindly done what was done in the Republican-dominated Constitutional Convention of 1920-22: produce a partisan document that was overwhelmingly defeated by the voters of Cook County. There had to be give and take somehow, and Witwer was the only one who could engineer it. He knew it meant that his fellow Republicans might regard him at times as a party traitor and that he would win no thanks from the Democrats for gaining them their basic needs.

In some respects, Witwer found it easier to deal with the Democratic Mayor Daley than with the Republican Governor Richard Ogilvie. Perhaps it was because Daley could be more outgoing and friendly than the more reticent Ogilvie. Or perhaps Ogilvie had more reservations about what ultimately could be accomplished and knew his mind less well than did his Democratic opposite number. The fact that fewer Republicans owed allegiance to the Governor than Democrats owed support to the Mayor may have been a factor. Daley was demonstrably the boss of the Democratic Party, but Ogilvie was not really the ruler of the Republicans; he could not control Attorney General William J. Scott, nor the Republican leader in the state Senate, W. Russell Arrington, nor others in positions of power, local or statewide. Witwer felt that the Governor did not bestir himself sufficiently when he should have, as in connection with the issue of merit selection of judges and other convention issues. There was no warmth in the relations of Witwer and Ogilvie. Indeed, there was a kind of coolness, if seldom hostility. It is not unlikely that the Governor was led by his staff to believe that the president of the Convention was too aloof, too independent, unwilling to take on Republican coloration. Yet, at the conclusion of the Convention, Ogilvie awarded a newly struck medal to Witwer called the Illinois Distinguished Service Medal.

During the period of the Convention, W. Russell Arrington was the leader of the Republicans in the Illinois Senate, and Witwer had to reckon with him, no easy task, particularly when it became apparent that an appropriation of more funds would have to be sought for the expenses of the Convention. To say that Arrington was the leader of the Republicans in the upper House of the General Assembly is, perhaps, an understatement. There was no more exigent a person in state politics than Arrington. Naturally bright and self-assured, his confidence soared because of his personal fortune. He was the attorney for W. Clement Stone in Stone's rapidly rising insurance domain and prospered as that company prospered. A multimillionaire, he was probably the wealthiest man in Illinois politics. He was not dependent upon anyone, and he showed it sometimes by scarcely concealed disdain for lesser men. He could be arrogant and insolent, and he rode herd upon his cohorts; but he was effective. His word was law. He could make deals with the opposition, because he understood their language. The question was whether or not Witwer, as presiding officer of the Convention, could deal with him. Witwer was not a rough and tumble politician, and he was a gentleman — a sometimes impossible situation in trafficking with the wheelers and dealers. But he was as strong-willed as Arrington, if gentler; and he was a fighter, who concealed his bellicosity with a mask of reasonableness. Witwer's relationship was also tempered by the fact he knew he would have to submit a budget to the General Assembly because of a prospective deficit due to the legislature's own failure to appropriate sufficient funds in the first instance. He would need Arrington's support. He feared that he would be depicted to the public as a spender and would have to appear hat in hand, like a mendicant.

To his consternation, he learned from his close confidant, Richard Lockhart, that the Arrington staff had not followed through on the filing of a bill for a deficiency appropriation of the Convention, the excuse being that the matter had originated in the House. This was contrary to what Arrington had promised Witwer. He raised the matter again with Arrington, who now told him that Paul Elward would have to handle the situation in the House. This was, for Witwer, like pouring salt on wounds. What followed can best be told in Witwer's own diary account of his further discussion with Arrington:

> I said to Arrington: 'I spoke to you four months ago about this in your office in Chicago. You had Senator Harris there at the meeting, you had Senator Coulson there, and you said that you were going to go ahead and have a legislative commission study this matter, consisting of some of the members of the Constitutional Study Commission' — I said that Coulson told me that the matter didn't have to be presented until April or May and as recently as last night he told me everything was fine about securing the appropriation. So I said to Arrington, 'Don't tell me you haven't been alerted; I have followed your advice.' 'Well,' he said, 'I'm only trying to help you — if you don't take my advice you won't get anything.' I said, 'That that may be, but I am telling you that we followed your advice before and we have gotten nothing out of it.'

Not long afterwards, Arrington's attitude seemed to change for the better.

Where Witwer had varying difficulties with the leaders and members of both parties, he might have counted on the small, but decisively placed, group of independents to assist him; but the independents seemed as devisive at times as the others. They were not really a unified group. Each was a law unto himself. They were united only in the desire to produce a good Constitution, but what made up such a package was not clear at all. Witwer was often as harassed by the independents as by the Democrats.

Subjectively, almost all of the delegates, regardless of party affiliation, thought they were seeking to write the best possible Constitution. Here the independents were united. It seemed clear that none of them was determined to defeat anything that came out of the deliberations. There were circumstances in which they might oppose the proffered Constitution — if it were regressive as a whole, dangerous or no better than the charter of 1870. But given a real choice, they would support the proposed Constitution of 1970. Witwer knew this, and it enabled him to work with the independents, even when they were insolent, arrogant and heart-breaking.

There was a small bi-partisan group that seemed unhappy with the Convention's prospects for a new Constitution. The Republicans Thomas C. Kelleghan and Dwight P. Friedrich were thus clearly identifiable from the outset. Less certain in opposition were the Democratic trade unionists James H. Kemp and William F. Lennon; they would sometimes suggest that they might come along in the end since they were Daley loyalists. A kind of ambiguity existed in Paul Elward, a spokesman for the Democratic Party. Where he would go, no one knew to a certainty. And it was increasingly clear that thwarted young Republican John Alexander, disappointed and disappointing, would toss aside any support that might have resulted from his being one of the vice presidents of the Convention and that he would campaign against adoption of the Constitution. There were a few others who were opponents in the end, more who were obstructionists during the course of deliberations. Witwer would have to learn how to deal with each of them.

In Witwer's mind and often in reality, there was a struggle between the younger delegates and the older ones, such as himself. He saw the young at times as much too sure of themselves, contemptuous of age and experience, arrogant, inconsiderate, determined to prevail at any cost, even if it meant the wrecking of the Convention and the defeat by the voters of its product. The young Republicans, such as Charles W. Shuman and William A. Sommerschield, wanted Witwer to be leader of the Republican bloc, to hold caucuses and the like, this despite his reasonable fear that it would weaken if not destroy his usefulness. They wanted Witwer to aid them in the effort to transform the lower house of the General Assembly from multi-member districts elected by cumulative voting to single-member districts with elections without cumulative voting. They would not be persuaded that if they succeeded in this effort they would drive Mayor Daley and his cohorts into opposing the entire proposed Constitution. Their attitude was that the Democrats could be fought tooth and nail and have their noses rubbed in the dirt without ill effect. In short, compromise could not be understood by them most of the time. If, in the end, some of them went along with the compromises that were worked out largely by Witwer, it was not with any enthusiasm or confidence.

Young or old, each of the 116 members of the Convention was a distinct personality, requiring continuing study and courtship by the president. It was not in his nature to be a hail-fellow-well-met. He was too tense at times to unbend because of his overriding desire to succeed in his high assignment. He tried desperately to understand young and old of both sexes and all races, creeds and ethnic groups. He was successful enough to weld them, for the most part, into a body determined to do its best and to produce an acceptable basic charter and to fight for its adoption by the voters.

The gratifying totality was that with the few exceptions above, virtually all of the 116 delegates favored the new Constitution in the end and fought for its adoption. But as the Convention went on, Witwer could not be sure that this would be the end result. Throughout the proceedings, he could never become over-confident or, indeed, reasonably confident. He had to be on guard all the time, and handle each delegate as an individual with distinct values, problems and goals. Witwer could take no one for granted. He had to probe, pry, encourage. The situation was not a constant, unchanging one. What seemed true one day was untrue the next, or uncertain. Battles once won were later lost or in doubt. His was a brand of politics based on floating coalitions. If Witwer were a completely stolid character he might have weathered all difficulties philosophically. But he was too concerned, committed, and this made him fearful and sometimes near the point of illness.

A number of incidents dramatize the strain of this pressure on Witwer.

One night, during debate on the proposed new Legislative Article, the convention recessed for a dinner break and resumed its deliberations after dark. It became obvious to Witwer and to observers in the press box that several of the delegates had by-passed dinner in favor of beverages. These delegates prolonged debate with superficial questions. A roll-call fever infected the small band of delegates, who pressed for time-consuming roll-calls on the most inconsequential of points. After an hour or so of suffering these dilatory tactics, Witwer, usually the most patient of men, had had it. He accused the delegates of "playing games."

Several delegates reacted furiously. How dare the president question their motives? What did he mean by such an outrageous accusation? At this point Witwer removed his glasses, peered solemnly at the delegates, and sounded every bit as admonishing as Roscoe Pound had sounded at Harvard Law School so many years previously. "No one," Witwer said, "no one can truthfully say there has not been some playing of games this night." He pressed for adjournment to the next day.

Now delegates were on their feet shaking their fists at Witwer, while the majority of their colleagues watched them in deep disgust. Several delegates shouted at Witwer, and it appeared for an instant that some would rush the president's rostrum. While he could have side-stepped the abuse by yielding the chair to a vice president, Witwer chose not to do so and remained to hear out each blistering attack.

Order was restored, through the ministrations of Vice President Smith, who exercised his talent for soothing ruffled feelings. After presiding through the turmoil to the adjournment,

Witwer wearily wended his way through the chambers and passed the press box. He came within a few feet of Edith Herman, a reporter for the *Chicago Tribune*. Herman, a writer of great sensitivity, had been appalled at the mistreatment of Witwer. She reached out a hand and rested it briefly on Witwer's arm, "Don't let them get you down," she whispered.

"That word of comfort gave me a greater lift than anything that had been said all week," Witwer recalled. "I remember the look in her eyes, so compassionate. She must have thought I looked as though I had been beaten over the head with clubs. That gesture helped sustain me. It really did."

Witwer remembered the lesson he had gleaned from that episode. He never again convened the delegates after a prolonged dinner break.

Another incident had a humorous ending. The afternoon of July 1, 1970, Witwer became aware of a general hustle and bustle as delegates scurried from their seats to the back of the hall or out of the chamber. He also noticed a number of delegates' seats were unoccupied. As floor debate droned on, it distressed Witwer that delegates, otherwise preoccupied, were oblivious to the proceedings.

Witwer chose this occasion to lecture the delegates on their obligations to the taxpayers, who expected them to devote full attention to the convention and be in attendance at all times. He got carried away. Unless delegates would remain in attendance, he threatened to send the sergeant-at-arms into nearby barrooms if need be to bring them back to their duties.

When the president had finished the sternest speech he would ever deliver from that rostrum, there was an uneasy silence. Then delegate Dawn Clark Netsch, an independent Democrat from Chicago, rose to speak. She calmly moved to have the convention recess to the downstairs lounge where other delegates had been busy setting up a party to celebrate President Witwer's sixty-third birthday. Witwer was flabbergasted. His face turned crimson. He moved with his fellow delegates to the downstairs lounge almost shame-faced about his remarks. When he saw that everybody else found the incident exceedingly funny, he succumbed to its humor, too, and enjoyed laughing at himself. Nonetheless, the admittedly trivial incident provided Witwer with his most personally embarrassing moment of the nine months of proceedings.

The convention always was erupting in crises of varying seismic proportion. As often as not, the crisis at hand was all consuming for a day, then quickly faded. Two incidents fall into this category.

First, there was an uproar over a prank involving a full-length oil portrait of George Washington, one of the state's works of art, that hung behind the speaker's rostrum in the Convention Hall. When delegates arrived one morning, they found a black and white cut-out photograph of Witwer's face superimposed on the head of Washington. Accepting the prank in good humor, nevertheless Witwer was most appreciative when one of the delegates suggested closing the drawn drapes that hung on each side of the portrait so that the gag could be hidden from view until there was time to remove Witwer's face from on top of Washington's. Later, when workers sought to peel off the offending photograph, they found it had been affixed with an inferior brand of transparent tape. Archivists reported to Witwer that had the tape been of superior quality, the removal could not have been accomplished without also peeling off George Washington's nose, a development that would have transformed a practical joke into an expensive act of vandalism and conceivably a threat to voter respect for the Convention. Gossip inevitably traced the prank to three of the younger delegates, who were grateful they had not caused irreparable damage to the state-owned portrait. Witwer was grateful that publicity was limited to one wire-service photograph of the Sam-on-George face that was published in half a dozen newspapers around the state. Witwer was not so much personally offended as he was worried that public perception of the Convention would suffer.

Second, Witwer was scheduled to deliver a Law Day address before a downstate service organization on May 1, and he prepared a text boasting of the openness of the Convention, which prided itself on never having held a closed meeting, either in general session or on the committee level. The day before Witwer was to deliver this speech, the Convention's Bill of Rights Committee, headed by Elmer Gertz, went into closed session to discuss a furor that had broken out over one of the committee's aides, Larry Miller. Gertz wanted to spare the young aide embarrassment by agreeing to the closed meeting. It was a futile gesture, because the entire Convention quickly learned what transpired behind the closed doors. It had been an overblown tempest. Several delegates had been angry over reports that Miller was keeping notes to write a book about the Convention and they thought this involved a breach of confidentiality. Others were angry that Miller reportedly favored one of the ideological factions over another on the committee. The ruckus ended with Miller's setting a date for resigning. As far as Witwer was concerned, the effect was to undermine his claim to a 100 percent "open" Convention, something he prized greatly.

To his extreme exasperation, not to say shock, Witwer experienced his worst hours at the Convention in connection with an incident having no tangible connection with the real work of the Convention. Being persuaded that John Gardner had considerable knowledge of urban problems as they impinged upon the law, Witwer invited him to address a session of the Convention on the issue of urban crisis, a subject much in the public eye in the late sixties and of importance in writing a home rule article. Gardner was a Republican who had served as the head of the Department of Health, Education and Welfare in a Democratic administration, and he was president of the Urban Coalition, a lobbying organization concerned with the new order of municipal concerns. The night before Gardner's appearance, a telex arrived containing his speech — not on the assigned topic, but one in which he intended to deliver a blistering attack upon the Nixon administration and the national commitment to the war in Vietnam and involvement in Cambodia. Witwer felt that such a talk would serve to fracture the Convention badly and would have no relevance to the matters properly before the Convention. He could foresee the loss of thousands of Illinois voters who would not understand Gardner's foreign policy blast in a convention setting, a matter which could defeat the Constitution at referendum. He foresaw disastrous consequences if Gardner spoke in a divisive vein. Through a series of phone calls after arrival of the telex, Witwer tried to persuade Gardner to return to the original theme of urban problems, and he personally offered to find another spot in Springfield where Gardner might speak on Vietnam. Witwer was also agreeable to printing Gardner's text in the proceedings of the Convention. He would do almost anything to placate Gardner, except to permit him to address the delegates on the unpopular war. Gardner refused all suggestions for he wanted this particular forum. Witwer then withdrew the invitation and advised Gardner not to come to Springfield.

Witwer's mistake was that he did not consult in advance with a representative segment of the delegates, even though the late hour at which Gardner's plans became known would have made such consultations difficult. Witwer did not take into sufficient considera-tion the psychological aspects. The American people do not like suppressions of speech. The logical impresses them too little in this area. Witwer lost the battle of the national media, but not Illinois newspaper support. The *New York Times, Fortune,* the *Chicago Sun-Times,* the national television networks and others blasted him. His attempts at replying were ineffective. Some of the delegates turned on him — including committed liberals like Albert Raby, Dawn Clark Netsch and even some of the Daley people. Lieutenant Governor Paul Simon was critical. It was a real mess. True, many delegates supported him, saying that although they agreed with Gardner on Vietnam, it had nothing to do with subjects properly before the Convention, and Witwer was right in cancelling his talk. When it was reported that Witwer might be censured by the Convention, Witwer contemplated resigning if such action were taken. Fortunately, it was not. The Convention would survive this mini-crisis, like it had so many others. It is even likely that substantial conservative support for the Constitution was won by the withdrawal of Gardner's invitation without loss of so-called liberal support. But the rancor remained, and at least for Witwer, the wounds remained unhealed and the fallout was to be felt by him even after adjournment of the Convention.

Several months after the delegates completed their task, but before the vote on ratification, the Board of Governors of the Chicago Press Club became embroiled in controversy over whether to give Witwer its award as "Man of the Year" for 1970. Ralph Otwell, an executive of the *Chicago Sun-Times* who later became its editor, argued Witwer's "censorship" of Gardner disqualified him from consideration. Otwell was joined by only two other Board members, but seventeen members voted favorably to make Witwer their Man of the Year in recognition of his constitutional and other civic accomplishments.

It must not be assumed that the success of the Convention was due exclusively to Witwer, monumental although his contribution was. As he is the first to say, the ultimate success, despite many difficulties which at times appeared to be insurmountable, was due, as well, to the officers, committee leadership and staff in the first instance, and, in the last analysis, to the 116 members of the Convention as a body. Generally speaking, they were an indefatigable group. Their attendance at all sessions of the Convention proceedings, including committee meetings, was almost perfect. Absence was a rarity, and, when it occurred, it was readily excusable. Even when the money ran out, and the delegates were serving without compensation, at the most critical culminating stage, they worked as if their very lives depended upon it. In the last days they labored interminably from early in the morning to late at night. Their meals were irregular; their rest periods few. But they worked, and worked, and worked, scarcely needing the prodding of Witwer at this stage.

Peter Tomei's Committee on Suffrage and Amendment was the first to respond to Witwer's often reiterated plea for some proposals to be considered on first reading. He did a brilliant job in presenting the proposal to the Convention, and it was a model for subsequent presentations by other committees. Tomei was clearly one of the most promising delegates. His campaign for election as a delegate had been one of the best conceived and effectively carried out in the state. He had every index of continued success. One could not predict how far he would go. Then, like a meteor, he plummeted in sudden death, in his 35th year, shortly after the ratification of the Constitution by the voters.

John C. Parkhurst's Committee on Local Government was the last to submit its proposals on first reading, much to everyone's disappointment. At the beginning of the Convention, Parkhurst who had been a leader in the General Assembly and was one of the most gregarious men alive, was looked upon as the outstanding delegate. Although he remained a mover and shaker, some of his luster faded as delay followed delay in the work of his committee.

Each committee was a short microcosm of the whole Convention. There were powerful personalities in principled and unprincipled disputes that often seemed without solution. In the end, every committee produced a product for discussion and approval or disapproval by the whole body of the Convention. Witwer sweated over the contentions and the resulting delays. He never ceased to prod each chairman and each committee.

The Bill of Rights Committee, under the leadership of its chairman, Elmer Gertz, was possibly the hardest working and most dedicated committee of the Convention. There were moments when Witwer felt that Gertz pressed the committee too hard and that they might resent his efforts. The committee was constantly publicized. The media seemed to regard it as good copy. Visitors to Springfield attended its sessions for entertainment as well as enlightenment. The disruptions, such as when Father Lawlor brought a bottled fetus to the committee room to dramatize his anti-abortion position, bothered Witwer. But the greatest stir occurred when the committee overwhelmingly voted to support a constitutional right to possess arms, subject only to the police power. The chairman and Witwer were greatly alarmed and conferred as to ways to reverse this recommendation. In the end, they failed, but gradually, it was realized that the gun adherents had gained little, as the police power qualification written into the measure was a very inclusive umbrella and imposed marked limitation on the gun authorization measure.

The agrarian society which produced the Illinois Constitution of 1870 feared the banks, warehouses and corporations generally, and provisions were placed in the document to protect farmers against the real or imagined evils. As time went on, it became apparent that the constitutional protective measures were unnecessary, that they were appropriate to a statute rather than a constitutional provision. Witwer and other purists at the Convention constantly bore in mind that it was a constitution they were writing and not a statutory code. Still, some on the General Government Committee balked at the excision of the warehouse provisions, although in the end they were eliminated. One begrudged interval at the Convention made Witwer and, perhaps, others wince when Victor Arrigo staged a mock protest, almost an hour long, against the elimination of the obviously dead provisions with respect to the World Columbian Exposition of 1893. The delegates were persuaded that corporation law ought to be left to the legislature, rather than the Constitution. For the same reason, it was voted to expunge the section prohibiting lotteries. Even opponents of gambling felt that it was a statutory matter.

But for a variety of reasons, many delegates were unwilling to eliminate all references to banking in the basic charter. Indeed, the subject led to possibly the strongest display of emotion on any issue other than judicial selection and, at most, one or two other matters. The banking community was divided between strongly contending forces, each lobbying more than they had ever done and making threats to defeat the proferred Constitution if they did not succeed. The currency exchanges, which had a vested interest in preventing branch banking, fought bitterly. In an earlier period of activity in the General Assembly, before the start of the Convention, there was evidence of something approaching legislative bribery in their behalf; and, long after the Convention was over, though unconnected with it, there were indictments of currency exchange lobbyists, leading to fines and imprisonment.

The General Government Committee, to which was assigned the subject of banking, had several bankers in its ranks. The committee, however, decided to entrust the presentation to one of its most vocal non-bankers, Mary Lee Leahy, much to her subsequent embarrassment. Mrs. Leahy accepted the assignment because, in her initial innocence, she thought that banking was a legislative, not a constitutional matter. Then, to state it in the vernacular as the only appropriate language, hell broke loose. Charges and counter-charges were shouted out. The atmosphere was nothing less than feverish, much to Witwer's dismay. It reached a boiling point when George Lewis, chairman of the Committee on the Legislature, who was increasingly vocal on all matters on the floor of the Convention, made a fiery speech in which the clear implication was that there had been improprieties, bribery even, of delegates. This was too much for Witwer, who felt that the very integrity of the Convention was impugned. As soon as possible, he questioned Lewis in private and learned, to his relief, that Lewis had no evidence whatsoever of wrongdoing. He forced Lewis to come before the Convention and admit as much, which Lewis did in a rather convoluted fashion that did neither Lewis nor the Convention any good.

Mrs. Leahy was outraged, as were many others. Henceforth, they were more careful not to get involved in matters beyond their control. In the end, the language requiring a popular referendum on all banking changes was removed and, instead, the General Assembly was given the right to authorize branch banking only by a vote of three-fifths of those voting or a majority of the members elected in each house, whichever is greater. This was not one of the nobler aspects of the Convention, but it was the sort of situation that arose throughout the proceedings, time and again to put Witwer and his Convention colleagues to the test.

Fortunately, the tests were not such that Witwer was in so despondent a mood as when he confided these words in his diary:

> Regrettably, the work of this Convention, which should be a joy to me considering the years over which I have sought a Constitutional Convention, has gotten so burdensome and so irritating that I am always relieved when Thursday arrives and I can plan to get back home. It is almost like an escape. I certainly hope that as time goes on I will develop a better feeling about the whole project. There are a number of delegates who can be identified as spoilers and trouble-makers, and they can be counted on one hand. The difficulty is that

there are so many other well-intentioned delegates who, either because of their lack of sophistication or by their complete independence, create just about as many problems as do the troublemakers. The outcome of this Convention may well turn on our ability to bring these people into line. I know that we will never bring into line the spoilers who are intent on destroying this Convention. But the ones who mean well and who are 'technical experts' given to long speeches, disinclined to trust other people's judgements, never willing to let a matter be settled once and for all, are the ones who will make or break this Convention. The outcome will largely turn on our ability to get them to see the light before it is too late.

His burden would be somewhat eased when one who was not always considerate would offer words of encouragement, as Witwer recorded:

Wayne Whalen called to say that he thought we had had a good week. He said that so often people will speak critically when things do not go perfectly, but he said he thought he would call to accent the affirmative. I thanked him very much and told him I too thought it had been a good week, but that he should not think for a minute that we are entirely 'out of the woods' in terms of the irritations and interruptions which have been caused by the handful of delegates who seemingly forget why they are in Springfield.

Witwer enjoyed excellent relations, for the most part, with editors and publishers, but his relations with the working media were never especially warm. Because Witwer could not affect personal intimacy with anyone of short acquaintance, he impressed many reporters as aloof. Witwer did not socialize with newsmen as they joined delegates and convention staff in barroom camaraderie, and his one-on-one interviews with the media usually were quite formal. Close to 15 reporters covered the convention full-time (this number tripled on days of white-heat controversy). Their attitudes toward Witwer and the Convention ran a wide gamut. There was Charles N. Wheeler III, of the *Chicago Sun-Times,* who was so imbued with the need to help the convention produce a new constitution that he refused to write about bizarre events which he

thought trivialized the work of the Convention. Wheeler had a
strong regard for Witwer as a leader of high purpose and
conviction. There was Charles Scolare, of the *Springfield Register
Journal,* who thought Witwer was so mesmerized by the historic
majesty of the occasion that he was ineffectual in leading the
Convention; Scolare tended to write stories indicating the Convention was headed for disaster. Most of the media fell somewhere
between Wheeler and Scolare in their attitude and coverage. Most
hued to the factual and newsworthy. Most underrated Witwer's
impact on the proceedings, although they did not go out of their way
to denigrate his role, either.

His relationship with the media notwithstanding, it seems
that everyone wanted to interview Witwer or to hear him speak. He
held many news conferences during the course of the Convention.
He made himself available to individual reporters of the press,
radio and television. He made appearances before live audiences. In
all, Witwer devoted countless hours to the task of informing the
public about the work of the Convention and selling its product.
This was in addition to the work in that area done by Jim Bradley,
the staff press representative, and David Stahl, the chairman of the
Convention Committee on Public Relations. This created an
enormous burden for the president, as he was determined not to
slight any of his duties because of media or other public demands
upon his time. He could, and did, on occasion turn over the duty of
presiding at sessions of the Convention to the three vice presidents;
but he could not turn over to them his other duties and responsibilities. He could, and did, consult with them and take them into
his confidence, less so Alexander than Lyons and Smith. But in the
last analysis, he had to hold a tight rein over everything that
happened publicly and privately. He felt, wisely it turned out, that
only he could assure the success of the Convention. He felt that he
could not distribute leadership responsibility without endangering
the outcome. The others, with the partial exception of Alexander,
had personal and leadership qualities, but they did not have the
unadulterated devotion and drive that were necessary. Personal
amiability, gregariousness and political considerations were too

operative, it seemed to Witwer, when he was not in charge. Tormented by fatigue and frustration, he often welcomed respite from the duty of presiding; but despite any personal pains, he had to be in charge and he was.

Rubin Cohn, an astute observer, long associated with Witwer in constitutional matters, summed up some aspects of Witwer's character and performance at the Convention:

> Witwer functionally is repelled by the crasser aspects of the political process. The politics of intrigue, of deals between disparate interest groups, of log-rolling and backroom negotiations, of compromise which offends his conceptions of principle, of effective discourse with persons whose attitudes offend him or contradict his views, these are not political tools within his arsenal of skills. Thus, when needled by experienced practitioners of the political art like Elward, Friedrich, Lyons and others, his responses from the podium at times were flustered and indecisive and sometimes, unfortunately, demonstrative of personal pique as well as political naivete. This combination of factors, e.g., his psychological and professional tendencies to remain above the battle, and his inexperience in dealing with the harsh realities of the political process, led many delegates and observers to view Witwer as an ineffective leader. I believe there is truth in this evaluation but I also believe that the compulsive drive with which he pursued his constant goal, e.g., a document which made significant improvements in governmental structures, powers and limitations, overcame to a large extent the weakness he portrayed. That he ultimately compromised on several important issues and vacillated on others reflected the conflicting forces which shaped his motivations as well as a developing maturity in his perceptions of the harsh realities of the political process. I believe that on this issue of leadership history will vindicate him to a greater extent than contemporary assessments condemn him.

Yet other occasions, as in his book *To Judge with Justice* on the Judiciary Committee of the Convention, Cohn had commended the political skill of Witwer.

As the deliberations went on, and particularly as the campaign for the adoption of the Constitution proceeded, Witwer knew increasingly that the document would stand or fall by its Revenue Article. Battles were waged over other provisions of the

Constitution, but these seemed to recede as the partisans confronted the issue of taxation. It is clear that increasingly the popular mood was to revolt against taxes, while demanding at the same time no diminution of governmental services. This led to a struggle against any and all kinds of taxes — income, personal property, real property and sales. There was also an insistence that governmental indebtedness be reduced, that bond issues be curtailed. Perhaps the most insistent demand was the abolition of personal property tax, at least for individuals. Just weeks before the start of the Convention, a constitutional amendment to that affect was ratified by the voters. It only complicated the task of the delegates. Cook County and Chicago had special needs with respect to the funding of the public schools and the classification of real estate. And, Witwer had to concern himself with every effort to work out the problems.

It was thought that one solution was reached when a section was included for the abolition of all personal property tax by January 1, 1979, with a required simultaneous adoption of replacement taxes on those relieved of the personal property tax. Ironically, it should be added, the Illinois Supreme Court, citing Witwer as an authority in support of its decision, ultimately held that abolition of the personal property tax was required, regardless of any simultaneous replacement. The delegates would not stand for a graduated income tax, but they did agree that, to a certain extent, a greater burden could be placed on corporations, possibly on the theory that corporations could not vote for or against politicians, except indirectly through pressures, propaganda and contributions. In any event a compromise Revenue Article was agreed upon, and was debated by the voters. It was the specified reason for opposition by the AFL-CIO and NAACP, who chose to ignore provisions that they should have applauded. Mayor Daley, while joining in the criticism of the Revenue Article and pledging to fight for its reformation, supported the proposed Constitution, in the referendum of December 15, 1970, to Witwer's continuing relief.

As the Convention neared its end, Witwer, after conferring with his two top staff, Joe Pisciotte and Dorothy Nadasdy, confided a refreshingly reassuring state of mind, in marked contrast with his often lugubrious attitude in the past:

> In talking with Dorothy and Joe tonight, I said that it was not until two weeks ago that I started to enjoy my experience as president of the Constitutional Convention. This is a rather strange fact because here's something I've been working on for about half of my adult life and yet I didn't enjoy the presidency until recently. I think the enjoyment came about when I first felt assured of the passage of the Article on Local Government giving Chicago and other cities home rule; that we had perhaps done what was essential to having a relevant Constitutional Convention. Also, that we had done what had almost made it imperative that Mayor Daley support the end-product. This is a peculiar thing. I think I have slept better at nights, I think I have been less irritable and a lot of things have changed since that happened.

The change in Witwer had not gone unnoticed. Elmer Gertz' wife, Mamie, who attended all of the Convention proceedings, approached Witwer outside the elevator in the Old State Capitol and told him, "You have undergone a metamorphosis. You're so genial and so friendly and you're doing such a great job as presiding officer."

The implication in her compliment did not escape Witwer. If he had undergone a change, and if he *now* was friendly and genial, that meant there had been times in the past when his personality was unfriendly and aloof. "Well," he responded to Mamie Gertz, "maybe I've undergone some change, but there have been some changes in the Convention to cause the change in me." Witwer referred to growing evidence that the Convention would hammer out a salable product. His optimism was premature.

The Convention's most serious crisis came during the third or final reading of the proposed new charter. It presented Witwer with a dilemma of make-or-break intensity. The crisis arose out of the two most divisive issues that faced the delegates — methods of judicial selection and the manner of voting for members of the lower house of the General Assembly.

The Daley Democrats and many of their allies, downstaters of both major parties, were committed to maintaining what had been traditional in Illinois for the judiciary, from the Supreme Court down to the lowest rungs — a method of selecting judges, which is nominally elective, but which, in effect, vests the politicians of both parties with the right of nominating the only candidates to run for judgeships. In Cook County this has meant that the Democratic organization has rewarded deserving party loyalists who are lawyers with the plums of certain election to the bench where they can subsequently protect the party's interests. These people would not tolerate any proposed new Constitution which deprived them completely of this time-honored opportunity. If the document provided for a non-partisan, merit selection of judges with no possible alternative, then Daley and his people would surely vote it down. On the other hand, there were those who saw judicial merit selection as so important that they would risk the consequences of thwarting the Daley forces completely even if it meant defeat of the whole Constitution. The vote on this issue flip-flopped from first reading to second, and it was perilous to contemplate what would happen ultimately.

With the same intensity, there were vast differences over the composition of the House of Representatives which were being vigorously and continually debated. The Constitution of 1870 had provided for three members of the House to be selected from each of the designated districts, and had instituted a system of selection unique to Illinois — cumulative voting. This meant that each elector could cast all three votes for one candidate, or one- and one-half for each of two candidates, or one vote for each of three candidates. In effect, this meant that if a citizen cast a so-called 'bullet' ballot — that is, all three of his votes for one candidate — and there were enough of such voters, they could elect their candidate even if he belonged to the minority party or an independent group, which often permitted some persons to serve in the House when they might otherwise not have been able to do so. The Democrats generally favored this arrangement, as it enabled them to achieve representation in areas where the majority party was Republican. Some Republicans also favored the system for the reason that they were able to get representation despite a Democratic majority. An increasing number of people, particularly downstate Republicans, wanted to discard the old system. They thought it more sensible for Illinois to follow the pattern of the rest of the states and to have single-member districts without cumulative voting. They argued that the smaller districts would result in better and more responsive representation. On this issue, too, the Convention flip-flopped between readings. Here, too, were unyielding adherents. If the advocates of single-member districts prevailed, as was likely, the Democrats would have added reason to defeat the proposed Constitution at the polls.

What was the solution? It would have to be a device that would not give final victory at the Convention to either side on either issue. It would have to place the ultimate choice in the hands of the voters. Witwer saw the answer as one that would not place in the new Constitution as a package either proposed solution — neither merit selection nor political election of judges, neither single-member House districts nor the current cumulative voting system — but would require those issues to be resolved in separate referenda aside from the vote on the Constitution as a package. In the closing days of the Convention he tried to win support with the media and with leaders of the contending forces, at first with no success. Then a coalition arose in the good government forces of the Convention and they, acting as if Witwer had never proposed such a solution, suggested to Witwer that, if he stood by them, they had the votes to bring about an answer that would save the Convention, placing alternatives in separate submissions outside the main package.

In token of the new union of forces, the sponsors of the stratagem (to become known as the KWW amendment) were listed as Lewis Wilson, a Republican; Betty Ann Keegan, a Democrat; and Wayne Whalen, an Independent. Having been burnt earlier and being skeptical of the vote count of the alleged coalition as to whether it would hold up in the face of the tempetuous reaction of the Daley forces, Witwer was not as committed on the surface as the new coalition desired; but as he sensed that these forces would hold together, he was as forthrightly for them as he could be without going completely overboard. The proposed arrangement meant that adherents of single-member House districts and of merit selection for judges would forego a direct convention victory of premature confrontation and be content to rest with the hope that at the polls they would prevail, if they educated the electorate. Rubin Cohn, in his fine book *To Judge With Justice* captured the drama of the rapidly developing events and the key role Witwer was to play on that crucial day:

The long session had begun with Witwer troubled and uncertain as to his stance. On the morning of 29 August, less than an hour before the convention was to reconvene, some half dozen representatives of the coalition, with Ladd as their principal spokesman, requested an audience with Witwer. They advised him of their plan, the KWW amendment, the parliamentary strategy they intended to pursue, and stated that the coalition had at least sixty-three votes, four more than necessary to achieve their goal. Witwer's open and "four square" support, however, was stated to be absolutely indispensable to the success of the plan. The group appealed for Witwer's support. He neither refused nor acquiesced, nor did he affirm neutrality, stating only that as presiding officer he would assure them fair treatment. He concluded with the non-committal observation that "We'll take it as it comes." With that he left to convene what he privately recorded as "probably the most decisive session of the convention."

He was now being asked to support the coalition "four square" in a plan which in essence he had proposed three days earlier only to suffer the embarrassment of cursory rejection. Moreover, to commit himself now to the coalition would place him in the political quandry of attempting to undo the victory of the multi-member district-cumulative voting adherents to which he had contributed so significantly just the evening before. When he concluded the meeting in his office with the ambiguous, "We'll take it as it comes," he was also reflecting not only the anamoly of his position, but also a lack of faith in the strength and firmness of the new coalition and in its ability to carry off its plan. He could not then be certain that the coalition plan would succeed, and he foresaw a chaotic denouement if it should fail. He knew the ferocity with which the Chicago Democrats and their supporters would oppose the coalition plan on the convention floor and the probable consequences of that opposition in the referendum upon the main document if the coalition should succeed. Harassed and weary after months of wracking tension and the oppressive burdens of leadership, suffering physical pain from a yet unrealized ailment which would soon require surgery, sustained only by the hope that the convention would produce a constructive document, Witwer's concern over the coalition strategy was further aggravated as he tried to assess his role as president in the resolution of an issue so explosive as to project the realistic possibility that it could cause the convention to collapse in total defeat and disarray, the most fearsome of all contingencies. It was a wrenching dilemma which Witwer confronted when he dismissed the coalition delegation, mounted the dais, and convened the session.

On the initial Lewis motion to approve Article IV and for enrollment Witwer voted aye. Since the defeat of the Lewis motion was the crucial first step if the coalition strategy was to succeed, Witwer's vote could be viewed as his decision to reject the coalition plan. Witwer disputes such an inference:

> That vote was consistent with a practice I had urged upon all delegates throughout the Convention of finally letting go of a matter on a "wrap-up" vote when once it had been demonstrated in the perfecting process, that the Article had been approved by a majority. My vote was not so much a vote in opposition to the coalition as an expression of my belief that the Convention just simply had to conclude its work and prepare to adjourn sine die.

The explanation, though not fully convincing, has plausibility. As presiding officer he was committed, though informally only, to a practice which he had not deviated. He could not logically explain or defend a vote opposed to the Lewis motion, or even a vote of abstention, either of which could be construed as a signal of commitment to the coalition and openly identify him as a member, and, more than likely, a leader of that group. It could trigger the disaster which he so feared. He was not at that moment ready to take that step. On the other hand, the coalition strategy would probably be effectively and irrevocably destroyed if the Lewis motion prevailed. To this extent Witwer's support of the Lewis motion appeared to be his negation of the coalition. It was a cruel dilemma.

As the day wore on, the evidence mounted that the coalition was a force with which to reckon, indeed that it might well achieve its goal. Subtly, without fully realizing it, Witwer moved toward the coalition. In this he was psychologically aided by the intemperate attacks of some of the Chicago Democrats upon his rulings, the numerous appeals from those rulings, and the consistent defeat of those appeals by the coalition. Finally, at the critical juncture, the roll call votes on Whalen's motion to suspend the rules, he openly joined the coalition by casting his votes in the affirmative. Witwer had crossed his Rubicon, throwing his support to the coalition, taking all the risks which had so deeply troubled him in his earlier speculations. He could have stayed above the battle, voting pass on the roll calls, maintaining an Olympian neutrality. He did not do so because his whole professional career had driven him to a preeminent leadership role on issues of constitutional reform. In the final analysis, he could betray neither his conscience nor his past. If this made him less the astute politician, it was a decision beyond his power. In the end he was to be vindicated, but before the final event he was to spend sleepless hours reassessing his role, reliving his doubts, experiencing the haunting torment of many anguished, uncertain decisions which had played so vital a role in the convention process.

Initially, the coalition prevailed in working out the device because some of the Daley Democrats were not present on the morning of the decisive vote. They were taken completely by surprise. Paul Elward, the Puritan, who was present, stormed in frustration. Later when Elward's cohorts appeared in force, they sought to undo the mischief. Their tactics were such as to antagonize the least committed of the coalition. All who had voted for the special kind of submission of the two controversial issues stood firm and the alternate method was adopted; and that was how the matter ended at the Convention. Later, at the referendum, the Daley position prevailed on both matters; but so did the package, which could be, and was, supported by Mayor Daley. To the surprise of many, the vote in Cook County was in favor of merit selection, giving heart to those who continued to fight for it. It failed by a narrow margin outside of Cook.

Despite his determination to succeed in welding together a workable new state Constitution, Witwer had moments, and even days of doubt, that he would succeed. In the end, there was a Constitution to submit to the people. At that time, and even later, Witwer could ask what he and his fellow members of the

Convention had really achieved. As a result of their combined labors, does Illinois have a charter that is superior to the century-old document that it superceded? True, they had deleted about 4,000 unnecessary words from the Constitution of 1870, but much that had been in that instrument is still present in the new document, albeit sometimes changed in language.

Witwer had said repeatedly that if only the new Constitution made it possible to effectuate change more easily than in the past, he would call it a success. Clearly, that purpose was achieved in various ways. The vote in the General Assembly and by the electors to convene a Constitutional Convention or to submit amendments to the Constitution was reduced from two-thirds to three-fifths. A provision was instituted for submitting to the voters the question of calling a convention every twenty years. In 1988 this question will be on the ballot. Provision was made for popular initiative relating to structural and procedural aspects of the legislature.

This was not all that was new and superior. Much needed, if somewhat limited, home rule was given to municipalities and counties. To Chicago this was reason sufficient for the ratification of the document. The protection of the environment was constitutionalized for the first time. New self-implementing measures guarantee freedom from discrimination, both in the private and governmental sectors, on the basis of race, color, creed, national ancestry, sex, and physical or mental handicaps in the hiring and promotion practices of employers and in the sale or rental of property. A right of privacy was indicated including protection from eavesdropping by electronic means. The residency requirements of voters were lowered. Provision was made for registration and election laws to be general and uniform and a bi-partisan board to supervise the administration of such laws was created. Agency reorganization by executive order was made possible. The governor was given enlarged veto power, including the reduction and amendatory vetos. A judicial inquiry board was created to hear complaints as to the official conduct of judges. For the first time, a finance article to assure financial disclosures and more responsible fiscal activity by state and local governments was added to the

Constitution, and provision was made for a new constitutional office of Auditor General to audit all public funds. Various revenue reforms involving income, personal property and sales taxes, were provided for. Constitutional mandates were created to educate all persons to the limit of their capacities, and to develop a state board of education.

And one might go through each article of the Constitution and find changes, some of them quite important, some less so.* Witwer could contend that Illinois was given, in the words of Gertz and Pisciotte, a charter for a new age. But was a successful convention and adoption of a new constitution for Illinois sufficient in itself to declare his quest a success? Was it worth the decades of persistence, the intermittent successes and failures through countless campaigns, meetings and speeches?

Surely the answer would have been "yes" based on the last regular session day of the Convention before the ceremonial closing. The politics and the compromises had been worked out, the document had gone through the final process of stylistic perfection, and Witwer had spent the day polishing the President's speech which would be the first official communication the Convention as a body would have with the public and the press on its newly proposed document. The address itself was an embodiment of the different interests of the delegates and the diversified state they represented. There had to be satisfaction in knowing he had provided the leadership for bringing about workable compromises and consensus such that the individual delegates and their interests could be sufficiently satisfied in a document that would replace a one-hundred year old constitution and serve as the rules of the game for the future.

---

*Witwer, in his closing "Address to the People" reprinted in the Appendix presents a precise narrative of each article. There is also a significant body of literature on the Convention — its politics, the participants, their accomplishments and failures — that discusses in-depth the new Constitution.

And certainly Witwer had to feel his unwillingness to quit was worthwhile on the last day of the Convention when the document was officially signed by the delegates and accepted by the Secretary of State. Newspaper accounts described it as Witwer's day of glory, the high point in a lifetime devoted to state constitutional reform. He was showered with accolades throughout the day. The warm feelings for Witwer enabled delegates who had been at each other's throats for months to embrace, exchange words of affection and depart Springfield in a state of euphoria. During the closing ceremony, delegates and hundreds of spectators grew hushed as Witwer descended from the rostrum and sat at the desk Abraham Lincoln used when the great emancipator was a legislator in the same chamber. Enclustered by a score of television cameras and newspaper photographers, Witwer signed the proposed new Constitution. As he arose, the assembly burst into applause. Shortly before adjourning, the Convention delegates and staff presented Witwer with a bronze plaque engraved with the words of the new Constitution's preamble.

There was undoubtedly deep satisfaction for Witwer on an individual level, a sense of personal accomplishment, but that which made the long struggle most worthwhile was the legacy for which he provided leadership and which was left to the state of Illinois, to its present and future generations. Millions have lived by the new Constitution since its adoption in 1971 and even more millions will be impacted by it during the course of their daily relationships to one another and in their relationship to government. The legacy was not only in the document itself, but in the process by which it came about and was adopted by the people on December 16, 1970 by a vote of 1,122,425 to 838,168.

Prior to the calling and holding the Sixth Illinois Constitutional Convention, a body of literature was created addressing the need for constitutional change and a state-wide network of supporters of that need was formed. A non-partisan, diverse group of delegates assembled with appropriate leadership, in a convention that was open, democratic in its deliberations, and fair to the delegates, the media, and the public. It gave opportunities for participation, and attention was paid to dissenters, without permitting obstruction. There was adherence to schedules and rules without enslavement by rigidity, but perhaps most important was a willingness, in the end, to compromise. There was acceptance of the certainty that no perfect constitution could be produced or ratified; that one must aim at the very best that is attainable. There was an understanding that a non-political, non-partisan convention did not operate in a vacuum. It is part of a social process, involving political and social issues; demography is part of democracy. There was a realization that the product of the convention had to be ultimately accepted and adopted by the electorate. Judged by these standards the Sixth Illinois Constitutional Convention succeeded admirably. The delegates took the Illinois constitution out of its century-old straightjacket and provided the state and its present and future citizens with a broad framework for change.

For most, the quest for a vastly improved constitution would have ended on July 1, 1971 when the new document went into effect. But for Sam Witwer, the man who understood that constitutional revision was not a game for the short winded, there was still work to be done. Implementation and interpretation of the Constitution's many provisions would require yet more speeches, meetings, writings, and struggles through the legislative and judicial processes. Witwer has remained involved throughout, and perhaps his greatest satisfaction has been that the product of his quest has withstood the challenge of rapid social and political change during the fifteen years since its adoption. It has been a servicable constitution through transitions of federal, state, and local political leadership, through good and bad economic times, through space travel, into the computer age and in anticipation of even greater advancements in technology. There have been no major challenges or criticisms of the basic document, but should the citizens of Illinois desire change, provision is made in the 1970 Constitution for revision without the long struggle undertaken by Witwer and others. The question of calling a convention shall automatically be placed on the general election ballot, by the Secretary of State, in 1988.

Witwer could be satisfied that his long quest for a vastly improved Constitution was successful. But for the time being, for the man who wouldn't quit, it is well to remember what wiley and wise old Benjamin Franklin said at the close of the debates over the federal constitution:

> When you assemble a number of men to have the advantage of their joint wisdom, you inevitably assemble with those men, all their prejudices, their passions, their errors of opinion, their local interests, and their selfish views. From such an Assembly can a perfect production be expected? It therefore astonished me, Sir, to find this system approaching so near to perfection as it does . . . . Thus, I consent, Sir, to this Constitution because I expect no better, and because I am not sure that it is not the best.

This could well have been Witwer's benediction.

SAMUEL W. WITWER ADDRESSES TO THE SIXTH ILLINOIS CONSTITUTIONAL CONVENTION

OPENING ADDRESS

December 9, 1969
On the occasion of his election as Convention President.

Distinguished Members of the Constitutional Convention:

Following my election yesterday, I expressed my deep and profound appreciation for the honor you have conferred on me, and the confidence which your vote signified. It is the highest possible honor that ever could have come to me. I also thank you for this opportunity to address you today. I particularly covet this privilege, mindful of the fact that as presiding officer I shall not participate in debate on matters other than questions of order, except infrequently when I may return to my seat as a delegate and participate in floor debate. I am going to depend on your help, your counsel, your patience, and your good will.

At the commencement of this Sixth Illinois Constitutional Convention, it is appropriate to note our historic role. That which we now undertake is the most solemn function of government a state can perform. Constitution-making is the fundamental and organic act of a free society, a task unequalled in importance in the life of a democracy. It is in constitution-making — to an extent

208

unequalled in any other activity — that the people are indeed the masters of their government. Every American state constitution clearly recognizes that all political power is derived from the people, as affirmed in the Declaration of Independence by the words "... to secure these rights, governments are instituted among men, deriving their just powers from the consent of the governed."

Our presence here in Convention assembled demonstrates Illinois adherence to this cardinal belief concerning the source of all political power. This Convention was indeed "called" by the people of Illinois, having been mandated by the largest numerical majority ever voted for a candidate or issue in the long history of the state. We come together not as partisans nor as representatives of special interest, but as "citizen-delegates" chosen by the electors of this state in order to "prepare such revisions, alterations or amendments of the constitution as shall be deemed necessary." These in turn will be submitted to the people for ratification or rejection. Our role is *to propose*. It is properly for the citizens of Illinois *to dispose*.

These facts alone must launch this great undertaking with a sense of high accountability and deep humility. But there are other reasons why it may be said we are indeed embarked on an historic mission. A century has come and gone since Illinois last held an *effective* Constitutional Convention, our only intermediate Convention, undercut by partisan and sectional strife, having failed to win voter approval of its recommended new constitution in 1922.

Recourse to the separate amending procedure under article XIV, section 2, has been almost as unproductive of meaningful and significant constitutional change as has the Convention route. Because of the built-in rigidity of the constitution and court rulings giving nonvoters in general elections the veto power of "no" voters, for decades Illinois has been trapped in a legal straitjacket from which we have escaped for the time being, at least, by reason of the Convention Call of November, 1968. That we make sure that Illinois never again returns to that entrapment and loss of self-determination is among the great duties of this body.

It is not my purpose today to speak to the substantive issues. Twenty-five years ago, the late Professor Kenneth Sears, a leading constitutional scholar, in analyzing our 1870 Constitution said, "Illinois, everything considered, is in the worst position of any state of the Union." In my considered judgment, his challenge remains substantially valid today. It is predictable that this Convention will review most of the articles of the existing constitution and find a number of them in need of revision. At this time, I should like to discuss, not substantive matters, but the kind and quality of Convention needed if we are to fulfill our historic role. The kind of Convention which I, as your president, will exert every effort to achieve should now be clearly stated to you.

I. I call upon you to make this an open Convention in every sense of the word. The people must ultimately accept or reject what we do here, and public interest in the convention will best be assured by open sessions of the Convention itself and of its committees. Arrangements should be made for committee hearings, not only at the seat of the Convention, where most committee meetings will be held, but on occasion in other sections of the state. Interested citizens will thus be able to attend such meetings without undue inconvenience. We must listen, and the people must be aware of our desire to listen.

Open debate is indeed essential. The best possible constitutional revisions will emerge from this body only as our differing viewpoints are fairly resolved in the give-and-take of full and open debate, conducted under the spotlight of public attention. We must make suitable arrangements for maximum participation of press, television, radio, and other media so that the Convention and the great issues are carried into every home.

Such a Convention also implies open attitudes and open perspectives. If we approach our work precommitted in thought or attitude, if we start in search of compromise and fail to pursue a constitution of excellence, little of lasting value will come from our efforts. A Constitutional Convention indeed should be an evolutionary, not a revolutionary process, but it should also be an encounter with an expanding future.

Openness also implies freedom from narrow partisanship and from domination by special interests. So far we have managed to stay reasonably clear of partisan conflict in the steps which have led us to this historic day. Both parties and their leaders have recognized that constitution-making must transcend transient policy considerations and problems, the things which are the grist of the mill of partisanship. Constitutional Conventions torn by either partisan or sectional strife or submissive to any interest other than the public interest may as well not take place, for nothing lasting will result. The time has long since passed for any separation between downstate and Cook County. We are simply too dependent upon each other to permit that to continue.

II. This convention must be an instrumentality by which Illinois can subject its basic political institutions to probing reexamination and reappraisal. As such, the Convention will be of the utmost importance and worth every cent it costs, aside from any revisions resulting from this Convention. It is important for a state to review its fundamental institutions at least once or twice in a hundred years. If our function is to be evaluative and involve a probing reexamination and reappraisal of Illinois government, not a superficial job of draftsmanship, we will certainly need all of the precious time at our disposal. That is why I urge immediate reference of the proposed rules prepared by the Constitution Study Commission to a Committee on Rules and a report back next week. If this is done, it will be possible during the holiday weeks to organize this Convention, appoint its committees, hire its staff, and "get the show on the road." Few Constitutional Conventions have faced more vexing and complex an assortment of constitutional problems than does our Convention. We had better recognize the fact that our task will not be light, that we face heavy burdens.

III. We need to remember that our responsibility is not to draft statutes and ordinances, but to propose the principles on which Illinois government will be structured in the decades ahead and the right of our citizens safeguarded and made meaningful. Our concern should be for basic principles, not detail and specification. The Federal Constitutional Convention held in Philadelphia in 1787 was of vast importance to our nation, mainly because the men who served in that Convention sought only to outline the basic and fundamental principles by which they thought this nation should be governed. Soon thereafter, Chief Justice John Marshall explained that the very nature of a constitution "requires that only its great outlines be marked and its important ingredients designated." A century and a half later, Mr. Justice Cardozo wrote, "A constitution states, or ought to state, not rules for the passing hour, but principles for an expanding future." The 1870 Illinois Constitution was not so drafted. It was fashioned to shackle the hands of those entrusted with public authority. It embodied, not only the wise federal system of checks and balances, but an inner structure of checks and balances which have hobbled every governor and every branch of government ever since. Let us not make the same mistake. Instead we must refuse to encumber the present or foreclose the future with precision and detail which have no place in a constitution worthy of the name.

IV. I shall strive for appointment of balanced and representative committees which will be free from domination by any interest group, faction, or party. The quality of the work of this Convention will largely depend upon the quality of our committees. Your officers in their performance of the manifold tasks of administration will need to employ the best possible staff the Convention is able to assemble. Some doubt has been expressed by members of the Illinois Constitution Study Commission whether the initial appropriation of the General Assembly will permit employment of such expertise and proper staffing. As you know, the search is on for adequate office facilities to meet the needs of the officers and members of this Convention. Both matters will require prompt action. I will present to you at an early date a review concerning finances and facilities so that we may plan accordingly for a meaningful Convention.

In conclusion, I ask of each of you that we approach our service in this historic Convention with the same enthusiasm, sense of historic mission, and commitment to excellence as fired the 33 men who drafted the first constitution of Illinois in 1818 and thereby set the stage for statehood. In a newspaper article which appeared in the September 2, 1818, issue of the *Illinois Intelligencer*, a fascinating account is given of an impromptu civic celebration held by the citizens of old Kaskaskia when they received word of the completion of the drafting of the 1818 Constitution and the adjournment of that Convention. After telling of the exciting events when the citizens of the town assembled, fired a federal salute in front of the old territorial capitol, and participated in other ceremonies in perpetuation of the remembrance of the day, the news story goes on to say:

> This was truly a proud day for the citizens of Illinois . . . a day on which hung the prosperity and hopes of thousands yet to follow . . . a day which will long be remembered and spoken of with enthusiastic pride; as a day connected with the permanent prosperity of our literary, political and religious institutions . . . as the main pillar in the ediface of our state independence, and justly the basis of our future greatness.

May history someday record that out of this gathering 150 years later came a sound and serviceable constitution, faithful to the traditions of Illinois and affording the main pillar for its future greatness and the fulfillment of the just hopes and aspirations of its people.

CLOSING ADDRESS TO THE PEOPLE
Adopted by the Convention on September 2, 1970

The Sixth Illinois Constitutional Convention has now finished its work and offers to the people of the State a proposed new Constitution.

In 1968, the people of Illinois were offered the opportunity to approve the calling of a convention to reexamine the basic structures, institutions and functions of their governments. For many in the State the convening of a constitutional convention at this time seemed particularly opportune. There was a great need to modernize an essentially nineteenth century constitution. Many had come to feel that few of the complex problems with which government must deal today can be solved in the national capitol, and that state and local governments, which are much closer to the people, must assume greater responsibilities.

At a time when the nation was troubled by unrest and dissension, Illinois had the opportunity to use the methods of democratic, peaceful, evolutionary change to improve systems that obviously were not working satisfactorily. The Convention gave to the people of Illlinois a chance to demonstrate to themselves, and especially to those who will inherit their responsibilities, that they could respond to a changing world. The scale was modest. It was not to be an attempt to remake the world; but only to rewrite one of fifty state constitutions of the United States. Nevertheless, how well the Convention did its work — and acceptance of that work by the people — is important not only to Illinois, but also to other states, as an inspiration to others to undertake the task of revitalizing state and local government in this country.

The Illinois Constitution of 1870 has been difficult to amend. It was written at a time when the fashion was one of detailed, restrictive constitutions which attempted to present legislative solutions to current problems. Agitation in Illinois for a constitutional convention in the late 1940s resulted in a proposal by the General Assembly of the Gateway Amendment, so-called because it was expected that it would open the way to easier constitutional change by Amendment. The Gateway Amendment was approved in 1950 and there was hope that other constitutional changes would follow. It was apparent by 1965, however, that constitutional change by the Gateway Amendment process was not adequate to bring the basic structures and procedures of Illinois government into the twentieth century. In fact the Constitution was hardly more amendable than it had been before 1950.

Constitutional rigidity forced citizens and officers of government to evade and violate constitutional statements, as changing conditions called for constitutional change which could not be secured by traditional means. Such evasion was largely responsible for much of the feeling in behalf of a convention which had developed by 1968.

In 1965 the General Assembly created a Constitution Study Commission which unanimously recommended that the question of calling a constitutional convention be submitted to the people in 1968. This call the General Assembly voted by an overwhelming majority. The ensuing referendum resulted in the largest popular majority ever given a candidate or a constitutional question in the history of the State. Of all who went to the polls in the general election of that presidential year, more than four persons out of every five voted upon the convention question. Almost three out of every four who expressed an opinion on the convention call were affirmative. The Convention which was authorized was the first in Illinois in fifty years and only the second since the Constitution was adopted in 1870.

The Convention sought to write a constitution which was acceptable to a majority. This process of democratic discourse was seldom easy. Intense disagreement was often encountered. Members differed with one another, in their efforts to find the the best constitutional course for the people of Illinois. The dominant themes throughout that search were three in number: greater protection of individual rights, increased responsiveness of government to the people, and heightened efficiency and effectiveness of government in its service to the public. The Convention sought, though not always successfully, to adhere to the principle that a constitution should deal with structure of government, its powers, and its relation to the individual citizen.

The members of the Convention were Black and white, were men and women, were young and not so young, were rich and not so rich, were urban and rural, were Republican and Democrat and Independent, were of many generations resident in the State and were foreign born, were in fact of the whole demographic mixture which makes Illinois at the same time so great and so perplexing a State. But of whatever persuasion, they take pride in describing here the most significant changes and additions which they propose in a new Constitution.

In the Preamble and Bill of Rights Article. The traditional Preamble is revised in order for it more fully to describe the aims of government in the State. Individual rights protected by the present Constitution are retained. There are additional new protections. All persons are guaranteed freedom from discrimination in housing and employment on the basis of race, color, creed, national origin, sex, and mental or physical handicap. Unreasonable invasions of privacy are prohibited; and the right of the citizen to keep and bear arms, subject to the police power is guaranteed. Equal protection of the laws is not to be denied on account of sex or for other reason. Prohibition of the death penalty is a separately submitted item, for acceptance or rejection by the voters, aside from the main body of the proposed new Constitution.

The Suffrage and Elections Article. Wider participation in elections, and greater protection of the integrity of the election process, were sought. The requirement for residence in the State as a prerequisite to voting is reduced from one year to six months; while the requirement for county residence is eliminated. The General Assembly may require residence in the election district of no more than thirty days, and may prescribe shorter periods of residence in both State and district for those wishing to vote in presidential elections. A State Board of Elections will supervise election law administration throughout the State. The question of reducing the voting age to eighteen is separately submitted to the voters.

The Legislative Article. In its consideration of the Legislative Article the Convention sought to achieve more meaningful representation of the people and to improve procedures in the General Assembly. The question of retaining the present system of 177 Representatives from multi-member districts with cumulative voting, with the addition that no party may limit its nominations to less than two, is offered separately to the voters. An alternative system of single-member districts for the election of members of the House of Representatives is also offered separately to the voters. In it each one of fifty-nine Legislative Districts, each electing one Senator, is to be divided into three House districts, for a total of 177, each electing one Representative. The plan which the electors favor will be placed in the new Constitution if it is approved. If the new Constitution is approved but neither plan of legislative structure is approved, then the applicable provisions of the 1870 Constitution will remain in effect.

Redistricting every ten years, in order to restore the equality of legislative district populations, is prescribed, with a "tie breaker" arrangement to reduce the likelihood of an at-large election. Annual sessions for the General Assembly are authorized; and the General Assembly is required to establish a uniform effective date for legislation. The minimum age for service in the General Assembly is reduced to twenty-one years.

The Executive Article. In the Executive Article, the Convention sought to make the executive branch more effective. In 1978 and thereafter, all state executive officers are to be elected for terms of four years. Thus the presidential election year will be avoided, and it is hoped there will be greater emphasis on state issues. The Superintendent of Public Instruction is no longer to be elected, and the Auditor is replaced by a Comptroller. The Governor and Lieutenant Governor are to be elected jointly, removing the possibility of their being of different political parties.

The Governor is to have greater veto powers — to reduce the amounts specified in appropriation acts, and to propose changes in acts submitted for his consideration. He also is to have authority to reorganize executive agencies and to reassign functions among them.

The Judiciary Article. Even though the Judicial Article of the present Constitution has been in effect only since January 1, 1964, the Convention sought to perfect it in the light of experience. A plan for judges of the Supreme, Appellate and Circuit Courts to be nominated by primary election or by petition, instead of party convention, and elected at general or special elections as the General Assembly shall determine, is offered as a separate question to the voters. The question of appointing judges at all levels, by the Governor from nominees submitted by Judicial Nominating Commissions, is also offered separately to the voters. The plan which the electors favor will be placed in the new Constitution if it is approved. If the new Constitution is approved but neither plan for choosing judges is approved, then the applicable provisions of the 1962 Judicial Article will remain in effect. The vote required to retain a judge in office at the end of his term is increased from a simple majority to three-fifths.

A Judicial Inquiry Board is to have authority to recieve or initiate complaints against judges, and to investigate the same. The Board may file such complaints with the Courts Commission, and if it does, the Board shall prosecute the complaint. The impeachment power of the General Assembly over judges is confirmed. The mandatory appellate jurisdiction of the Supreme Court is reduced; and the Supreme Court is given authority to assign constitutional appeals of lesser import to the appellate courts, thus relieving itself of this burden. Provisions for filling vacancies in judicial positions are prescribed. Permission is granted for two or more counties to join for the purpose of electing a single states attorney. The Clerk of the Supreme Court, and the clerks of the Appellate courts, shall be appointed by the respective courts. Circuit court clerks may be elected or appointed, as the General Assembly directs.

The Local Government Article. The heart of the Local Government Article is in its provisions for home rule, a concept not included in the present Constitution. Home rule units are defined as any county having a chief executive, elected by the voters, and any municipality having a population of more than 25,000. Any smaller municipality may in referendum elect to become a home rule unit; and any home rule unit may in referendum elect to give up home rule status. Home rule units have wide discretion as to the powers and functions each will exercise and perform. The General Assembly only by a three-fifths vote may limit or deny strictly local powers to home rule units; but by a simple majority may limit or deny to home rule units any power which is exercised concurrently or exclusively by the State. Home rule units may exercise much discretion in regard to their governmental structures and offices.

Changes other than those relating to home rule are included. All counties and municipalities have greater flexibility in providing services. Traditionally rigid county governments may be reorganized following referendum or Board action. Wide latitude in intergovernmental cooperation is permitted.

The Finance Article. This is a totally new Article which has no counterpart in the present Constitution. It is concerned with better management of the taxpayer's money. It declares financial records of State and local governments to be open to the public. It provides for a balanced executive budget, to be prepared each year by the Governor, and to extend to all the financial affairs of the State. The General Assembly is to appoint an Auditor General, for a term of ten years, who will have charge of the audit of all aspects of State finance. Uniform systems of local governmental accounting are to be provided by the General Assembly.

The Revenue Article. Here the Convention sought to provide a structure upon which the General Assembly could build an equitable and adequate tax system. Any income tax is limited to a non-graduated tax. A corporate income tax rate may not exceed the rate on individual persons by more than the ratio of eight to five. Neither of these limitations is contained in the present Constitution. Real property may be classified for ad valorem tax purposes in counties of more than 200,000 persons. With such classification the ratio of the highest to the lowest level of assessment may not exceed two-and-one-half to one, and real property used in farming shall be assessed at a level not higher than single family residential property.

The ad valorem tax on personal property is made dependent, insofar as individuals are concerned, on the amendment which is to be voted on at the November 3, 1970 general election, which would prohibit the personal property tax "as to individuals." Any remaining personal property tax is to be abolished by 1979, and the loss of revenue to local governments is to be replaced by a statewide tax, imposed on the class or classes relieved of ad valorem taxation upon personal property subsequent to any prohibition brought about by the adoption of the amendment to be voted on in 1970.

Exemption from and credits for taxation are authorized, such as food in relation to a sales tax, and homesteads and rent credits in relation to the tax on real property. Debt secured by the full faith and credit of the State requires approval either by three-fifths of the

General Assembly or in a popular referendum. Debt to be repaid from revenue generated by the object for which the debt was incurred, such as a dormitory or toll highway, is to depend on approval by a simple majority of the General Assembly.

The Education Article. The Convention was greatly concerned with improving and equalizing opportunities for education. The education of all persons to the limit of their capabilities is declared to be a fundamental goal of the people of the State. Education through the secondary school is to be free, with such further free education as the General Assembly may provide. The State is to have primary responsibility for the costs of public education. A State Board of Education is authorized, with members to be either elected or appointed, or a combination of the two, as the General Assembly may direct. The Board is to appoint the chief state education officer.

The Environment Article. Pressing needs of the time were recognized in this Article, which has no parallel in the present Constitution. The maintenance of a healthful environment is declared to be the public policy of the State, and the right and duty of each person. The individual is given legal standing so that he may enforce this right through appropriate legal proceedings.

The General Provisions Article. Here a miscellany of items considered to be in the public interest were brought together. A sworn statement of economic interests is required of all candidates for and holders of state office, and of all members of Constitutional Boards and Commissions. A similar requirement may be imposed by the General Assembly on local candidates and officials. All such statements are to be open to public inspection.

The provisions of state and local government pension and retirement systems shall not have their benefits reduced. Membership in such systems shall be a valid contractual relationship.

Public transportation is declared to be an essential public service, which the General Assembly may by law assist. Public funds may be granted to private agencies for the provision of public transportation services.

The requirement of a referendum for changes in the banking laws has been deleted. Any law authorizing branch banking, however, would require an extraordinary majority of the legislature.

The Constitutional Revision Article. A primary difficulty with the present Constitution is in amending it. Thus an effort is made to make the process of constitutional change more workable. By a three-fifths vote of each house, the General Assembly may propose amendments to the Constitution or place the question of calling a constitutional convention on the ballot. Either proposition may be approved by three-fifths of those voting on the question or a simple majority of those taking part in the general election. The greater ease of amendment which is proposed is clear, since the present Constitution specifies a two-thirds approval in the General Assembly for such questions, and also requires for adoption, two-thirds of those voting on a proposed amendment, or a simple majority of those voting in the election. The question of calling a convention shall automatically be placed on the general election ballot, by the Secretary of State, at the end of any twenty-year period in which it has not been submitted to the people by the General Assembly. No such provision is in the present Constitution.

Amendments to the Article on the Legislature, of a structural or procedural nature, may be proposed by petition, with signatures at least equal in number to eight percent of the total vote for Governor in the preceding election. Thus a reluctance on the part of the General Assembly to propose changes in its own domain can be overcome.

The Deletion of Sections and Articles. In preparing a new Constitution the Convention deleted much material because of its obsolescence or constitutional irrelevancy. The Boundaries Article is deleted because determination of the boundaries of the State is a matter of Federal Law, not of the State Constitution.

In addition to deletions, the Convention has improved the directness and simplicity of the language of many of the provisions carried over into a new Constitution. The proposed document is shorter by 5,000 words than the one now in effect. While no member of the Convention would insist that it has written a perfect

Constitution, most are of the opinion that their product is an attempt to better meet the needs of their era.

The Convention asks the People for their support of the proposed new Constitution in the coming referendum. For all items which are separately submitted it recommends, in addition, the most careful public scrutiny. Throughout the Convention, its members have been obliged, while seeking to serve the public interest, to realize that no single point-of-view could dominate any question, nor could any interest or faction have its will consistently prevail. In a State so diverse as Illinois, only the spirit of compromise has made it possible for may problems to be solved. The Convention asks the People to view its product in the same spirit — with the idea that while it is not in every respect ideal from a given point-of-view, it is from any vantage point far better suited than is the Constitution of 1870 to serve the future needs of the State.

INDEX

A

Adams, Rolland L., 59, 61
Alexander, John, 163, 182, 194
Ancel, Louis, vii, 47, 48, 49, 52, 113, 164, 165
Arrigo, Victor A., 170, 177, 191
Arrington, W. Russell, 173, 180-81
Arvey, Jacob, vii, 73, 84, 85, 87, 106, 107

B

Banks, Samuel A., vii, 64-65, 66
Banks, Mrs. Samuel A., 66
Benes, Eduard, 30
Bentley, Richard, 72
Bigley, Harold, 18
Birch, A.T., 81, 117
Black, John D., 82
Blue Ballot, 48, 94, 96, 108, 111; campaigns, Witwer's role in, 74, 85, 89, 95, 100, 103, 112, 116, 117, 132. *See also* Witwer, Samuel W., and Con Con; and the Gateway campaigns; and the Joint Committee for a Constitutional Convention
Borah, Senator William E., 118
Bauler, Paddy, 90
Bradley, James T., 194
Brand, Lenora, 145
Brooks, Senator C. Wayland, 84
Brussells, Abraham, 110
Burditt, George M., 153

Burgess, Kenneth F., 156
Burlage, Thomas D., 42
Bush, Vice President George, 50

C

Campbell, Mortimer B., 23
Carey, Philip J., 175
Carpentier, Charles, 77, 81, 126
Cedarquist, Wayland B., 81
Chambers, Carl C., 59, 61
Chapman, John, 138
Chicago Bar Association: and Witwer's *University of Chicago Law Review* article, 80; role in constitutional reform, 86, 88, 89, 90, 92, 109; Witwer's work for, on Gateway amendment committee, 72-74, 76-80; 86, 88, 89, 90-92
Chicago Daily News: and Witwer's *University of Chicago Law Review* article, 81; position on Witwer's U.S. Senate Candidacy, 122, 127. *See also* Witwer, Samuel W., and the media
Chicago Tribune: opposed to call for a constitutional convention, 78, 82, 90, 92, 97, 165 (conversion of, 95); position on Witwer's U.S. Senate candidacy, 122, 125, 128. *See also* Witwer, Samuel W. and the media
Clare, Carl P., 51-52

223